THE SCARLET THREAD OF SCANDAL

THE SCARLET THREAD OF SCANDAL

Morality and the American Presidency

CHARLES W. DUNN

ROWMAN & LITTLEFIELD PUBLISHERS, INC.
Lanham • Boulder • New York • Oxford

ROWMAN & LITTLEFIELD PUBLISHERS, INC.

Published in the United States of America
by Rowman & Littlefield Publishers, Inc.
4720 Boston Way, Lanham, Maryland 20706
www.rowmanlittlefield.com

12 Hid's Copse Road
Cumnor Hill, Oxford OX2 9JJ, England

Copyright © 2001 by Rowman & Littlefield Publishers, Inc.
First paperback edition 2001

British Library Cataloguing in Publication Information Available

**The hardback edition of this book was catalogued by the Library of Congress as
follows**

Dunn, Charles W.
    The scarlet thread of scandal : morality and the American presidency / Charles W.
Dunn
        p.   cm.
    Includes bibliographical references and index.
    ISBN 0-8476-9606-5 (cloth : alk. paper)
    1. Presidents—United Sates—History—20th century.   2. Political corruption
United States—History—20th century.   3. United States—Politics and
government—20th century.   4. United States—Moral conditions.
    5. Presidents—United States—History.   I. Title.
    E176.1.D86   2000
    973'9—dc21   99-41012
                                                                                                          CIP

ISBN 0-8476-9696-5 (cloth : alk. paper)
ISBN 0-8476-9607-3 (pbk : alk. paper)

Printed in the United States of America

⊖™ The paper used in this publication meets the minimum requirements of American
National Standard for Information Sciences—Permanence of Paper for Printed Library
Materials, ANSI/NISO Z39.48-1992.

CONTENTS

PREFACE

Above all, it should never be forgotten that Watergate first became known because there was a watchman in the night, not because of the vigilance of the Congress, the courts, or the press. Each helped to expose the web of Watergate in its turn, but later!

—Charles W. Dunn, *The Future of the American Presidency*

Has any subject commanded more public attention in recent years than presidential morality? Scandals involving Johnson and Vietnam, Nixon and Watergate, Reagan and Bush and Iran-Contra, and Clinton and Lewinsky erupted one after another on the political landscape, permanently marring the American political panorama for Democrats and Republicans and, indeed, for all America. Shortened presidencies; damaged leadership potential; increased partisanship; protracted legislative, judicial, and press investigations; and reduced public trust now scar the political terrain. In response, *The Scarlet Thread of Scandal: Morality and the American Presidency* purposes to help interested citizens understand this controversial subject of presidential morality and to help presidents understand the relationships between presidential morality and presidential leadership.

Neither President Clinton's problems nor market demand prompted me to write this book. My interest in presidential morality began long before the revelations related to Whitewater and Monica Lewinsky's stained dress. My first book, *The Future of the American Presidency,* published in 1975, addressed this subject.

THE PUZZLE OF PRESIDENTIAL MORALITY

Writing about presidential morality is like completing a jigsaw puzzle. The issues of presidential morality often arise in mysterious and unexpected ways, not just through thorough investigations by Congress, the courts, and the press. Without the discovery of the Watergate break-in by a night watchman, President Nixon would have served two full terms, his illegal and unethical actions unknown to the nation. Without the stain of his semen on Monica Lewinsky's dress, President Clinton would not have had his immorality exposed and his leadership limited. Fitting more pieces into the puzzle should help us see the picture more clearly.

Many anecdotal books have appeared on presidential morality, especially following the eruption of such issues as Nixon and Watergate and Clinton and Lewinsky. While these books play a useful role in clarifying the story line, they do not generally rise to the level of analysis and explanation. I have used anecdotes in this book, not to tell an interesting story, but to illustrate my analysis and conclusions. My concern is with what and why, not with who, where, and when.

Liberals and conservatives, Democrats and Republicans may debate whether this volume says too much or too little about Clinton, just as they could have debated that issue regarding Nixon in *The Future of the American Presidency*. Regardless, all must agree that Clinton's record on this subject is the most recent and one of the most controversial. Although *The Scarlet Thread of Scandal* raises questions about presidential morality in every administration from Washington through Clinton, public awareness of current history dictates a disproportionate emphasis on recent presidencies.

This book offers my interpretation of presidential morality. I did not write it to please everyone but rather to help interested citizens—and presidents—improve their understanding of the subject. I intend this book as an exploratory inquiry into a subject fraught with controversy. I offer suggestive and indicative analyses and conclusions rather than definitive and decisive answers. I hope this book will prompt others to add to the debate on this important topic, whether in agreement or disagreement with my analysis.

By following the thread of presidential morality as it weaves its way from Washington through Clinton, *The Scarlet Thread of Scandal* is also intended to serve as a librarian's resource on the subject. From here, librarians and interested readers can turn to individual presidential autobiographies and biographies for more information.

Bridging the Gap

In 1975 Watergate provided grist for the mill of my analysis in *The Future of the American Presidency*, which explored the abuse of presidential power. From then until now, I have analyzed American politics in a variety of ways, from academic books to popular commentary on network television. In my books, running the gamut from text, to trade, to scholarly, I have tried to explore uncharted waters, focusing on issues generally ignored by my colleagues. In the electronic media I have analyzed political issues on such programs as NBC's *Today Show* and ABC's *World News Tonight*. My political analysis has also appeared on the pages of *Time*, the *New York Times*, the *Wall Street Journal*, the *Washington Post*, *Congressional Quarterly Weekly Report*, and other publications. Three important lessons stand out from a quarter-century of academic and popular political analysis.

First, for most of the twenty-five years since the publication of *The Future of the American Presidency*, morality and such related subjects as religion and ideology have had the stature of an orphan child among scholars and the mass media. Only in recent years has there been a broader attempt to understand the impact of these subjects on American politics. I vividly remember when political scientists interested in these subjects could fit inside the proverbial telephone booth during meetings of the American Political Science Association. As in the scholarly community, only in recent years have the media begun to offer in-depth analysis of morality, religion, and ideology. For example, just a few years ago ABC-TV became the first network to employ a full-time reporter to cover religion.

Second, morality, religion, and ideology are unsettling and uncomfortable subjects, especially to scholars who tiptoe about them as though they were minefields, afraid that addressing these topics may damage their scholarly careers. When I began to study the relationship between the American presidency and morality, religion, and ideology during the 1970s, my closest friend and colleague among political scientists strongly admonished me not to undertake this research. He said, "Chuck, you will hurt your career. No one studies those subjects." Perhaps scholars fear that they cannot write on these topics without bias, but in a sense no research is bias-free. Still, research on morality, religion, and ideology probably increases the danger of getting hit by the explosive charge of bias. Should that danger, however, prevent scholars from addressing three of today's most pressing issues? Moreover, how can we even pretend to understand the presidency without studying the intersection of morality, religion, and ideology?

Third, by usually writing in arcane language, scholars fail to perform an enormous public service. Certainly scholars should write for fellow scholars, but they should also write in language understood by a much larger audience of interested citizens and politicians. In short, they should balance the theoretical with the practical. Scholars have a profound public service obligation: communicating their knowledge to rank-and-file citizens interested in politics.

This book continues a professional lifetime of writing on American government and politics, integrating and applying much of what I have written in earlier books. I have attempted throughout my career to bridge the gap between professional and public service and between the theoretical and the practical, sometimes breaking new ground as I did so.

Every book, from my first in 1975 to those still in progress, bears the invaluable marks of outstanding research assistants. Ryan Teague, Meghan Graves, Chris Koon, and Natalie McDaniel contributed directly to this book, while David Page and Tommy Strickland indirectly influenced its direction through their research on earlier books. Authors, and certainly this one, walk through valleys of despair and doubt, wondering about the value of their work. Robert Louis Stevenson put it well: "I hate to write. I love having written." Many times Rowman & Littlefield editor Steve Wrinn lifted my spirits and renewed my vision to help me arrive at the love of writing. Copyeditors, like surgeons, wield their scalpels to heal and perfect a body. Cheryl Hoffman adroitly wielded her editorial scalpel on the body of this book, giving new life and vigor to its ideas.

I appreciate a timely grant from the Earhart Foundation to study how ideology, theology, and morality affect American politics. Long before the moral scandals of the 1990s dominated media attention, Earhart supported this research. Neither the foundation nor I could have anticipated how important this subject would become.

Finally, I would like to acknowledge other scholars who have contributed to the national debate on morality. "Reconstructing America's Moral Order" in the *Wilson Quarterly* (Summer 1999) presents the views of Francis Fukuyama and Paul Berman in this critical debate. Fukuyama wrote *The Great Disruption: Human Nature and the Reconstitution of Social*

Order (1999), while Berman wrote *A Tale of Two Utopias: The Political Journey of the Generation of 1968* (1996). Many other well-known analysts and thinkers have contributed to this continuing dialogue, including William Bennett, Charles Murray, Gertrude Himmelfarb, Daniel Patrick Moynihan, and James Q. Wilson. The autumn 1999 issue of *PS*, the journal of the American Political Science Association, contains a symposium "Scandal and Government: Current and Future Implications of the Clinton Presidency," to which Mark J. Rozell, Clyde Wilcox, Robert J. Spitzer, Louis Fisher, Molly W. Sonner, and Stephen J. Wayne contributed.

The Scarlet Thread of Scandal adds to this debate by focusing on the morality of the president, who, as the only nationally elected public official, more than anyone else represents all Americans and provides a window on American society.

1

THE SCARLET THREAD OF SCANDAL

The Presidency is preeminently a place of moral leadership.
— Franklin D. Roosevelt

As the twentieth century closes, discussions of morality and the presidency abound, prompted by the scandals and rumors of scandal in the administration of President Bill Clinton. But the Clinton presidency does not exist in a historical vacuum. It is part of the fabric of history.

The scarlet thread of scandal—personal, constitutional, and financial—boldly weaves its way through presidential politics. A cursory glimpse at just the modern presidents from Franklin D. Roosevelt through William Jefferson Clinton reveals a range of scandals, from Roosevelt's affair with Lucy Mercer, to Kennedy's alleged links with the Mafia, Reagan's involvement in the Iran–Contra arms-for-hostages deal, and Clinton's sexual peccadilloes.

Sex scandals excite great public interest, but other scandals may exact a greater toll on presidents, the presidency, and American politics, as the fates of Presidents Lyndon B. Johnson and Richard M. Nixon show. One was brought low by U.S. involvement in Vietnam and the other by his coverup of a bungled burglary of the Democratic Party's Watergate offices.

To be successful, presidents need a firm grasp of moral questions. How well they lead the country and how history assesses their performance depend on their handling of moral issues.

A number of factors influence what issues emerge at a given time and how presidents react. Among the factors that must be considered, especially in our own time, are:

- Cultural conflict in an adversarial society
- The intersection of moral character and moral issues
- The press and presidential morality
- Presidential strategies during moral combat
- Ideology
- Religion's moral lens
- Public policy's moral cloak
- Popular expectations of presidential behavior
- The constitutional cultivation of moral issues
- Historical revisionism and presidential greatness
- The national debate about moral decline
- Personal versus public policy morality
- Contrary definitions of morality

CULTURAL CONFLICT IN AN ADVERSARIAL SOCIETY

Some argue that America is in a state of cultural collapse, rendering traditional moral issues much less important. According to this argument, most Americans no longer view historic Judeo-Christian standards as controlling influences in American life. According to this line of thinking, America is in the midst of a great culture war between a fading culture of moral certainty and an emerging culture of moral relativism. The former emphasizes absolute standards of right and wrong, while the latter deemphasizes them.

Others argue that any president, Democrat or Republican, conservative or liberal, now faces intense moral scrutiny, unlike previous presidents, making governance more difficult. Presidents and candidates for the office know they will face intense scrutiny of every aspect of their public and private lives and will face allegations, both true and false. The laserlike focus on presidential morality can blind, debilitate, paralyze, and evict presidents.

Which view is correct? Perhaps both. Americans look at moral character through the lens of economic self-interest. Moral character looms larger in the public mind when the nation's economy is poorer, while a healthy economy stifles interest in moral scandal. Each view offers sound arguments and illuminates our understanding of moral scandals. In short, there is no simple explanation for the way the scarlet thread of scandal weaves its way through the modern presidency.

THE INTERSECTION OF MORAL CHARACTER AND MORAL ISSUES

Presidents may be called upon to confront major moral issues, as Abraham Lincoln did during the Civil War and as Franklin Roosevelt did during World War II. Lincoln and Roosevelt rank high on the scales of presidential greatness because of how well they dealt with these issues.

What constitutes a moral issue? What is the moral side of the issue? National consensus on the answers is not always easy to achieve. President Clinton, for example, supports abortion rights, affirmative action, feminism, and nondiscrimination against homosexuals as morally correct, while others take diametrically opposed views.

THE PRESS AND PRESIDENTIAL MORALITY

An industry of moralists and moralizers has emerged in the press, looking for the latest hot, headline-grabbing story. Sometimes they turn opinion into fact and a thin thread of evidence into a compelling case against a president. Reporters and commentators on the far left harass conservative and Republican presidents, while those on the far right irritate liberal and Democratic presidents. Conspiracy theories abound. *Who, what, when, where, and why?* These small words spark big questions and a litany of charges and countercharges. Nixon apologists and Nixon himself thought the press did him in, and that was also a major part of President Clinton's defense, as Hillary Rodham Clinton and other Clinton defenders took to the airwaves to charge that a right-wing conspiracy was at work.

Beginning in the late 1960s, the American press corps gradually became more adversarial to government and public officials and more willing to inquire into areas that were once off-limits. They turned a blind eye and a deaf ear to John F. Kennedy's immorality during the early 1960s but thoroughly exposed Clinton's during the 1990s. During the Watergate scandal and Whitewater scandals, the press became like a pack of hounds on the trail, each racing to get out front with the latest titillating revelation.

Presidents today can continue to govern effectively if attacks on their morality come only from reporters and commentators outside the mainstream. The mainstream press usually does not get into the fray until an event sparks their interest and lends credibility to the charges originally brought in other forums.

PRESIDENTIAL STRATEGIES DURING MORAL COMBAT

Presidents caught in the midst of a scandal can pursue a number of strategies. They can admit error, alter policies, change personnel, offer to cooperate with authorities investigating their administrations, and blame previous administrations. For example, critics suggested that if Nixon and Clinton had made early and full admissions of guilt, they would have bolstered their public support and negated the need for congressional and judicial investigations. When charged with complicity in the Chinese espionage scandal in 1999, Clinton immediately welcomed new policies and procedures; at the same time, he argued that the Bush and Reagan administrations had also permitted such incidents. President Reagan dismissed Secretary of Interior James Watt to remove the sting of a brewing scandal, and he also required his administration to cooperate fully with the investigation of the Iran-Contra affair.

During the Watergate and Whitewater scandals, Nixon and Clinton followed a fivefold strategy in their battles to survive moral scandal.

- **Delay.** Fighting for time, they hoped the public and the press would shift their attention to something else. Nixon refused to hand over subpoenaed documents until the U.S. Supreme Court ordered him to. Clinton filed many lawsuits and appeals, losing almost every one, to delay cooperating with the investigation.

- **Deny.** Recognizing that they occupied the most powerful and prestigious office in the world, they used the moral authority of the office to make forceful denials of moral turpitude. Nixon denied knowledge of the Watergate break-in, and Clinton denied having an affair with Monica Lewinsky until discovery of his DNA on the infamous dress.

- **Discredit.** Using the power of the presidential bully pulpit, they and their surrogates trashed the character of the opposition, calling them names, charging them with perpetrating falsehood and attempting to link them to conspiracies. Nixon and his supporters charged that Archibald Cox, the independent prosecutor, was part of a liberal Democratic conspiracy to get him. Clinton, his wife, and his supporters railed against an alleged vast right-wing conspiracy that wanted to evict him from the White House.

- **Deflect.** Knowing of a president's power to generate publicity, they deflected attention from their moral crises by taking the offensive on other issues, announcing new plans and policies that appealed to key groups in American society, and traveling extensively. Their image handlers showed them at work for the American people.

- **Diminish.** When President Clinton finally admitted to an affair with Monica Lewinsky, he said his actions were merely "inappropriate," not wrong, harmful, damaging, or sinful. His choice of words diminished the seriousness of the affair. Nixon attempted to play down the importance of charges against him by insisting that his actions were either in the public interest or outside his knowledge and purview. Supporters of both Nixon and Clinton offered the pragmatic argument that what they did was essentially no different from what other presidents had done.

In the end, this fivefold strategy failed Nixon but enabled Clinton to survive. The state of the economy was one of the factors that distinguished them. A sluggish economy created an undertow, weakening President Nixon's strategy and finally drowning his presidency. A booming economy buoyed President Clinton, raising serious questions about sacrificing the nation's economic health on the altar of impeachment.

IDEOLOGY

Ideology is a natural spawning ground of questions about moral character. Conservatism and liberalism, Right and Left, offer conflicting explanations of America's origins and competing visions of America's future. For example, conservatives usually advocate limited government and lower taxes, while liberals often advance causes associated with enlarged government and increased taxes. Taking their explanations and visions very seriously, the respective sides fight for advantage. Questions about moral character can deeply wound the opposition and limit the advancement of its cause. Conservatives and liberals advance conspiracy theories about their opponents' motives. Conservatives argue that a liberal bias in the mainstream media of network television and the nation's major newspapers gives liberals a distinct advantage in presenting the liberal case to the public. Liberals contend that conservative dominance of radio talk shows enables conservatives to foment opposition to liberals and their agenda.

RELIGION'S MORAL LENS

America's unique religious heritage causes many people to see morality through the eyes of religion. To them religion is the only lens for accurately viewing American morality. President George Washington stated in his Farewell Speech on September 26, 1796:

> Let it simply be asked where is the security for prosperity, for reputation, for life, if the sense of religious obligation desert the oaths, which are the instruments of investigation in the Courts of Justice? And let us with caution indulge the supposition, that morality can be maintained without religion. . . . Reason and experience both forbid us to expect that national morality can prevail in exclusion of religious principle.[1]

Just as ideology divides Americans, so too does religion. Persons of conservative religious persuasion normally identify with and defend ideologically conservative presidents, while the liberally inclined do the opposite. Typically, members of the Christian Coalition march in lockstep with conservative and Republican politics, while members of the National Council of Churches march heel-and-toe with liberal and Democratic Party politics.

Presidents use religious symbols to identify with important groups, a legitimate aim. Their use of these symbols, however, may enable them to capture unfairly or inappropriately the moral high ground, to appear like something they are not, to inoculate themselves against charges of immorality, and once charges of immorality occur, to help them weather the political storms.

In 1952, for example, Democratic presidential candidate Adlai E. Stevenson, a Unitarian, became a Presbyterian, while Republican presidential candidate Dwight D. Eisenhower, not belonging to any religious body, also became a Presbyterian. Both moved inside the symbolic comfort zone of mainstream Protestantism. Speaking before several thousand Southern Baptist preachers in Houston, Roman Catholic presidential candidate John F. Kennedy directly appealed to Southern Baptists in 1960 by promising there would be no papal influence over his administration.

In a more ecumenical mode, President Nixon held Sunday services in the White House featuring Jewish, Protestant, and Roman Catholic clergy. His successor, President Ford, seeking a larger slice of the Southern Baptist vote, attended church the Sunday before the election at the prestigious First Baptist Church of Dallas, where he had a photo-op with the then best-known Southern Baptist preacher, W. A. Criswell. President Carter proclaimed that he was "born again," a not-so-subtle appeal to evangelical Protestant voters.

President Clinton went to church, Bible in hand, during the height of revelations about his alleged affair with Monica Lewinsky. On the Sunday he allegedly met with her and suggested how she could cover up their affair, he waved his Bible to the crowd as he left church. He and his family also had the Reverend Jesse Jackson in the White House for prayer and counsel during this time. To help him overcome personal problems, he chose three prominent Protestant ministers to guide him. Almost every president from Kennedy through Clinton has employed evangelist Billy Graham for inaugural prayers and White House photo-ops. Nixon even attended one of Graham's crusades.

Rhetorically, presidents invoke religious language to put a moral gloss on their positions, policies, and campaigns. President Johnson, in defense of his Voting Rights Act of 1965, said to Congress: "For with a country as with a person, 'What is a man profited, if he shall gain the whole world, and lose his own soul?' Above the pyramid on the great seal of the United States it says in Latin, 'God has favored our undertaking.' God will not favor everything we do. It is rather our duty to divine His will. I cannot help but believe that He truly understands and that He really favors the undertaking that we begin here tonight." President Clinton used the biblical term "covenant" during his 1992 acceptance speech at the Democratic National Convention and later in his campaign.

Presidential candidates Barry Goldwater and George McGovern in 1964 and 1972, respectively, went so far as to claim: "In your heart, you know he's right," and "Right from the start." Even the successful presidential campaign slogans such as "New Deal," "Fair Deal," "New Frontier," and "Great Society" created a moral tone of right versus wrong, posing a disadvantage for opponents.

Analytically, writers about the presidency often turn to religious and moral language to capture their views of the institution. Roman Catholic scholar Michael Novak said: "Americans treat America as a religion. Hatred for political opponents waxes theological. Like separate islands, the political religions of the land are connected through a single office. The president is the one pontiff bridging all."[2] Political scientist Clinton Rossiter referred to Abraham Lincoln as "the martyred Christ of democracy's passion play."[3] New York Times journalist James Reston said that "the White House is the pulpit of the nation and the president is its chaplain."[4]

The presidency and presidents, encased in a cocoon of religious symbols and rhetoric, invite intense attention to moral questions. By creating high expectations for presidential candidates and presidents, the religiosity of American public life sets them up for a fall when they fail to measure up morally.

PUBLIC POLICY'S MORAL CLOAK

Presidents frequently wrap a moral cloak around their policy initiatives, placing the opposition in a morally defensive position. The moral cloak of slogans and symbols dresses up presidential policy initiatives, sometimes covering up serious policy defects. Opponents must not only debate the substantive merits of policy proposals but also undress them. President Eisenhower, for example, wrapped the moral cloak of national defense around several of his initiatives. He promoted the interstate highway system in the National Defense Highway Act and enlarged federal contributions to higher education through the National Defense Education Act. President Kennedy, inheriting Eisenhower's drably titled Public Law 480, renamed the program "Food for Peace" and greatly expanded its scope. He called his Latin American policy initiatives "Alliance for Progress," and his best known international policy initiative, "the Peace Corps." In the next administration, President Johnson used such titles as "War on Poverty," "Safe Streets," "Head Start," and "Model Cities" for his programs. More recently, proposals by President Clinton to put a hundred thousand federally funded police officers on the streets and a hundred thousand federally funded school teachers in the classrooms put opponents on the defensive, although they had sound fiscal and other arguments against the ideas.

A moral tone may generate stronger support and higher expectations for a policy, but also create greater risk if a policy fails. Johnson trumpeted his "Great Society" policies with great moral fanfare, but gradually many critics and much of the public perceived them as failures. Had his policies succeeded, he would likely have ranked higher on the scales of presidential greatness used by public opinion pollsters and scholars. The failure of his policies to measure up to enlarged moral expectations probably magnified their failure and contributed to his diminished stature.

POPULAR EXPECTATIONS OF PRESIDENTIAL BEHAVIOR

Just as failure of policies to meet high expectations can harm a president's standing in the public eye, so can failings in personal morality. For example, critics marvel at how well and how long Bill Clinton survived the high winds of moral hurricanes, while George Bush could not weather the light wind of adversity from his "read my lips" reversal. Differing expectations may provide an explanation. Apparently the public expected more of Bush and less of Clinton. Bush offered a highly moral persona to the American public, but Clinton issued several confessions even while campaigning for president. He confessed, for example, to using marijuana and to causing "pain" in his marriage. Jimmy Carter faced a problem similar to George Bush's when he stated in his 1976 campaign that "You can trust me." Early in his administration, however, his closest and most trusted adviser, Bert Lance, then the director of the Office of Management and Budget, was caught in a banking scandal. For a while that rocked public confidence in Carter, as he failed to meet the expectations he had created.

THE CONSTITUTIONAL CULTIVATION OF MORAL ISSUES

American government and politics include structures and principles that cultivate questions about moral behavior. The Constitution's First Amendment guarantee of freedom of the press gives a broad grant of authority and immunity to reporters and columnists to pursue moral questions. They can win Pulitzer Prizes, promotions, and book contracts by reporting tantalizing tales about presidential morality. Rush Limbaugh makes a fortune by his attacks on liberals and Democrats. Questions about Bill Clinton's morality served as fodder for his radio talk show. During the Nixon presidency, then little-known *Washington Post* reporters Bob Woodward and Carl Bernstein became internationally famous with their titillating front-page stories about "Deep Throat" and the Nixon character.

America's two-party system with its emphasis on winning the grand prize, the presidency, ensures that each party explores and exposes moral weaknesses in the candidates and office holders of the other party. In their zeal for victory candidates, campaigns, and parties sometimes cross the line between legal and illegal activities. President Clinton's campaign apparently engaged in substantial fund-raising efforts outside the law, notably foreign fund-raising through several East Asian conduits. President Nixon's Watergate scandal broke when a night watchman discovered a White House–sponsored break-in at the Democratic Party's headquarters. Separation of powers, especially when Democrats and Republicans divide control of the Congress and the White House, ensures the airing of dirty linen through prolonged committee investigations. The Senate Watergate Committee did that with Richard Nixon. Both House and Senate committees turned the searchlight on Bill Clinton.

The American judiciary is also a participant in the process. Democrats wanting to investigate President Richard Nixon and his aides gave birth to the statute creating the position of independent counsel. Republicans opposed its creation. Then when Republicans used the office to investigate President Bill Clinton, Democrats wanted to abort it. In the end, the office of independent counsel died at the hands of both parties.

The federal courts also have a role to play. In *U.S. v. Nixon* in 1973, a unanimous Supreme Court ruled that the doctrine of executive privilege does not allow a president to withhold evidence that is material to a criminal trial. Then, in over a dozen cases, federal courts denied efforts by President Clinton and his associates to refuse to testify and provide evidence.

HISTORICAL REVISIONISM AND PRESIDENTIAL GREATNESS

A treasure trove of archives in presidential libraries and elsewhere enables historians, journalists, and political scientists to subject presidential legacies to the pen of criticism and correction. President Truman left office with one of history's lowest popularity ratings. Now, however, he enjoys a much higher ranking on the scales of presidential greatness. Most historians, journalists, and political scientists concluded that President Truman made more courageous foreign policy decisions than perhaps any other president. Fred Greenstein's *Hidden-Hand Presidency* put a new gloss on President Eisenhower.[5] Charged with moral weakness in failing to publicly challenge Senator Joe McCarthy, Eisenhower's reputation suffered until Greenstein revealed that he had a successful behind-the-scenes strategy of challenging McCarthy. Other presidents, including Kennedy and, to a lesser extent, Franklin Roosevelt, have seen their standings fall over time, as sexual involvements surfaced that were unreported during their administrations.[6]

THE NATIONAL DEBATE ABOUT MORAL DECLINE

Intense national debate now centers on the state of morality in America. Many analysts believe that America is in a state of moral decline. The publisher and editor in chief of *U.S. News and World Report,* Mortimer B. Zuckerman, concludes: "There is a great yearning in the country to provide our national life and institutions with a larger moral dimension."[7] Former U.S. secretary of education William J. Bennett argues: "The real answer to the perils of our time is that we simply must become more civilized. We must pay attention to something that every civilized society has given preeminent importance: instilling in our children certain fundamental traits of character—traits like honesty, compassion, courage, perseverance, altruism, and the fidelity to one's commitments."[8] Dr. Benjamin Spock stated: "This century has seen a progressive relaxation of many of our standards of behavior and the souring of many commonly held beliefs. Taken one by one, most are of little importance. Taken together, I believe they show that we have lost our way."[9]

Since presidents occupy a unique position as the only nationally elected leader, they more than anyone else can serve as a moral anchor. Little wonder, then, that presidents become embroiled in debate about America's moral condition. Critics and pundits often expect them to act as a bulwark against moral decline. According to this analysis, moral scandal in the White House tears at the fabric of society by shredding our belief in heroes. People depend upon presidents for moral guidance and leadership; they are like stars in the sky, providing moral direction and light. When presidents no longer cast light along the moral pathway, Americans stumble and fall in the moral darkness.

PERSONAL VERSUS PUBLIC POLICY MORALITY

Is a president's private morality a proper subject for public debate? Is there a relationship between a president's private morality and public policy? Should presidents lie about their personal lives if that would help them pursue a greater good for the American public? Some argue that a president's private morality should always remain private; others vehemently disagree. Some argue that the public interest always outweighs and overrides questions of personal morality; others believe the opposite.

Apologists for Presidents Nixon and Clinton, for example, staunchly defended their moral integrity, decrying the immorality of political foes. Central to their defense is this argument: Americans should judge its presidents, not by their personal morality, but by how well they lead the country. Do their public policies benefit Americans at home and abroad? What is good for America then becomes the measure of morality, not a president's personal behavior. Geraldine Ferraro, the 1984 Democratic Party vice presidential candidate, put it this way in her 1998 defense of President Clinton: "Morality is how you deal with the problems of the country."[10]

Nixon apologists argue that he got America out of the Vietnam War, defined a new American foreign policy that led to diplomatic relations with China, and began the needed rebalancing of government power, shifting more responsibility to the states and away from the national government. Clinton advocates consistently point to his high public approval ratings and the strength of the American economy. His private life, they argue, is not our business.

Countering the moral morass of the Nixon era, Jimmy Carter campaigned in 1976 on the theme "You can trust me." This not-so-subtle indictment of Nixon's personal immorality helped pave the way for Carter's defeat of Gerald Ford, whose approval rating plummeted after he pardoned Nixon.

Attacking the moral quagmire of the Clinton administration, critics cited links between personal morality and public policy. They pointed out that Clinton's defense against charges of personal immorality engulfed him and his staff, preventing him from effectively leading the Congress and the nation. Clinton, like Nixon, won a major reelection victory, but charges about his personal immorality torpedoed his opportunity for significant public policy leadership. He lacked the personal moral standing necessary to fight for major changes in public policy. Ironically, the public approved of his job performance, but not his personal character. They distinguished between Clinton the president and Clinton the person.

CONTRARY DEFINITIONS OF MORALITY

As a system of ideas about good and bad, right and wrong, morality appears to have an easily defensible definition. The problem arises, however, when different systems are used to define good and bad, right and wrong. Conflicting systems produce competing definitions. The increasing diversity of American society now produces more systems and, therefore, more conflict. Seven varying definitions can be identified in today's society:

- **Divine Morality.** God defines morality through positive and negative decrees, such as the Ten Commandments and the Sermon on the Mount.

- **Utilitarian Morality.** Morality depends upon whether an action or a decision will increase human happiness.

- **Natural Rights Morality.** Since all humans possess natural rights, actions and decisions bear the mark of moral approval if they do not violate the natural rights of others.

- **Contractual Morality.** When humans agree to live together, such as through a social contract or a covenant, they establish binding moral standards to govern the conduct of their relationships.

- **Legal Realism Morality.** Morals and laws do not depend upon a widely shared sense of justice among the citizenry, but rather they are the arbitrary enactments of the politically powerful.

- **Values Clarification Morality.** People derive their moral standards through discussing the merits of moral alternatives.

- **Primitive Morality.** According to each of the above definitions, morality depends upon a source or a process. Primitive morality, believing that moral analysis is impossible, merely declares that rightness is rightness and wrongness is wrongness: no explanation is necessary or warranted.

Competing definitions of morality not only complicate presidential leadership but also offer more lines of moral defense for presidential decisions. Presidents come to the White House consciously or unconsciously influenced by one or more of these definitions of morality. Then knowingly or unknowingly they draw upon them to strengthen their leadership. President Clinton understood and used these competing definitions. Depending upon his political and public policy needs, he reinforced his leadership by appealing to different kinds of morality. For example, he used the language of natural rights to support his military intervention in the Balkans and the language of utilitarianism to support his calls for federal funds to hire police officers and teachers for local governments and school districts. In the first instance, he wanted the American military to protect the natural rights of besieged Kosovo Albanians, and in the second, he wanted to increase human happiness by enhancing public safety and improving public schools. And he used the doctrine of love and forgiveness from divine morality to invite the public and political leaders to overlook his transgressions.

Conclusion

The presidency is a place of leadership conditioned by personal moral character, the constraints and pressures that mold the nation's moral condition, and moral issues themselves. Together they shape the exercise of presidential leadership. History records how well a president's moral character intersects and interacts with the nation's moral condition and moral issues. On that hinges the political life span and the legacy of presidents.

2

THE MORAL KALEIDOSCOPE

Many Americans worry that the moral order that once held the nation together has become unraveled.

—James Q. Wilson, *Moral Judgment*

American morality has become kaleidoscopic, reflecting an increasing variety of competing ideas about morals and religion, blurring the lines separating right and wrong. Although total agreement about American morality never existed, basic agreement was once more common. The directions of American morality have shifted from uniformity to diversity, from simplicity to complexity, and from singular to plural. Sociologist Robert N. Bellah says that

> any coherent and viable society rests on a *common set of moral understandings* about good and bad, right and wrong, in the realm of individual and social action. It is almost as widely held that these common moral understandings must also in turn rest upon a *common set of religious understandings* that provide a picture of the universe in terms of which the moral understandings make sense. Such moral and religious understandings produce both a basic cultural legitimation for a society which is viewed as at least approximately in accord with them, and a standard of judgment for the criticism of a society that is seen as deviating too far from them.[1] (emphasis added)

KALEIDOSCOPIC MORALITY AND PRESIDENTIAL LEADERSHIP

Kaleidoscopic morality makes presidential leadership more difficult. Presidents can no longer count on widely accepted moral standards to guide their actions and must try to accommodate, appease, and appeal to differing moral interests. Today's moral issues, such as abortion, feminism, homosexuality, crime, public education, juvenile delinquency, and family breakdown, contrast sharply with those in earlier eras. Historically, presidents faced such controversial issues as the Civil War, but neither the quantity nor the diversity of those issues matched those that presidents confront today. Moreover, even on such issues as the Civil War, the two sides generally looked to the same source—the Bible—as their guiding moral authority, although they differed on its interpretation and application.

Morality manifests itself in many ways, but its foundation is truthfulness. Thomas Henry Huxley said that "Veracity is the heart of morality." Questions about morality swirl around many issues, including public policy, money, power, and sex, but no matter the issue, without truthfulness, the very foundation of morality and society crumbles.

What determines truthfulness? Does truth have an absolute and unalterable standard? Or does it turn on situations and circumstances? The contemporary debate pitting absolute truth against relative truth offers scholars ample fodder for articles and books. More important here, however, are the origins of that debate and how it influences presidential morality. In the shifting kaleidoscope of our diverse culture, Americans see truth through many lenses, including politics, religion, ideology, and language.

Moral storm clouds hang over every major presidential decision. Presidents daily confront division and discontent about definitions of the morally acceptable, both in their public and in their private lives. People and groups fight to define what is moral and right for the family, art, education, law, domestic politics, and foreign policy, as well as about the intersection and relative weights of the president's private and public moral decisions.

POLITICS AND THE MORAL KALEIDOSCOPE

Politics floods American society today. People and groups clamor for governmental solutions to their problems, and the government treads on territory previously off-limits. Big government is now the norm. Under the banner "Don't Tread on Me," American colonists fought against governmental intrusion in their lives. They wanted freedom from excessive governmental encroachment in society. The Founders believed that government is at best a necessary evil that requires restraint. An examination of their beliefs places in stark relief the issue of why today's moral conflicts differ in quantity and quality from those faced earlier in the life of the Republic.

The Founders' Distrust of Man and Government

The Founders' distrust of both man and government manifested itself in three important ways. First, by separating the national government's power into three branches and by dividing power between the national and state governments, the Founders revealed their distrust of power concentrated in man's hands. Second, by adopting the Bill of Rights to protect man from the capricious exercise of the national government's power, they expressed their distrust of government. Third, by allowing the people as a whole to directly elect only one part of the national government, the House of Representatives, they exhibited their distrust of the people. The Founders allowed the people only indirect influence in the selection of presidents and members of the Senate and Supreme Court. Alexis de Tocqueville put this interpretation on their actions:

> The greatest part of British America was peopled by men who, having shaken off the authority of the Pope, acknowledged no other religious supremacy. They brought with them into the New World a form of Christianity which I cannot better describe than by styling it a democratic and republican religion.[2]

According to Bellah,

> The Bible was the one book that literate Americans in the 17th, 18th, and 19th centuries could be expected to know well. . . . Biblical imagery provided the basic framework for imaginative thought in America up until quite recent times and, unconsciously, its control is still formidable.[3]

Political historian Richard Hofstadter spoke of the grip that Christian morality had on the Founders:

> To them a human being was an atom of self-interest. They did not believe in man, but they did believe in the power of a good political constitution to control him. . . . From a humanistic standpoint there is a serious dilemma in the philosophy of the Fathers, which derives from their conception of man. They thought man was a creature of rapacious self-interest, yet they wanted him to

be free—free, in essence, to contend, to engage in an umpired strife. . . . They had no hope and they offered none for any ultimate organic change in the way men conduct themselves. The result was that while they thought self-interest the most dangerous and unbrookable quality of man, they necessarily underwrote it in trying to control it.[4]

The three authors of the *Federalist Papers* make that clear. James Madison spoke of the "degree of depravity in mankind which requires a certain degree of circumspection and distrust,"[5] the "caprice and wickedness of man,"[6] and the "infirmities and depravities of human character."[7] John Jay believed that "dictates of personal interest"[8] govern man. Alexander Hamilton spoke of the "folly and wickedness of mankind."[9] Even Thomas Jefferson, who was not a Christian, held to a Christian view of the nature of man:

> Free government is founded on jealousy, not in confidence; it is jealousy and not confidence which prescribes limited constitutions, to bind those we are obligated to trust with power. In questions of power, let no more be heard of confidence in man but bind him down to mischief by the chains of the constitution.[10]

The Founders' Belief in Higher Law

Besides espousing limited government, the Founders also believed that the laws of man should conform to the laws of God. For example, the phrase "the laws of nature" in the Declaration of Independence refers to divine law. John Locke declared in his *Second Treatise on Government:* "Thus the law of nature stands as an eternal rule of all men, legislators as well as others. The rules that they make for other men's actions, must . . . be conformable to the law of nature, i.e., to the will of God."[11] Locke also stated, in "The Reasonableness of Christianity as Defined in the Scriptures": "As Christians we have Jesus the Messiah for our king, and are under the law revealed by Him in the Gospel."[12] William Blackstone's *Commentaries on the Laws of England*, the most important influence on the American legal system and required reading in American law schools through much of the last century, states: "As man depends absolutely upon his Maker for everything, it is necessary that he should at all points conform to his Maker's will." Blackstone also carefully distinguished between natural law and the law of nature: "The revealed law is of infinitely more authority than what we generally call the natural law. Because one is the law of nature, expressly declared to be by God himself; the other is only what, by the assistance of human reason, we imagine to be that law."[13] The Declaration of Independence holds that man's rights come not from man but from God and that they are unchangeable: "We hold these truths to be self-evident, that all men are created equal, that they are endowed by their Creator with certain inalienable rights." According to the Declaration of Independence, government should protect God's ordained rights for man: "That to secure these rights governments are instituted among men."

The Founders' Use of Covenant

The Founders liberally borrowed the idea of covenant from the Bible. The Mayflower Compact, the first and best-known example, says: "We . . . do by Presents, solemnly and mutually in the Presence of God and one another, covenant and combine ourselves together into a civil Body Politick." In the biblical tradition, a constitution, or covenant, functions as a solemn agreement between parties to reflect God's divine covenant with his people. The Founders covenanted under God to establish governments answerable to God and his law. Political scientist Daniel Elazar concludes that:

> The constitutions of the American states in the founding era were perhaps the greatest products of the American covenant tradition. . . . The creation of new states, even new towns, across the United States throughout the 19th century reflected the covenanting impulse.
>
> For Americans, covenant provides a means for a free people to form political communities without sacrificing their essential freedom and *without making energetic government possible.*[14] (emphasis added)

The Founders' Confidence in Gradual Change

The Founders wanted change to occur gradually and incrementally within the bounds of existing institutions. They believed that gradual and incremental change conserves the best of society's customs, foundations, and traditions. Rapid change, they believed, threatens society with instability. British parliamentarian Edmund Burke put it this way: "A state without the means of some change is without the means of its conservation."[15]

The Founders wrote a Constitution that frustrates advocates of rapid change. Separation of powers, division of powers between state and national governments, and obstacles to amending the Constitution help ensure that change comes through deliberate and thoughtful action. These constitutional principles and procedures create a multiplicity of decision-makers, and complexity and diversity in decision-making.

A primary intellectual architect of the New Deal, Rexford Tugwell, conceded that the Constitution hampered Franklin D. Roosevelt's New Deal efforts to reduce liberty and increase equality in public policy.

> The intention of the eighteenth and nineteenth century law was to install and protect the principle of conflict; this [principle], if we begin to plan, we shall be changing once for all, and it will require the laying of rough, unholy hands on many a sacred precedent, doubtless calling on an enlarged and nationalized police power for enforcement. We shall also have to give up a distinction of great consequence, and very dear to a legalistic heart, but economically quite absurd, between private and public or quasi-public employments. There is no private business, if by that we mean one of no consequence to anyone but its proprietors; and so none exempt from compulsion to serve a planned public interest.[16]

Tugwell admitted that New Deal advocates wanted rapid change but that they had to conform to constitutional restraints.

> Organization for these purposes was very inefficient because they were not acknowledged intentions. Much of the reluctance stemmed from the constantly reiterated contention that what was being done was in pursuit of the aims of the Constitution of 1787, when in fact the New Deal actions contravened those aims.[17]

To achieve rapid change, New Deal advocates redefined the Constitution without amending it. Supreme Court Justice Felix Frankfurter, for example, said that words in the Constitution are "so restricted by their intrinsic meaning or by their history or by tradition or by prior decisions that they leave the individual justice free, if indeed they do not compel him, to gather meaning not from the Constitution but from reading life."[18] Justice Oliver Wendell Holmes echoed Frankfurter's belief: "When we are dealing with words that also are a constituent act, like the Constitution of the United States, we must realize that they have called into life a being the development of which could not have been foreseen by the most gifted of begetters."[19]

By redefining words and terms in the Constitution, the New Deal increased the power of the national government and advanced more rapid economic, political, and social change. In 1936 the Supreme Court changed the meaning of "general welfare" (Article I, Section 8) by declaring that Congress no longer had to limit appropriations to the purposes spelled out in the Constitution. The Court said in *U.S. v. Butler:* "The power of Congress to authorize expenditure of public moneys for public purposes is not limited by the direct grants of legislative power found in the Constitution." This broadening of the meaning of "general welfare" enabled the national government to extend its power over many more areas of American life. In 1937 the Supreme Court (in *NLRB [National Labor Relations Board] v. Jones and Laughlin*) expanded "interstate commerce" (Article I, Section 8) to include intrastate commerce if it substantially affects interstate commerce. By blurring the distinction between interstate and intrastate commerce, this decision allowed the national government to encroach upon powers and public policies historically established by the states. In 1942 the Supreme Court again extended the meaning of "interstate commerce" (Article I, Section 8), this time to allow the national government to regulate products even if the producer did not intend to sell them. According to the Court's decision in *Wickard v. Filburn,* if a producer keeps a product off the market, other producers must grow, raise, or manufacture substitute products. More recently, the national government has used the Fourteenth Amendment clauses "equal protection of the laws" and "due process of law" to increase its regulatory authority over education and criminal law. For well over a century, the states had retained control over these areas.

Judicial action to redefine and reinterpret the Constitution rather than amend it vacated the traditional relationships between the national and state governments and violated the intentions of the Founders. James Madison stated in the *Federalist Papers* that:

> The powers delegated by the proposed Constitution to the federal government are few and defined. The former will be exercised principally on external objects, as war, peace, negotiation, and foreign commerce, with which last the power of taxation will, for the most part, be connected. The powers reserved to the several states will extend to all the objects which, in the ordinary course of affairs, concern the lives, liberties, and properties cf the people and the internal order, improvement, and prosperity of the state.[20]

The national government's expanded powers have broken the

Founders' mold for federal-state relations. Architects of these changes did not trust state and local governments either to do what they wanted or to do it as fast as they wanted. Undergirding the bold national programs of the New Deal, the Fair Deal, the New Frontier, and the Great Society was an implicit moral impulse. Presidents Roosevelt, Truman, Kennedy, and Johnson wanted to expand the national government's regulatory power in American society to achieve their moral vision of equality.

Harvard University political scientist Harvey Mansfield points out the repercussions of that moral vision: "A society of natural equals . . . needs government of unlimited scope, that is, an enormous inequality of political power, in order to protect its equality."[21] The Founders believed in both liberty and equality but emphasized liberty much more. As equality rose in importance, beginning with the Civil War and continuing through the social and economic reforms of the twentieth century, the national government's power greatly increased. It became the big umpire, the moral arbiter of disputes about equality in America.

In the 1960s, leaders such as Senator Barry Goldwater and then-governor Ronald Reagan arose to challenge this expansion of power and to restore the traditional understanding of American government and its purpose. They called for reduced national government power, restored state and local government power, renewed emphasis on personal responsibility and individual liberty, and decreased emphasis on personal rights and individual equality.

RELIGION AND THE MORAL KALEIDOSCOPE

From the schoolhouse to the White House, religion sharply seasons American politics. Religious differences on such issues as abortion and prayer in the public schools ignite political controversies, forcing presidential candidates and presidents to tiptoe through moral land mines to gain election and keep popular favor. For example, Presidents Jimmy Carter and Bill Clinton stated their personal opposition to abortion but did not press their position on the Democratic Party, where support for abortion is high. President George Bush and presidential candidate Bob Dole modified their religious positions to appeal to religious conservatives. George Bush switched from pro-abortion to anti-abortion, and Bob

Dole left a liberal United Methodist Church, ironically the same one that Clinton began attending. Finding himself uncomfortable in conservative Southern Baptist circles, Clinton attended his wife's church, Foundry United Methodist. Republican candidates for the 2000 presidential nomination positioned themselves to avoid the wrath of religious conservatives in the party.

Presidents and presidential candidates also weave together personal faith and politics. Carter and Reagan accepted the "born again" label. In 1988 two ministers were candidates: the Reverend Jesse Jackson campaigned for the Democratic Party's nomination, while the Reverend Pat Robertson, founder of a Christian television network and university, did the same in the Republican Party. Roman Catholic Cardinal O'Connor sternly rebuked two ranking Democrats, 1984 vice presidential nominee Geraldine Ferraro and 1988 national convention keynote speaker Mario Cuomo, for failing to oppose abortion. In 1992 a promotional video at the Democratic National Convention showed Bill Clinton as a young boy with Bible in hand at a Southern Baptist church.

The issues are real. The emotions are intense. The solutions are problematic. From the schoolhouse to the White House, religious interests play for high stakes. They influence American politics, but politicians also move them as pawns on the political chessboard. From any perspective, however, religion no longer plays its original role in American politics.

Creation of the Christian Consensus

Layers of dark dust now cover Roman Catholic Alexis de Tocqueville's conclusion in 1831 about religion's original role in the United States.

It was religion that gave birth to the English colonies in America. One must never forget that. In the United States religion is mingled with the national customs and all those feelings which the word evokes. For that reason it has peculiar power.... Christianity has kept a strong hold over the minds of Americans, and ... its power is not just that of a philosophy which has been examined and accepted, but that of a religion believed in without discussion. ... Christianity itself is an established and irresistible fact which seeks not to attack or defend.[22]

Sixty years later, in 1892, the U.S. Supreme Court echoed Tocqueville's conclusion in a unanimous decision, *Church of the Holy Trinity v. United States*. The Court held that:

> Our laws and our institutions must necessarily be based upon and embody the teachings of the Redeemer of mankind. It is impossible that it should be otherwise; and in this sense and to this extent our civilization and our institutions are emphatically Christian. . . . This is a religious people. This is historically true. From the discovery of this continent to the present hour, there is a single voice making this affirmation. . . . [W]e find everywhere a clear recognition of the same truth [that] . . . this is a Christian nation.

Tocqueville's analysis in 1841 and the U.S. Supreme Court's decision in 1892, though now long forgotten, reveal several conclusions about the once dominant impact of Christianity on American life. First, Christianity greatly influenced America's moral standards, education, culture, and society. Second, the principles and structures of American government bore the indelible marks of Christian influence. Third, Christianity set an absolute standard, separate from the democratic majority, for judging the actions of government and the behavior of individuals. Fourth, Christianity emphasized the personal responsibility of the individual. America's widely acclaimed discoverer, Christopher Columbus, put a personal touch on this legacy when he wrote:

> It was the Lord who put into my mind . . . the fact that it would be possible to sail from here to the Indies. . . . I am the most unworthy sinner, but I have cried out to the Lord of grace and mercy, and they have covered me completely. . . . [N]ot one should fear to undertake any task in the name of the Saviour, if it is just and if the intention is purely for His holy service.[23]

Largely ignored in modern scholarship and textbook writing, this telling story of America's religious heritage contrasts starkly with religion in America today.[24] Religious changes have sharply altered the view through America's moral kaleidoscope. No one could imagine leaders and documents today speaking with clarity and force that they did in colonial and early American life.

During the 1600s King James I (1606) dedicated Virginia's founding in its charter with these words: "to the glory of his divine Majesty, in propagating the Christian religion to such people as yet live in ignorance of the true knowledge and worship of God." Virginia's Second Charter (1609) says that "the principal effect which we can expect or desire of this action is the conversion and reduction of the people in those parts unto the true worship of God and the Christian religion." The Mayflower Compact (1620) records this purpose: "to the glory of God and the advancement of the Christian faith." In its First Charter (1629), Massachusetts's stated purpose was that its citizens "maie wynn and incite the Natives of County to the Knowledg and Obedience of the onlie true God and Savior of Mankinde, and the Christian Fayth." Citizens of Exeter, New Hampshire (1629), organized with these words: "In the name of Christ and in the sight of God, [we] combine ourselves together to erect and set up among us such government as shall be, to our best discerning, agreeable to the will of God." Harvard College (1636), founded to train ministers of the gospel, stipulated in its rules and precepts for students, "Everyone shall consider the main end of his life and studies to know God and Jesus Christ, which is eternal life." The people of Connecticut (1638) organized "into Combination and Confederation togather to mayntayne and presearve the liberty and purity of the Gospell of our Lord Jesus, which we now professe."

Residents of New Haven, Connecticut (1644), specified in their charter "that the judicial laws of God, as they were delivered by Moses . . . be a rule to all the courts in this jurisdiction." The Maryland Toleration Act (1649) declared, "No person or persons whatsoever within this province . . . professing to believe in Jesus Christ shall . . . henceforth be any ways troubled, molested (or disapproved of) . . . in respect of his or her religion nor in the free exercise thereof." The Great Law of Pennsylvania (1689) proclaimed, "Whereas the glory of Almighty God and the good of mankind is the reason and the end of government . . . therefore government itself is a venerable ordinance of God."

During the 1700s, a similar pattern emerged. Philadelphia's Liberty Bell (1752) had inscribed thereon the words of Leviticus 25:10: "Proclaim liberty through all the land and to all the inhabitants thereof." Meeting in Philadelphia (1774), the Continental Congress authorized payments to chaplains to open their sessions with prayer. Members of Congress (1776) set aside a day of fasting and prayer that they might "by sincere repentance and amendment of life, appease God's righteous displeasure, and through the merits and mediation of Jesus Christ, obtain His pardon and forgiveness." The Virginia Bill of Rights (1776) stated: "It is the mutual duty of all to practice Christian forbearance, love and dignity towards each other." Pennsylvania's legislators took this oath of office (1776): "I do believe in one God, the creator and governor of the universe, the rewarder of the good and the punisher of the wicked. And I do acknowledge the Scriptures of the Old and New Testament to be given by Divine inspiration." Delaware's legislators pledged in their oath (1776): "I do profess faith in God the Father, and in Jesus Christ His only Son, and in the Holy Ghost, one God, blessed for evermore; and I do acknowledge the holy scriptures of the Old and New Testament to be given by divine inspiration." Congress authorized the purchase of twenty thousand Bibles (1777) because the domestic supply was short and also provided for army chaplains. Congress (1782) recommended to the people "the Holy Bible as printed by Robert Aiken of Philadelphia" as "a neat edition of the Holy Scriptures for the use of schools." The Virginia Statute of Religious Liberty (1786) proclaimed that "Almighty God hath created the mind free; that all attempts to influence it by temporal punishments or burdens, or by civil incapacitations . . . are a departure from the plan of the Holy Author of our religion." The Northwest Ordinance (1787) stated, "Religion, morality, and knowledge being necessary to good government and the happiness of mankind, schools and the means of education shall be forever encouraged." James Madison wrote in the *Federalist Papers* (1788), "We have staked the future . . . upon the capacity of each and all of us to govern ourselves, to sustain ourselves, according to the Ten Commandments of God."

Evidence of this pattern continued during the 1800s, although contrary points of view became more evident, as we shall see later. John Quincy Adams illustrated the historical pattern (1821) when he said: "The highest glory of the American Revolution was this: it connected, in one indissoluble bond, the principles of civil government with the principles of Christianity. . . . From the day of the Declaration . . . they [the American people] were bound by the laws of God, which they all, and by the laws of the Gospel, which they nearly all, acknowledged as the rules of their conduct."

Noah Webster's first dictionary (1828) contained many biblical definitions, and he subsequently wrote that "the religion which has introduced civil liberty, is the religion of Christ and his apostles . . . this is genuine Christianity, and to this we owe our free constitutions of government . . . the moral principles and precepts contained in the Scriptures ought to form the basis of all of our civil constitutions and laws." *McGuffey's Reader* (1836), which sold 122 million copies between 1836 and 1920, contained this foreword to the first edition: "The Christian religion is the religion of our country. From it are derived our prevalent notions of the Character of God, the great moral governor of the universe. On its doctrines are founded the peculiarities of our free institutions."

Alexis de Tocqueville wrote in *Democracy in America* (1841), "In the United States of America the sovereign authority is religious." He also concluded that "there is no country in the world in which the Christian religion retains a greater influence over the souls of men than in America." Supreme Court justice Joseph Story stated in his *Commentaries on the Constitution of the United States* (1851):

> Probably at the time of the adoption of the Constitution, and of the first amendment to it . . . the general if not the universal sentiment in America was that Christianity ought to receive encouragement by the state so far as was not incompatible with the private rights of conscience and the freedom of religious worship. Any attempt to level all religions, and to make it a matter of state policy to hold all in utter indifference, would have created universal disapprobation, if not universal indignation.

Acknowledging Puritanism as the fountainhead for much of the pattern that emerged from early colonial times into the 1900s, Harvard University historian Samuel Eliot Morison said in *The Oxford History of the American People:*

> Puritanism was a cutting edge which hewed liberty, democracy, humanitarianism, and universal education out of the black forest of feudal Europe and the American wilderness. Puritan doctrine taught each person to consider himself a significant if sinful unit to whom God had given a particular place and duty, and that he must help his fellow men. Puritanism, therefore, is an American heritage to be grateful for and not to be sneered at because it required everyone to attend divine worship and maintained a strict code of ethics.[25]

A Jewish rabbi, Joshua O. Haberman, concurs, but offers a different emphasis. The former senior rabbi of the Washington Hebrew Congregation of Reformed Judaism and visiting professor at Washington Theological Union, Rabbi Haberman believes America's religious heritage is a safeguard against totalitarianism:

> The suspension of the Bible's moral "barriers" has made possible all the atrocities of Hitler, Stalin and other totalitarian rules. The veneration of the Scriptures as supreme law, superior to the laws of kings, potentates, or magistrates,

was the germ of the all-important political philosophy—the very heart of our democracy—which recognizes "a government of laws and not of men." The Bible gave our nation its moral vision. And today, America's Bible belt is our safety belt, the enduring guarantee of fundamental rights and freedoms.[26]

Erosion of the Christian Consensus

Although Christianity remained dominant in America until the mid-twentieth century, challenges emerged, beginning early in American history. These challenges gradually escalated until they eclipsed the Christian consensus, moving America into a post-Christian era as the new millennium approached. In 1801 Yale University President Timothy Dwight foresaw the looming conflict.

> You must take your side. There can be no halting between two opinions. . . . Between them and you there is, there can be, no natural, real, or lasting harmony. . . . Will you imbibe their principles? Will you copy their practices? Will you teach your children, that death is an eternal sleep; that the end sanctifies the means? that moral obligation is a dream? Religion a farce? . . . will you burn your bibles? Will you crucify anew your Redeemer? Will you deny your God?
>
> COME out, therefore, from among them, and be ye separate, saith the Lord, and touch not the unclean thing; and I will receive you, and will be a father to you: And ye shall be my sons and daughters, saith the Lord Almighty.[27]

In inaugural addresses and Thanksgiving Day proclamations, presidents shifted their emphasis. Nowhere is this more evident than in the opening lines of two presidential Thanksgiving Day proclamations. Until Franklin Roosevelt's presidency, all presidents followed George Washington's emphasis on the providence and grace of God. Roosevelt began a new emphasis on the works of mankind. In his opening lines, George Washington said: "Whereas it is the duty of all nations to acknowledge the providence of Almighty God, to obey His will, to be grateful for His benefits, and humbly to implore His protection and favor . . ."[28] Roosevelt said:

> In traversing a period of national stress our country has been knit together in a closer fellowship of mutual interest and common purpose. We can well be grateful that more and more of our people understand and seek the greater

good of the greater number. We can be grateful that selfish purpose of personal gain, at our neighbor's loss, less strongly asserts itself. We can be grateful that peace at home is strengthened by a growing willingness to common counsel. We can be grateful that our peace with other nations continues through recognition of our own peaceful purpose.[29]

Roosevelt's proclamation reflected many emerging challenges to the historic Christian consensus. The Christian consensus did not collapse through revolution overnight, but rather through evolution over time. First, Deists and Unitarians challenged traditional Christian thinking during the founding era, particularly on such doctrines as the divine inspiration of the Bible and the deity and virgin birth of Jesus Christ. They did, however, agree on the importance of individual liberty and personal responsibility. Benjamin Franklin and Thomas Jefferson were the best known adherents of Deism. Second, transcendentalism, springing up in the mid-nineteenth century, taught that everyone has a spark of divinity within and that no one is born into sin. Various utopian faiths also emerged then, desiring to establish perfect communities and emphasizing, of course, the perfectibility of mankind. Third, social gospel advocates surfaced around the turn of the twentieth century to advocate creating the kingdom of God on earth through the lever of governmental social action. The Methodist Social Creed of 1908, an early example of social gospel theology, contained seeds that germinated during the New Deal. Fourth, after the social gospel came neo-orthodoxy with its redefinition of traditional Christian words and doctrines, including sin, Heaven, Hell, righteousness, and salvation. These changes focused more on temporal and earthly concerns and less on eternal and heavenly matters. Social gospel and neo-orthodox forces combined to capture control of historically conservative Christian institutions and denominations. For example, they took control of Princeton Seminary and the northern Presbyterian denomination during the 1920s. Fifth, secular humanism came along to argue that humans are capable of self-fulfillment without divine help. Lamenting the rise of humanism, Aleksandr Solzhenitsyn said in his 1978 Harvard University commencement address: "The humanistic way of thinking . . . started Western civilization on the dangerous trend of worshipping man and his material needs."[30]

Paralleling these challenges were changes in the composition of America. Large numbers of newly arriving Jewish and Roman Catholic immigrants during the 1800s and early 1900s challenged the dominant orthodoxy of Protestant Christianity.[31] More recently, Muslims have numerically eclipsed Episcopalians.

Religiously, America changed from a homogeneous to a heterogeneous society. The changes challenged long-standing customs and precedents, shaking the foundations of what had been considered America and American. Notable changes occurred during the 1960s when the U.S. Supreme Court either limited or denied historically accepted religious practices in the public schools. For example, the Court forbade school boards and school officials from sanctioning prayer and Bible reading.[32] Implementing Thomas Jefferson's idea that a wall of separation should stand between church and school, religion and government, the Court severely restricted the public practice of religion. John Dunphy, writing in the *Humanist*, put the changes in bold relief: "The [public school] classroom . . . will become an arena of conflict between the old and the new—the rotting corpse of Christianity . . . and the new faith of humanism."[33]

Two interesting political, religious, and social changes have resulted from the decline of mainline Protestantism and the rising power of Judaism and Roman Catholicism. First, to fight for preservation of their values, conservative Protestants have joined with conservative Jews and Roman Catholics in common efforts. Such organizations as the Moral Majority and the Christian Coalition illustrate this cooperation, especially among Catholics and Protestants. Second, the growing strength of the Roman Catholic Church has ushered in a new era, "the Catholic moment" in America. Catholics now constitute the largest force among church bodies in American politics. For example, more Catholics serve in Congress than adherents of any other religious denomination. These two dramatic changes occurred during the last hundred years.

Dissension and the Eroding Christian Consensus

The tensions generated by the emerging beliefs and groups magnify a larger question: Should modern America take religious principles into account? Can or should a divided religious community expect society to take its views seriously?

At one extreme stand humanists, who believe that religion damages American society by keeping people tied to religious faith. At the opposite extreme stand conservative Protestant and Roman Catholic Christians, conservative Jews, and Mormons who believe that a godless society will fall because it has no moral foundation. Between are many points of view. The two sides have different views of America's past, different perceptions of the present, and different visions for the future. They disagree about the nature of God and man and about what government should do and how. In this light, all the individual issues—of education, abortion, sexual practices, clergy in politics, and so on— become rallying points for debate.

Did America begin as a secular state, as some contend, or as a Christian nation, as others argue? Today's scholars usually believe in a secular-state interpretation, offering several arguments. First, the *Federalist Papers,* the fundamental explanation of the government established, contain no references to God or to the Bible. Second, the only person of major significance during the Founding era to refer to the Bible, Thomas Paine, was not a Christian. Third, James Madison and Thomas Jefferson, leading architects of America's founding, generally refrained from invoking the Bible in their writings. Fourth, the U.S. Constitution contains no references to the deity, while the Declaration of Independence contains only a few. Fifth, the Founders emphasized "natural law" rather than "divine law," believing that man has rights just because he is man and not because he is a creature of God.

Christian-nation advocates set forth their counterarguments. First, they argue, John Jay, one of the three authors of the *Federalist Papers*, was an ardent Christian, and other prominent Founders, such as James Madison, received strongly Christian theological educations that influenced their perception of the role of government. Second, leading deists such as Thomas Jefferson and Benjamin Franklin recognized and responded to the dominant Christian consensus of the Founding. Third, the term "law of nature," used by Jefferson in the Declaration of Independence, came from Blackstone's *Commentaries,* where the term clearly refers to the laws of God and is synonymous with "divine law." Fourth, today's scholars understandably offer a secular-state explanation, because that is the dominant view of our day, while scholars in the last century usually upheld the Christian-nation view, because that was the received wisdom of their day.

Some try to steer a middle course through the rocky shoals of these two views. One group contends that the Declaration of Independence and the U.S. Constitution represent, respectively, the secular-state and Christian-nation viewpoints. Deists, such as Thomas Jefferson, Samuel Adams, and Thomas Paine, had more influence over the Declaration of Independence, while almost every delegate to the Constitutional Convention was a Christian. Another group argues the reverse, pointing out that the Declaration of Independence contains several references to the deity while the Constitution contains none.

The issue is crucial. If secular-state adherents are right, the United States continues to give undue deference to Christianity. If Christian-nation advocates are right, then America has substantially removed the Christian underpinnings of its founding.

What standards should govern public policy decisions, and how should American democratic institutions assess their results? Should a democratic government respond solely to the will of the people, or should it look to an external reference point? These questions are much in dispute. If there is an external reference point, who defines and applies it? In the name of divinity, many argue that democracy should have ethical and moral measurements of divine origin as its ultimate guide for decision-making and judgment. Both the Christian Coalition and the National Council of Churches claim to know what those ethical and moral principles are, but they come up with different answers. Earlier in America's history, consensus came more easily.

Today many groups compete to define what is moral. Religion, once the moral glue of American society, now is a divided and divisive force in politics and government. Religious interests compete on the same political terrain with nonreligious interests in trying to define American morality and public policy. Religion occupies a role no more exalted than that of any other interest in the secularized politics of America's pluralistic democracy.

In the nineteenth century, Alexis de Tocqueville could write of America: "In the United States religion exercises little influence upon the laws and upon the details of public opinion, but it directs the customs of the community and by regulating domestic life, it regulates the state."[34] Religious groups no longer control the customs of the community, so they fight today to influence the laws. Presidents and presidential candidates face the whiplash of religious forces trying to influence them and to woo their support. Religion sounds not a clarion call of moral certainty but rather a cacophony of moral inconsistency.

IDEOLOGY AND THE MORAL KALEIDOSCOPE

Jesse Jackson and Jesse Helms, Ted Kennedy and Pat Robertson, Dick Gephardt and Newt Gingrich support the foundational principles and organizational structures of American government contained in the U.S. Constitution, but they disagree on their visions for America. They work under the same government to pursue sharply contrasting visions. Loosely, we call these differing visions conservatism and liberalism, or the Right and the Left.

Most Americans place themselves in the center, however, neither to the right nor to the left. But since the 1950s, the center has lost some of its dominance. Many Americans have shifted to the right or to the left, but especially to the right. Barry Goldwater in 1964 and then Ronald Reagan in 1980 and 1984 offered conservative visions for America that contrasted sharply with the liberal visions of Lyndon Johnson, Jimmy Carter, and Walter Mondale in 1984. From 1964 to 1980 the liberal vision lost substantial appeal in America, making way for the success of Ronald Reagan's conservative vision. During that same period, contrasts between the Right and the Left have become sharper.

These contrasting ideologies (see table 2.1) and their different visions for America make presidential leadership more difficult. As the ideological pattern of the moral kaleidoscope shifts, presidents cannot rely as much on centrist America to govern and must appeal to, and compromise with, sharply contrasting ideological values. The differences are not absolute, but represent the directions and inclinations of conservative and liberal thought. Table 2.1 indicates that conservatives are more likely than liberals (1) to hold orthodox and traditional religious views; (2) have less faith in the goodness, reason, and perfectibility of mankind; (3) prefer state and local government to the national government; (4) believe nationalism rather than internationalism should govern American foreign policy; (5) emphasize personal responsibility rather than personal rights; (6) trust free markets or capitalism in economic policy; and (7) desire gradual and incremental change economically, politically, religiously, and socially.

Within both conservatism and liberalism are sharp contrasts, further altering America's moral kaleidoscope. Economic conservatives usually want to reduce the size and scope of government and to implement free-market economics. Typically religious conservatives want to use, even enlarge, government to strengthen morality by abolishing abortion and banning

TABLE 2.1

CONSERVATISM AND LIBERALISM: VALUES AND VISIONS EMPHASIZED

	LIBERAL	CONSERVATIVE
GOVERNMENT		
Primary focus	Individual	Community
Preferred government	National	State and local
Direction of sentiment	Internationalist	Nationalist
Method of influence	Direct	Indirect
Accountability	To man	To God
Rate/type of change	Faster/utopian	Slower/ prescriptive
Relative importance	Equality	Liberty
Justice achieved by	Governmental reform	Spiritual regeneration
ECONOMICS		
Source of authority	Central government	Free markets
Growth sector	Public	Private
Government function	Regulate	Foster competition
Tendency	Socialism	Capitalism
CULTURE AND RELIGION		
Ultimate source of knowledge	Reason	Nature/Bible
Biblical interpretation	More symbolic	More literal
Moral standards	Relative/situational	Absolute/ orthodox
Relative emphasis	Man	God
Moral emphasis	Social	Personal
Relative importance to man	Rights	Responsibilities
Origin of evil	Unjust society	Original sin

homosexuality. Economic and religious conservatives play tug-of-war for control of the Republican Party's vision for America. When seasoned with too much economic conservatism, the Republican Party subjects itself to attacks that it lacks compassion for the downtrodden. Too much seasoning by religious conservatives gives the party the image of self-righteous zealots. Republican presidential candidates must unite the party's conservative base to win the nomination, while Democratic candidates must unite the party's liberal base. Both must then move to the center to win the election. In 1980 and 1984 Ronald Reagan united the various strands of conservative thought and successfully appealed to the center of the American electorate. George Bush accomplished that feat in 1988 but failed in 1992. Bill Clinton's campaigns united liberals behind him and then appealed to the center. Clinton also borrowed such popular conservative ideas as welfare reform to increase his political appeal.

In short, America's moral kaleidoscope displays sharply contrasting ideological visions. Choosing the visions most appealing to the public is a key to successful presidential leadership.

LANGUAGE AND THE MORAL KALEIDOSCOPE

Language slides down a slippery slope in democracies. Public opinion and political realities combine to undermine the certainty of language. Over time, words lose consistent and coherent meaning, no longer serving as dependable points of reference or anchors of stability. Allan Bloom put it this way in *The Closing of the American Mind*: "In politics, in entertainment, in religion, everywhere, we find the language connected with Nietzsche's value revolution, a language necessitated by a new perspective on the things of most concern to us. Words such as 'charisma,' 'life-style,' 'commitment,' 'identity' and many others, all of which can easily be traced to Nietzsche, are now practically American slang."[35] Examining the dynamics of public opinion and political reality in the mid-nineteenth century, Tocqueville pointed out that the redefinition of words

is simple, quick, and easy. No learning is needed to make use of it, and ignorance itself can make it easier. But it involves great dangers for the language. In thus giving a double meaning to one word, democratic peoples often make both the old and the new signification ambiguous. A writer begins by the slight deflection of a known expression from its original meaning and he adapts it, thus modified, as best he can for his purpose. A second writer twists its meaning in a different direction. Then comes a third, taking it off down a new track. Then, since there is no accepted judge, no permanent court to decide the meaning of a word, the phrase is left to wander free.

. . . . [I]t is not at all tyrannical, but it hinders, restrains, enervates, stifles, and stultifies so much that in the end each nation is no more than a flock of timid and hardworking animals with the government as its shepherd.[36]

In 1992 Vice President Dan Quayle introduced "family values" as a new term in political debate. Defining family as historically understood—father, mother, and children living together in a home—he argued that the subversion of the traditional family undermines society and its stability. Reflecting on the Los Angeles riots that year, Quayle stated:

In a nutshell: I believe the lawless social anarchy which we saw is directly related to the breakdown of family structure, personal responsibility and social order in too many areas of our society. . . . [M]arriage is a moral issue that requires cultural consensus, and the use of social sanctions. Bearing babies irresponsibly is, simply, wrong. Failing to support children one has fathered is wrong. We must be unequivocal about this. It doesn't help matters when prime time TV has Murphy Brown—a character who supposedly epitomizes today's intelligent, highly paid, professional woman—mocking the importance of fathers, by bearing a child alone, and calling it just another "lifestyle choice."[37]

In a later speech, Quayle said:

Americans try to raise their children to understand right and wrong, only to be told that every so-called "lifestyle alternative" is morally equivalent. That is wrong. The gap between us and our opponents is a cultural divide. It is not just a difference between conservative and liberal. It is a difference between fighting for what is right and refusing to see what is wrong.[38]

Democrats, realizing the advantage this gave Republicans, strenuously objected to their use of the term "family values." Candidate Clinton said:

I'm fed up with politicians in Washington lecturing Americans about "family values." Our families have values. Our government doesn't. I want an America where "family values" live in our actions, not just in our speeches. An America that includes every family. Every traditional family and every extended family. Every two-income family and every single-parent family, and every foster family.[39]

Rather than uphold the traditionally accepted definition of family, Clinton not only broadened the definition but also failed to admit a relationship between the breakdown of the family and social chaos. Of course, acceptance of variant definitions of the traditional family represents votes. Four years later, Democrats embraced, but redefined, "family values." Mrs. Clinton showcased their new definition at the 1996 Democratic National Convention.

For Bill and me, there has been no experience more challenging, more rewarding and more humbling than raising our daughter. And we have learned that to raise a happy, healthy, and hopeful child, it takes a family. It takes teachers. It takes clergy. It takes business people. It takes community leaders. It takes those who protect our health and safety. It takes all of us. Yes, it takes a village. And it takes a president. It takes a president who believes not only in the potential of his own child, but of all children, who believes not only in the strength of his own family, but of the American family; who believes not only in the promise of each of us as individuals, but in our promise together as a nation. It takes a president who not only holds these beliefs, but acts on them. It takes Bill Clinton.[40]

Mrs. Clinton and the 1996 Democratic platform enlarged the traditionally understood definition of the family and called for new and expanded national government programs for the newly defined family.

Confucius said: "When words lose their meaning, peoples lose their liberty." The gradual redefinition of moral words and terms is like taking down the sails and removing the rudder and compass of a boat. There remains no way to steer the boat in the right direction. In these circumstances, morality becomes a matter of political assertion and will, not of accepted definitions and standards.

Democracy by its very nature subverts language and its moral content. As words and terms become empty vessels void of moral content, presidents and presidential candidates define and redefine words and terms to suit their political purposes. The person with the broadest and most encompassing definition usually wins, because that is where the votes are. Opposing family values or any other broad and encompassing term becomes politically untenable.

CONCLUSION

Politics, religion, ideology, and language have changed the view through America's moral kaleidoscope. Not only does it now reflect more divergent and divisive ideas about morality, but it also represents less historically acceptable moral content. The foundation of presidential leadership now rests on moral quicksand rather than solid rock.

3

ORIGINS OF MORAL CONFLICT IN THE MODERN ERA

What is past is prologue.
—Inscription, National Archives, Washington, D.C

Americans often see early presidents through rose-tinted glasses. First, fables, legends, and myths place presidents on pedestals above the reach of reality. Tarnishing such presidential icons as Washington, the father of our country, and Lincoln, the Great Emancipator, who preserved the Union, usually rests in the realm of the impossible or improbable. People seem to like the stuff of legend. Second, lack of historical literacy also contributes to misunderstanding of early American presidents. Greater familiarity with recent presidents means Americans see more of both their good and their bad sides. Early presidents are not as easily analyzed. Third, fables, myths, and legends have not yet had time to develop for contemporary presidents. Only after decades did Washington and Lincoln become fixed points in the galaxy of folklore. Fourth, the mass media did not exist early in American history. Without radio, television, and mass-market magazines, early Americans lacked instant insights into presidential character and conduct. The mass media, largely a product of the post-1930s period, give Americans greater opportunity to know more about modern presidents. Small wonder, then, that moral questions about presidents now appear to occur more frequently.

However, immoral, corrupt, incompetent, arrogant, and scandalous presidents sometimes occupied the White House before the modern era. Even some of the revered Founding Fathers cast ominous moral shadows over their presidencies. Dark allegations of moral scandal dot presidential history: Thomas Jefferson's black mistress, Andrew Jackson's adultery,

Andrew Johnson's drinking, Grover Cleveland's illegitimate son, and Warren Harding's alleged affairs. Americans of the nineteenth and early twentieth centuries heard tales of moral scandal. Some of the tales were false; some, questionable; and some, true.

If history serves as the best predictor of the future, then it is important to understand the past. Did moral issues and scandals before the modern era differ from those of the contemporary period? Did they occur less frequently? Have changing moral standards altered the number and type of scandals? Or does history speak with the same tone regardless of the era? To place contemporary moral scandals in context, these and other questions bear examination. A comprehensive treatment is beyond the scope of this book; the following discussion offers an illustrative cross section.

THE PRESIDENTIAL FOUNDING FATHERS, 1789–1824

Five Founding Fathers served as president: George Washington, John Adams, Thomas Jefferson, James Madison, and James Monroe. In type and tone, their scandals foreshadowed today's, but they did not have the same impact. Generally, their public reputations overshadowed their private reputations, thereby limiting the damage of allegations about personal scandals.

George Washington, 1789–1797

George Washington formed the presidency's moral mold. A "dominating, fair, and brilliant man" whom no other could rival, he remains America's greatest symbol of moral integrity in politics. But even he could not escape gossip, potential scandal, and moral questioning. Although modern presidents would beg to differ, Washington claimed that the press abused him more "than any man in history."[1]

Rumors swirled around Washington that he had illegitimate children.[2] Even his fellow Founding Fathers spread jealous rumors against him. John Adams considered Washington just an ordinary man with very little intellect.[3] Others intimated that Washington was "practically illiterate," suggesting he could not even count his change for a purchase.[4] Since public reputations mattered more in those days than private reputations, personal moral problems had only minimal effect on politics.[5]

Documentary filmmaker Ken Burns suggests that Washington may have "fudged his Revolutionary War expenses . . . [which today] would undoubtedly bring a special prosecutor and constant press attention."[6] Little evidence, however, supports the alleged war-expenses scandal. If Washington had a few moral slips, he definitely made up for them with majestic acts of patriotism by refusing absolute power and providing stability in our first eight years under the Constitution.

John Adams, 1797–1801

John Adams's presidency echoes the theme that the presidential Founding Fathers faced greater scrutiny of their public reputations than of their private problems. Adams confronted allegations that he had connections with the British, and the XYZ affair haunted him as he faced war with France. The press also pummeled him.

The American people feared British control of the government, so Adams's Federalist views aroused rumors of the administration's allegiance with the mother country. Apparently Adams had no ties with Great Britain, but the United States Senate found North Carolina Senator William Blount guilty of conspiring with the British on the issue of Spanish Florida.[7] The Senate's action in the Blount case led to scrutiny of the entire government.

Facing a possible war with France, Adams built up the armed forces while attempting to negotiate with the French. In the XYZ affair, French prime minister Talleyrand allegedly demanded $250,000 and a $10 million loan to prevent war. Adams refused the attempted extortion.

Adams demonstrated moral courage and public integrity by firmly holding to his personal beliefs despite pressures from his own Federalist Party. He refused to cave in to those who wanted war with France, and his personal political philosophy steered a separate course from both Jefferson's common-man philosophy and the Federalists' elitist ideas.[8]

Because of his views, allegations in the press abounded. Benjamin Bache, otherwise known as "Satan" by Abigail Adams, accused Adams of nepotism in naming his son, John Quincy Adams, as minister to Prussia. This and many other attacks, though frequently false, made life uncomfortable for Adams.

Without the limitation of libel laws and with First Amendment protection, the press relentlessly pursued Adams. In response, Abigail Adams pushed the president to approve legislation limiting the First Amendment. When Congress passed the Alien and Sedition Act, which severely restricted criticism of government officials, Adams signed it. Containing fines of up to $2,000 and imprisonment of up to two years upon conviction of seditious acts, as well as allowing the deportation of foreigners deemed a threat to the United States, the Alien and Sedition Act prompted a public outcry.[9]

Shortly after passage of the Alien and Sedition Act in 1798, a court convicted and imprisoned Bache. Adams viewed his actions as a proper defense of his family, not as an infringement upon constitutional liberties. The public differed, and the government scrapped the Alien and Sedition Act.

John Adams found himself trapped in a vise between competing forces: (1) constitutional and personal, and (2) his own dying Federalist Party and the emerging party of his successor. On balance, conflicting pressures constrained this president, reducing the impact of his personal integrity and patriotism.

Thomas Jefferson, 1801–1809

Advocacy of states' rights and the common man—ideas that he inconsistently defended—paved Thomas Jefferson's path to the presidency. There he faced personal and political moral issues. His personal life did not conform with the moral standards of his time, and he also faced difficult decisions about national expansion and foreign policy.

Although serious political scandals hardly dented Jefferson's reputation, they scraped around the edges. Historians suggest that Jefferson's Democratic-Republican Party "manipulated the methods of selecting electors in Virginia and Pennsylvania and . . . enjoyed the skill of Aaron Burr's ward-heeling in New York City."[10] Jefferson probably played no part in those scandals, but they occurred on his watch.

Jefferson said slavery is "contrary to the rights of man," but he defended slavery in the South and in the territory acquired in the Louisiana Purchase.[11] However, Jefferson encouraged passage of laws prohibiting the slave trade from coming into the United States.

Fearing his Federalist Party rival, Alexander Hamilton, Jefferson hired Phillip F. Calendar to print bad stories about him.[12] Jefferson, the esteemed gentleman from Monticello, stooped to throwing political mud in response to the Federalists' mudslinging at him. His political actions did not always measure up to his exalted place on the shelf of presidential icons.

For example, Jefferson's personal moral scandals sometimes dwarfed his political problems. Calendar finally turned against Jefferson, writing scandalous information about his former boss.[13] Calendar claimed that Jefferson had a slave mistress by the name of Sally Hemings, an allegation ostensibly verified in 1998 by DNA tests. Calendar also wrote that Jefferson liked to "dabble to some extent in African merchandise." According to contemporary writer Gail Collins, Calendar's evidence appeared reliable. Other prominent Americans and visitors from Europe commented that some of Jefferson's slaves looked remarkably similar to their master.[14] Another scandal involved large amounts of personal debt.[15] Under today's laws, Jefferson's money troubles might have merited an investigation by an independent counsel.

Writing to his nephew Peter Carr, Jefferson said: "Fix reason firmly in her seat, and call to her tribunal every fact, every opinion. Question with boldness even the existence of a God."[16] Even today, such advice conflicts with what most Americans believe. Many still consider Jefferson's religious views heretical. Ironically, his political party included many orthodox Christians, especially Baptists, who liked Jefferson's views on the separation of church and state.

Among the presidential Founding Fathers, Jefferson set off more moral fireworks than anyone else, just as Bill Clinton has done among the modern presidents. Both are brilliant men whose lives present many enigmas, paradoxes, and ironies. Jefferson, however, retains a high rank on the ladder of presidential greatness, something Clinton is unlikely to manage. Moral scandals exploded in Clinton's face but hardly singed Jefferson.

James Madison, 1809–1817

George Washington recognized James Madison's leadership skill and integrity by personally asking him to lead the Virginia delegation to the Constitutional Convention in Philadelphia. His integrity and skill as a political leader helped produce the final version of the most important document in American history.[17] Madison brought an earnest moral dedication to the convention and to the document's ratification.

Madison, along with John Jay and Alexander Hamilton, wrote the *Federalist Papers,* urging ratification and promising a Bill of Rights. Madison, as a man of uncompromising integrity, kept his word by leading the Congress to propose the first ten amendments to the Constitution. Oddly enough, Madison then retired from politics until passage of the Alien and Sedition Act under John Adams.[18] Wanting to protect individual liberties, he joined Thomas Jefferson's cabinet as secretary of state after the election of 1800.

Madison became Thomas Jefferson's presidential heir in 1808, an election won without campaigning. When Madison first entered the executive office, France under Napoleon and Great Britain were at war, and many "war hawk" congressmen wanted to expand America's borders into Canada. Feeling pressure for war, Madison caved in to a war with Great Britain when negotiations might have prevented it.[19] The Federalists promptly dubbed the War of 1812 "Mr. Madison's War."

After the war, the country enjoyed economic prosperity and westward expansion, and Madison savored high popularity. Madison apparently did not rush into war to gain popularity, but the war benefited him politically and Americans economically.

Although Madison respected both political parties, not unexpectedly he sided with his own, the Democratic-Republicans. He compromised on the Federalist idea of a Bank of the United States, and he imposed higher tariffs on imports. Throughout, his administration appeared remarkably free of corruption and scandal.

As president, Madison wanted the Constitution "strictly interpreted."[20] He vetoed a bill by John C. Calhoun to fund a "perfect system of roads and canals" throughout the nation. Although a national system of roads and canals would help the nation, Madison stood by the words he wrote in the Constitution and left such funding to the states. He did approve a bill sponsored by Calhoun to build a national road, now known as U.S. 40.

Madison opposed slavery more strongly than the other presidential Founding Fathers. He wrote to the Marquis de Lafayette that "the continuance of slavery in America impaired the influence of our political example."[21] Proposing the sale of excess land in the United States to pay for the purchase of all slaves, Madison would have had the freed slaves live in an African colony.[22] He also urged Congress to find some method of ending the practice of slavery and the slave trade.[23]

Hemmed in by the politics of his day, however, Madison did not actively oppose slavery during his presidency nor its spread later in the Missouri Compromise. Thus, Madison joined many others in opposing slavery morally but accommodating it politically. This moral pragmatism defined his career and his success.

James Monroe, 1817–1825

James Madison placed the presidential mantle on James Monroe, making his election a formality, and left the slavery issue on the White House doorstep to greet him, as it would every new president through Reconstruction. Like them, Monroe compromised on this moral issue. He performed well on the foreign policy stage, however, leaving a lasting legacy. Like Madison, Monroe had no obvious moral moles or warts.

James Monroe appeared incapable of corruption. His attorney general, William Wirt, said: "He is a man of soft, polite, and even assiduous attentions. . . . there is often in his manner an inartificial and even an awkward simplicity, which, while it provokes the smile of a more polished person, forces him to the opinion that Mr. Monroe is a man of a most sincere and artless soul."[24] Monroe agreed to the Missouri Compromise with the realization that compromise meant a prevention of distress in the Union. For the same reason, like presidents before him, he did not actively oppose slavery.

Monroe's foreign policy as president helped form national boundaries and protect the United States from European aggression. Monroe, who as Jefferson's secretary of state had negotiated the Louisiana Purchase, as president negotiated the acquisition of Florida and the demilitarization of the boundary with Canada.[25] The Monroe Doctrine helped to establish the United States as a world power and may have prevented wars with its warning to the nations of Europe.[26]

Monroe built the moral foundation of his foreign policy on the goal of making the United States more powerful and prosperous. Serving in an "Era of Good Feeling," he had the opportunity and latitude to pursue his aim. His early political career marked him as a follower of Jefferson and Patrick Henry, waiting in turn for his time to serve. He was not known as a political opportunist. By waiting and then wisely using his time and opportunities, he achieved more than most of his contemporaries.

PRESIDENTS AND THE COMING OF THE CIVIL WAR, 1825–1861

Transition and turbulence define the ten presidents serving between 1825 and 1861. Slavery, the pervasive moral issue of the time, cast a shadow over presidents because they failed to contest its legality. Some would not morally justify slavery, but neither would they politically oppose it. Valuing political peace over political turmoil, they avoided addressing slavery's moral questions. Political pragmatism trumped political principle.

As an entrenched and unquestioned social institution throughout large parts of America, especially the South, slavery was not a moral issue in the minds of many people. By accepting slavery, presidents of the era did not incur their moral wrath. Lacking the willpower to oppose slavery, these presidents postponed its ultimate resolution, the Civil War.

John Quincy Adams, 1825–1829

John Quincy Adams faced personal and political dilemmas similar to his father's. As was the case with his father, the strength of his morals may have precipitated his failures. Descriptions of John Quincy Adams paint him as a stern man bent on perfection. Other politicians referred to him as the "Iron Mask," capable of infecting others with psychic frostbite.[27]

Although stern and cold to many, as a president he worked hard to overcome his political difficulties. Adams rose at four in the morning, read his Bible, and worked a full day.[28] He demanded perfection in himself, those around him, and his nation, but these demands ultimately left him with the feeling that "the great object of my life . . . has failed."[29]

Adams's toughest political problem was the same as his father's: he was a president without a party. He considered himself a representative of the nation, letting his political party take a backseat. Adams seemed to favor whoever could help him become president. In 1824, in one of history's closest presidential elections, Adams beat Andrew Jackson in a race decided by the House of Representatives. Adams received many crucial votes from allies of Henry Clay of Kentucky. He then named Henry Clay secretary of state, prompting press claims of "bargaining and corruption."[30]

Adams also waffled on some important moral issues. While he supported the abolition of slavery, he favored admitting Texas and Florida into the Union as slave states. In another case, Adams abandoned moral principle by recognizing the treaty to send Creek and Cherokee Indians on to the Trail of Tears.[31] He later remarked that "we have done more harm to the Indians since our Revolution than the British and French nations before."[32]

Like John Adams, John Quincy Adams, who was married to a British woman, faced criticism as a loyalist to Great Britain and the monarchy. He incurred Southern wrath when he proposed new tariffs inimical to the South. Southern states' rightists, such as John Randolph of Virginia, called Adams "John the First."[33] On balance, however, Adams was less lenient to the British than many other politicians. In fact, his divorce from the Federalist Party stemmed from his opposition to Great Britain.[34]

During the 1828 election, another moral issue arose when the press reported alleged adultery by Andrew Jackson, Adams's opponent.[35] Adams's supporters exploited the news, which Adams himself did nothing to stop. Some believe these allegations led to Rachel Jackson's premature death. Although Adams did not exploit the stories, he benefited from them. Since some papers falsely referred to Adams as a "pimp, gambler, and spendthrift,"[36] his failure to thwart rumors about Andrew Jackson is understandable, if not justifiable.

Adams's wife, Louisa, believed that the "Adams men were peculiarly harsh and severe with their women. . . . [T]here seems to exist no sympathy, no tenderness for the weakness of the sex."[37] Perhaps this offers an explanation of her own depression. Although Adams's coldness is not the definitive reason for either Rachel Jackson's death or his wife's depression, the two cases show his disregard for personal emotions.

On a lighter note, John Quincy Adams could have faced scandal in the press over his summer swims. Adams' enjoyed waking before dawn and swimming in the buff in the Potomac River. He would walk to the river and swim alone, until once a reporter caught him and forced an interview by holding the president's clothes ransom.[38]

Adams also exacerbated his political and moral difficulties by advocating a stronger central government when that was no longer popular. Whatever the reason for Adams's political and moral troubles, he continued to fight for his political views by returning to the House of Representatives. This move may have momentarily diminished respect for the presidency and possibly for himself. Opinions differ as to whether John Quincy Adams was a moral politician, a moral opportunist, or just a political failure.

Andrew Jackson, 1829–1837

Washington insiders held the Jackson administration in low esteem. Jackson's 1828 campaign reached out to the common man, going over the heads of the Washington establishment. John Quincy Adams's campaign avoided average citizens; instead, Adams held social gatherings in his home and with the Washington elite. By mobilizing a new political base in American politics, Jackson activated new moral forces and changed perceptions of presidential power, igniting a firestorm about what powers a president had and how he could use them.[39]

Jackson's campaign and philosophy of presidential power should have come as no surprise. His career as a military general mirrored his use of presidential power. Jackson, in an attempt to gain political popularity, invaded Spanish Florida without the consent of President James Monroe.[40] A tough man with a military approach to problems, Jackson ordered the hanging of two British subjects for aiding militant Native Americans.

Jackson not only represented the common man but also sometimes acted like his followers, showing toughness and at times a disregard for human life. While dueling with Charles Dickinson over a horse racing debt, after being shot himself, Jackson shot and killed Dickinson.[41]

Jackson had great impact on American government and public policy on such issues as banking, the presidential veto, and the use of the military. He played a dominating role, creating new precedents for presidential action. For example, after he had boldly asserted his veto power, his opponents tagged him as "King Andrew I."[42]

Jackson directly opposed what he considered morally wrong, and when he took a stand, he did not back down. For example, he steadfastly stood by his position on the national bank. Devotion to his beliefs, a part of his moral character, served him well, but other uncompromising presidents, such as John Tyler and Woodrow Wilson, did not enjoy similar success.

On slavery, Jackson had an easier job than other presidents, but still he staked out his position. He hated abolitionists. In a modern-day spin move, Jackson transformed his support of slavery into support for the common man by claiming that the elites wanted to use abolition as a way to end democracy.[43]

Personal scandals hurt Jackson more than political scandals. During the 1828 election, Adams's supporters discovered that Andrew Jackson had lived with his wife, Rachel Robarbs, before her divorce from her first husband was final.[44] Robarbs's first husband had divorced her in 1793 on grounds of adultery. Although the affair was only a dim memory in 1828, publisher Charles Hammond printed the expose to inform Americans of Andrew Jackson's immorality.

Rachel Jackson, who disliked politics, died after suffering two heart attacks after she learned about the scandalous stories. Jackson blamed his political opponents for Rachel's death, declaring that "those vile wretches who slandered her must look to God for mercy."[45] Jackson's close friends realized that Jackson never recovered from Rachel's death, which may have caused Jackson to become more stubborn and uncompromising.

Jackson's campaigns attacked Adams in several ways. For example, Jacksonians accused Adams of gambling away $25,000 in tax money on a billiard table in the White House. In reality, Adams only played billiards to relax after work.[46] Other absurd stories also attacked Adams's personal morality.

After becoming president, in retaliation for the scandal against his wife, Jackson protected the reputation of Peggy Timberlake.[47] Timberlake married Senator John Eaton of Tennessee after her first husband committed suicide. The Washington press labeled the new Mrs. Eaton as a longtime, married mistress of Senator Eaton. Recognizing the similarities between Mrs. Eaton's dilemma and his deceased wife's scandal, Jackson defended her against the ill-will of Washington's social establishment, including members of the Jackson cabinet.

Although other issues, such as the national bank and a state's right to nullify acts of the national government, created serious problems, Jackson's handling of the Eaton episode created a great divide in his cabinet. Jackson promoted Martin Van Buren, who helped him in the Eaton case, and shunned John C. Calhoun, who opposed him. Had this split between Jackson and Calhoun not occurred, Calhoun might have risen to the presidency and prevented civil war. As it was, Calhoun became an architect of the South's position on slavery and its separation from the Union.[48]

Since the Peggy Eaton case lacked sufficient importance to divide the government, Jackson's inability to compromise on it was a moral injustice to the government and the nation. Like all men, Jackson made moral errors in his life and during the presidency, but his decisions and actions are not in the same category as the previous presidents. Perhaps Jackson's errors are more noticeable because he alienated the Washington establishment by bringing a new look to the presidency and American politics.

Martin Van Buren, 1837–1841

Martin Van Buren received the presidency as a gift from Jackson, who appreciated his loyal service. He had helped Jackson in many ways, including his defense of Peggy Eaton. The worst scandals of Van Buren's presidency came during his two presidential campaigns. Despite Van Buren's humility in comparison to Jackson's confidence, he made significant moral decisions.

Van Buren's attitude toward the presidency may have lowered its moral standing. In his inaugural address, he said: "In receiving from the people the sacred trust twice confided to my illustrious predecessor, and which he has discharged . . . . so well, I know that I can not expect to perform the arduous task with equal ability and success."[49] Assuming a "caretaker" role for Jackson instead of asserting his own platform, Van Buren retained Jackson's cabinet.[50] However, without Jackson by his side, he failed to command respect.

During his presidential campaigns, critics said Van Buren was elitist and effeminate.[51] Congressmen Davey Crockett described Van Buren as "laced up in corsets such as a woman in town where . . . it would be difficult to say from his personal appearance whether he was a man or a woman, but for the large red and gray whiskers."[52] In his campaign against Harrison, the Whigs painted Van Buren, whom they labeled "Martin Van Ruin," as a "lily-fingered aristocrat" who ate his meals off golden plates. Van Buren's decision to spend public funds for a hot-water tank for the White House also drew sharp criticism.[53] Van Buren's appearance prompted many jokes and false accusations. Morally, however, on public policy, Van Buren earned credit for beginning to reform labor conditions, including limiting federal employees' workday to ten hours.[54] Beyond that, Van Buren did not have an overwhelming moral impact for good or ill.

William Henry Harrison, 1841

Harrison's death shortly after his inauguration limits analysis of him primarily to his campaign. Despite his short term, however, he had an impact on the presidency.

Harrison, who was more than a poor common man, demonstrated how an image can create a national following. John Quincy Adams described Harrison's popularity as "demonstrations of popular feeling unexampled since that of Washington in 1789."[55] Propaganda, pro and con, laced his campaign. Whigs portrayed him as a "plain living cabin liver on the Tippecanoe River" who led the army patriotically against the Indians.[56] Critics called him a coward who took improper credit for victories. They nicknamed him "Granny Harrison" and the "Petticoat General."[57] Whigs described Harrison's home as a one-room log cabin; in reality it was a sixteen-room house.

In his long-winded inaugural address, Harrison promised to let Congress have more power in making national policy, but his death cut short his intent. His successor, John Tyler, did not always follow Harrison's ideas.

The next four presidencies, covering twelve years, dodged America's greatest moral issue, slavery, thereby prolonging its resolution. John Tyler, perhaps America's most stubborn president, faced the government's financial issues. James K. Polk, perhaps America's most underrated president, influenced western expansion. Zachary Taylor, the nineteenth-century version of General Dwight D. Eisenhower, was immensely popular, but he let Congress decide most moral issues. Finally, Millard Fillmore, the least known of the four, faced the toughest decision of war or peace.

John Tyler, 1841–1845

John Tyler encountered an uncommon situation for presidents. He was a man without a party.[58] Some argued that Tyler acted unethically by turning against the people, Whigs, who elected him. In Tyler's defense, the Whig Party did not help him become president but rather used him as a political ploy to get Southern votes. Although Tyler had bitter enemies who created rumors to embarrass him, he remained firm in his beliefs. Congressmen tried to impeach Tyler for not voting with the Whigs, but they lacked grounds for even starting an impeachment committee. Tyler, a slave owner who later served in the Confederate Congress, refused to attack slavery, preferring to stay within the safe confines of accepted practice and tradition. Whether with Whigs or with slavery, he stubbornly remained bound by his own sense of integrity.

James K. Polk, 1845–1849

James K. Polk's administration, focusing on foreign policy and westward expansion, greatly influenced the nation's future. The new territory created questions about whether to allow slavery's expansion, which Polk managed to finesse. While advocating protection of slavery in the South, he opposed its extension into the western states. He believed each state should decide slavery's fate.[59]

Polk's acquisition of new lands raised another moral dilemma. Was expansion justified? "Manifest destiny" was his answer: "We must ever maintain the principle that the people of this continent alone have the right to decide their own destiny." Manifest destiny allowed the acquisition of new lands as a necessity for security. Some believe Polk, who was nicknamed "Napoleon of the Stump," manipulated events to start a war with Mexico, claiming it was necessary for security, but tension on the Texas border had existed for some time. Polk negotiated the Oregon boundary with the British without recourse to war. Accomplishing most of his goals during his four-year term, Polk retired in the eyes of many as America's most underrated president.

After his presidency, Polk endorsed an eccentric political endeavor, the new Know Nothing Party, becoming its presidential candidate. The Know Nothing Party endorsed strict separation of church and state and opposed the Roman Catholic Church.

Zachary Taylor, 1849–1850

The Mexican War transformed Zachary Taylor into a military hero, an image he rode to the White House. Before his election, Taylor had never even voted.[60] The Whigs used Taylor as a mythical character, "Old Rough and Ready," to appeal to the voters. Taylor was kinder than Andrew Jackson, though, even earning the praise of Chief Black Hawk, whom he captured during the Black Hawk Indian War.

Taylor, an intelligent general, had received very little education as a child in Kentucky. He definitely was not a politician swayed by the current of political opinion. When Southern politicians claimed that they would run federal troops out of New Mexico, Taylor said, "I will command the army in person and hang any man taken in treason."[61]

Taylor inherited from Polk vast new territories and the slavery controversy. Before becoming president, Taylor owned a Southern slave plantation, but as president, he stood more on neutral ground. Taylor, like Polk, focused more on how the states would enter the Union and left the slavery issue to Congress. He opposed a compromise on slavery, causing Daniel Webster to suggest that "Taylor's death prevented civil war."[62] The difficult decision of compromise fell to Millard Fillmore.

Millard Fillmore, 1850–1853

Like Lincoln later, Fillmore had to decide whether to compromise his moral convictions or to start a civil war. Like Tyler before him, Fillmore provided geographic balance for the Whig ticket, which wanted to woo Northern voters.[63] Fillmore, one of the only presidents of his time to publicly denounce slavery, believed that states should decide the issue. Unlike Tyler, Fillmore compromised his moral convictions by signing the Fugitive Slave Act and the Compromise of 1850. Fillmore's moral compromise became the Whig Party's death warrant. He foolishly believed that compromise would end problems between the North and the South, and he infuriated abolitionists by using federal troops to enforce the Fugitive Slave Act. In his final presidential speech, Fillmore proposed moving all slaves to another country and then solving the labor shortage through Asian immigration. On balance, Fillmore shifted the burden of slavery and an impending Civil War to another decade and another president. Although he compromised his personal conviction about slavery's immorality, his opposition highlighted the issue. More important than slavery as a moral issue was the prevention of civil war. This concern guided Fillmore's decisions.

Taylor, Polk, Tyler, and Fillmore faced serious moral issues, but personal moral scandals hardly dotted the landscape of their administrations. They governed during important times morally, but moral scandal did not distract their attention from the nation's pressing issues.

Franklin Pierce, 1853–1857

Pierce, who looked like a president but lacked a president's resume, had bouts with alcoholism and a reputation as a second-rate soldier. In some critics' opinions, his presidential campaign attempted to mislead the American people into thinking they were voting for a distinguished military general. Nathaniel Hawthorne, on the other hand, praised Pierce as an upright executive.[64] Pierce's pro-slavery policies angered slavery's moral opponents. Although Pierce lacked the strongest moral convictions, he was not totally out of sync with the 1850s.

A recovering alcoholic, Pierce served as a general in the Mexican War, where he had a record of fainting and dizzy spells during battles. Although

Hawthorne claimed that Pierce had a "noble gift of natural authority" and that he was great patriot, his personal friendship may have biased his judgment.[65] Pierce was the first presidential candidate to use photography in his campaign, causing some to say he emphasized personal appearance and an exaggerated patriotism to become president rather than campaign on issues and ideas.[66]

Pierce supported pro-slavery "Border Ruffians" in the new government of Kansas. He signed the Kansas–Nebraska Act, which violated the Missouri Compromise by allowing slavery in Kansas. He unsuccessfully tried to obtain Cuba so that slaves could not escape by sea to a free territory. To his credit, he supported slavery out of a belief that the Constitution permitted it and that his job was only to stand by the Constitution.[67]

After his presidency, he supported slavery even more strongly. In his home state of New Hampshire, he made speeches against the use of force on the South. Pierce may have expressed his true views on the morality of slavery when he denounced the Emancipation Proclamation. Pierce condemned Lincoln's act as an attempt to "butcher" the white race so as to "inflict" freedom on Negroes who did not understand how to use it.[68] Pierce refused to fly the American flag after Lincoln's assassination, and he died a hated man in his New England home.

James Buchanan, 1857–1861

James Buchanan, like Pierce, was pro-slavery, and even defended the extension of slavery into new states. A variety of other moral issues also clouded his reputation.

For example, Gail Collins claims that James Buchanan was not only the first bachelor president but also the first homosexual president.[69] He lived with Senator William King, and the two, known as the "Siamese Twins," always attended parties together. A Tennessee congressman called King "Buchanan's better half," and Andrew Jackson referred to Buchanan as "Mrs. Nancy." Buchanan also had a great attachment to his secretary of the treasury, Howell Cobb. Kate Thompson, the wife of another cabinet member, believed there was "something unhealthy in the president's attitude." However, because homosexuality was so unthought of and unheard of then, Collins believes that few people even knew the characteristics of a homosexual.

Another tale of corruption with Buchanan involved the president's abuse of power in a court case.[70] A friend of Buchanan, David Sickles, killed his wife's lover. Sickles, an immoral character anyway, regularly used prostitutes even while married. But Buchanan wanted to help Sickles escape a murder conviction, so the president "convinced" crucial witnesses to leave town. Today, that action would probably qualify as obstruction of justice.

Buchanan protected slavery in several ways, including allegedly influencing the Supreme Court in the Dred Scott decision.[71] He also supported the Lecompton Constitution in Kansas, which only represented the interests of pro-slavery supporters.[72] When South Carolina decided to secede from the Union, Buchanan declared that although a state did not have the legal right to secede, the federal government did not have the right to stop secession.[73]

After South Carolina occupied Fort Sumter, Buchanan refused to take action against the secessionist movement. Following Lincoln's inauguration, Buchanan stated: "Sir, if you are as happy in entering the White House as I shall feel on returning to Wheatland, you are a happy man indeed."[74]

CIVIL WAR POLITICS AND RECONSTRUCTION PRESIDENTS, 1861–1897

Civil War and Reconstruction presidents served during the most tumultuous period of American history. Facing the intractable issues of slavery and preservation of the Union, they were America's most morally vulnerable presidents. Acute conflicts divided fundamental pillars of society: families, communities, churches, and schools. Sources of unity and loyalty became weapons of enmity and hostility. Presidents in this era confronted charges and countercharges of personal and public immorality.

Abraham Lincoln, 1861–1865

Abraham Lincoln burnished his image with brilliant rhetoric, compassion for people, and America's two greatest presidential successes: preservation of the Union and abolition of slavery. He did not enjoy a meteoric rise to political sainthood, however. Only after many years did Americans make him the highest-ranking president on most presidential greatness scales.

Lincoln tiptoed carefully through moral minefields to avoid explosions that would destroy him and the country. He did not always take the moral high road. Long forgotten by most Americans is the fact that Lincoln violated individual liberties and democratic principles more than any president since John Adams signed the Alien and Sedition Act. He suspended the writ of habeas corpus, declaring that persons aiding the Confederacy were subject to indefinite confinement without judicial hearing or indictment.[75] Chief Justice Taney said Lincoln's actions were unlawful and warned that if such "usurpation continued the people of the United States are no longer under a government of laws."[76] Lincoln also recognized Republicans in each state instead of duly elected state governments.

When peace advocates met to plan the war's end and to oppose Republicans, Lincoln sent General Ambrose Burnside to maintain their loyalty. Burnside abused the treason law and violated the freedom-of-speech laws, arresting a leading Peace Democrat, Clement L. Vallandigham, for calling the president "King Lincoln." The Democratic *New York Atlas* described the situation as "tyranny of military despotism . . . weakness, folly, oppression, mismanagement, and general wickedness of the administration."[77] Lincoln eventually released Vallandigham to the South. Burnside even suspended publication of the *Chicago Times,* but Lincoln overturned Burnside's decision.

Lincoln is, of course, renowned as the president "who freed the slaves." Yet he recognized the Fugitive Slave Act and accepted New Mexico as a slave state. Throughout the Civil War, as Lincoln said in an open letter to journalist and founder of the *New York Tribune* Horace Greeley, "My paramount object in this struggle *is* to save the Union and is not either to save or to destroy slavery." Still, he ended the letter by saying, "I intend no modification to my oft-expressed personal wish that all men every where could be free."[78] It is often forgotten that the revered Emancipation Proclamation of January 1, 1863, freed slaves only in states still in rebellion, as Lincoln had warned the Confederacy in a September 22, 1862, proclamation.[79]

Lincoln's crises and dilemmas reveal that presidents sometimes find themselves in a moral vise that squeezes out a compromise. His two great goals, preservation of the Union and abolition of slavery, did not always mesh. In the end he achieved both. But to do so he sometimes made less than perfect and just moral choices. Telescopes provide better pictures of presidential morality than microscopes.

In his personal life, Lincoln also met moral issues. Mary Lincoln's actions did not reflect well on the president. Her desire for social status and fondness for spending sprees produced a large debt, and she even accepted gifts from office seekers.[80] According to some, Lincoln would have trouble with today's feminists, because he referred to Mary as "child-wife," "little woman," and other condescending nicknames.[81] Lincoln's love of off-color jokes and stories also presented a moral problem for those who love innocuous speech. Lincoln's soaring rhetoric in the Gettysburg Address was not completely representative of his everyday jokes and stories.

Perhaps the most biased and hostile press in American history called Lincoln many vicious names and spread many malicious rumors. Confederate papers accused Lincoln of being part Negro, nicknaming him "Abraham Africanus the First."[82] Some papers called him a drunkard. According to another rumor that inflamed Americans in the North and the South, Lincoln had a less-than-serious black song played as he looked over the Gettysburg battlefield. To Southerners and most Northerners, this seemed disrespectful of those who died. Lincoln replied that the song was a "sad little song" instead of a comic one.[83]

Freezing the film on Lincoln at any given moment may reveal moral moles and warts, but when allowed to run until the end, the film reveals moral greatness. Early in his political career he defended the right of revolution, suggesting that later he might support secession. His defense of revolution, however, was finely honed and balanced. He defended revolution while allowing himself latitude to support preservation of the Union: "The right of revolution as a moral right must be exercised for a morally justifiable cause . . . without such a cause, revolution is no right, but simply a wicked exercise of physical power."[84] To Lincoln, the Confederacy failed to meet the moral justification of revolution.

Moral greatness also reveals itself in the aftermath of victory. Most critics believe that, had Lincoln lived, he would have healed the wounds of war through a charitable and a magnanimous reconstruction policy. As it was, harsh policies failed to bind up those wounds, leaving them open for generations.

Andrew Johnson, 1865–1869

When Andrew Johnson assumed the presidency, he was almost unknown, but Radical Republicans soon discovered him. Disliking his reconstruction policies, they plotted his impeachment. Johnson, a Tennessee Democrat running on the Union Party ticket with Lincoln in

1864, wanted a generous reconstruction policy that limited the military's role. Congress wanted a punitive policy. Johnson dismissed his secretary of war, Edwin Stanton, in 1868 for opposing his policy. Stanton claimed that Johnson violated the Tenure of Office Act, which forbade presidential removal of an official without senatorial concurrence. (Johnson believed the act to be unconstitutional, a view that was later upheld by the Supreme Court.) The House of Representatives impeached Johnson for violating that act, but the Senate failed by one vote to convict him.[85]

Johnson "remained constant to his beliefs regardless of the personal cost to himself."[86] Although he is often considered a mediocre president, Johnson's legacy includes several distinctions. Despite significant opposition in his home state of Tennessee, he stood for the Union during the Civil War. Later he refused to compromise with the Radical Republican Congress even in the face of political death. The Thirteenth Amendment, abolishing slavery, was ratified during his administration. The Fourteenth Amendment, guaranteeing citizenship to blacks, was also proposed and ratified during Johnson's administration, but without his support. Johnson had vetoed the 1866 Civil Rights Act, which declared freedmen were U.S. citizens entitled "to full and equal benefit of the laws"; Congress overrode the veto, but, fearing that the Supreme Court would agree with Johnson that the act was unconstitutional, proposed the amendment.

Rumors of drunkenness buffeted Johnson from his vice presidency through his presidency. Unfortunately Johnson himself provided the initial evidence. Whether to calm his nerves or for some other reason, he had became drunk and incoherent during his vice presidential inauguration. When asked about Johnson's problem, Lincoln replied, "Andy . . . ain't no drunkard." A Radical Republican opponent later described Johnson as "the person who defiled our chief council chamber on Saturday with the spewings of a drunken boor." When Johnson tried to rally Americans behind his Reconstruction policies, opponents heckled him as a drunkard.[87] But compared to his successor, Grant, Johnson was temperate.

Ulysses S. Grant, 1869–1877

After winning a name for himself as a Civil War general, Ulysses S. Grant was placed in charge of the five military districts in the Reconstruction-era South. In that post, he supported Radical Republican policies rather than those of his commander in chief, President Johnson. As president, Grant continued to support the Radical Republicans' agenda, including their refusal to allow Confederate supporters to vote. The Radical Republican reconstruction policy not only failed to restore national unity but also deeply hurt the South.

The Grant administration had more than its share of scandals, although Grant was never personally implicated in any wrongdoing. In perhaps the major scandal, the directors of Credit Mobilier, a company formed to divert railway-construction profits to Union Pacific's promoters, gave large blocks of railroad stock to members of Congress and others, including Vice President Schuyler Colfax, in exchange for covering up corruption. Grant's secretary of war in his second term, General William W. Belknap, was involved in a kickback scheme in the Indian agency and resigned rather than face impeachment. Corruption even reached into the president's office: his personal secretary, General Orville E. Babcock, was involved in the Whiskey Ring, which defrauded the government of at least $1.2 million in excise tax revenue it should have received from sales of alcohol.[88] Grant appointed a millionaire war contractor as secretary of the treasury, who eventually resigned because of obvious conflicts of interest.

While his personnel choices were bad, Grant was not without redeeming qualities. Political analyst Michael Barone argues that Grant himself was an able and intelligent person with noble ideas.[89] For example, he was the only president between Lincoln and Truman to enforce the rights of African Americans. He also proposed Santo Domingo as a haven for former slaves and suggested dividing it into three states so that blacks would have some political power.

Grant was arguably, however, the most notable drunkard in American history. While Johnson was rumored to have a problem with drinking, Grant was a drunkard.[90] Three things helped him survive politically. First, reporters covered up his problem, because they revered him as the "Savior of the Union." Second, even when drunk, he managed to appear sober. By 1872, however, newspapers printed the truth, nicknaming him "His Inebriated Excellency." Third, putting a spin on the story, Grant supporters drew pity for Grant from the American people by saying he could not help himself.

Although scandal, corruption, and drunkenness marked Grant's two terms, his popularity among the people was undiminished. It was even proposed that he run for a third term, but the 1876 Republican National Convention balked and instead nominated Rutherford B. Hayes. Only in the twentieth century did historians revise Grant's reputation downward, a direction that presidential historian Michael Barone and others have begun to reverse.

Rutherford B. Hayes, 1877–1881

The 1876 election was not a bright spot in American politics. The Democratic candidate, Samuel Tilden, had clearly won the popular vote, but the electoral college vote was in doubt. Louisiana, Florida, and South Carolina submitted two sets of electoral college votes, one Democratic and one Republican; the electoral votes of Oregon were also contested. With the electoral votes in those states, Tilden carried the electoral college 203 to 166; without them, the tally shifted to 185 for Hayes, 184 for Tilden. After three months of uncertainty, Congress created a commission to solve the problem. In exchange for counting the Republican rather than the Democratic votes, Republicans promised to remove troops from the South, end the Reconstruction governments, and give loans to Southern states to rebuild their economies.[91]

That compromise made Republican Rutherford B. Hayes president, but the irregularity of the election cast a shadow over his administration. There is some irony in this, for Hayes was one of the most morally upright, not to say straitlaced, men to be president. He and his wife, the former Lucy Ware Webb, "began each day by kneeling at morning prayers and closed each day by singing hymns."[92] "Lemonade Lucy"—a name she earned for her refusal to serve alcohol in the executive mansion, a move that brought ridicule from Washington society—was the first college-educated first lady and a strong supporter of the Women's Christian Temperance Union.

Hayes himself was not popular with the professional politicians in the Republican Party. His followers were disappointed when he did not reward them as they expected under the spoils system, which saw campaign contributors placed in many patronage jobs.[93] Considered a "high principled gentleman in politics,"[94] in the face of stubborn opposition from both Democrats and Republicans, Hayes pushed for civil service reform. He especially targeted jobs connected with tax collection, removing future president Chester A. Arthur (the number two man in Senator Roscoe Conkling's Republican machine) from his post as collector for the Port of New York.[95] He also issued an executive order forbidding federal civil servants from active political participation other than voting. The electoral deal that brought him into office included an agreement not to enforce the Fifteenth Amendment, which guaranteed the civil rights of blacks, leaving them essentially disfranchised for many years to come. Southern Democrats did not keep their promise to treat freedmen fairly, and segregation replaced slavery.[96] Hayes expressed sympathy for blacks both before and after his presidency, and in his last annual message to Congress called special attention to the oppression of former slaves.[97] But attempting to rebuild the Republican Party in the South, he compromised by advocating policies acceptable to Southerners.

Hayes did not seek reelection—in fact, he recommended amending the Constitution to give the president one six-year term. In his last executive order, perhaps to please his wife, Hayes banned the sale of liquor at army camps and forts. Somewhat in the fashion of Jimmy Carter a century later, in his retirement he devoted most of his time to charitable work.[98]

James Garfield, 1881

James Garfield looked like either a saint or a snake, depending on the source and the rumor. As a devoted Christian, he preached earlier in his life. As a person given to compromise, he helped negotiate the agreement that made Hayes president in 1876. Garfield supported Radical Republican reconstruction policies. Rumors linked him to the Credit Mobilier scandal, but the evidence was not conclusive.

A mixture of politics and morality probably motivated him on the issues of reconstruction politics and race. He recognized that emancipating blacks and giving them the freedom to vote could increase Republican majorities. Regarding reconstruction, Garfield "gave his assent to every Congressional bill adopted to complete the program of Reconstruction in the South."[99] But Garfield did not hold African Americans in the highest regard, referring to them as "the great mass of ignorant and degraded blacks."[100] After the Civil War, Garfield successfully defended a Confederate loyalist, L. D. Milligan, from execution.

During his brief presidency, Garfield began cleaning up fraud in the postal service. The investigations that he started saved millions, but Garfield died before he could have more impact. Charles Guiteau, a disappointed office seeker, shot Garfield. Today's medical practices could have healed Garfield's wounds. As it was, he died seventy-nine days after the shooting, leaving a significant legacy despite his short presidential career. His assassination etched an indelible moral imprint on history. Magnifying the problems of political patronage, this tragedy led Congress and the next administration to adopt civil service reforms.

Chester A. Arthur, 1881–1885

Chester A. Arthur, who had gained the vice presidency as a sop to the "Stalwart" faction of the Republican Party and Roscoe Conkling's New York machine, came accidentally to the presidency as a result of Garfield's assassination. During his brief tenure as vice president, he continued to support the spoils system. But as president, he espoused the cause of civil service reform.

When he became president, he appointed most of his friends from New York to high positions in the government. He even asked Roscoe Conkling to become a Supreme Court Justice, but Conkling declined. During the first two years of his term, Arthur acted like a spoils politician, although professing support for civil service reform. When the Democrats took control of Congress at midterm, Arthur became a leader in the fight for such reform. Arthur kept all his friends in their good jobs until the day before the Pendleton Act became effective, suggesting that his commitment to reform was not heartfelt.[101] With low popularity in the Republican Party, he could not win renomination.

As a representative of the Republican Stalwarts, Arthur used the spoils system to their advantage. Yet he signed into law a moral change in government that undermined the foundation of a political machine's success, political patronage. So, the one major accomplishment of the Arthur administration appeared more moral than the president himself.

Grover Cleveland, 1885–1889, 1893–1897

Charges of immorality and political corruption threatened to drown Grover Cleveland, but his personal integrity kept him afloat. As governor of New York, Cleveland cleaned up the corruption of political machines, and as president, he tried to clean up the federal government. He was nicknamed the "Veto President." Standing for what would help the common man, Cleveland advocated low tariffs, and he returned eighty-one million acres of illegally confiscated railroad land to citizens. Despite his good deeds as governor and president, Cleveland had an illegitimate child, and he became the goat of an uncompromising press.

Cleveland, the first Democratic president since Buchanan (1857-1861), felt the sting of the Washington press, which did not give him a presidential honeymoon. Unlike in the early 1800s, the American people had more interest in the private lives of politicians than in public corruption.

The *Buffalo Evening Telegraph* printed "A Terrible Tale" about Cleveland's illegitimate child with Maria Halpin. The story said that Cleveland cold-heartedly put the child in an orphanage.[102] Only partially accurate, the story failed to point out that the bachelor Cleveland put his son in an orphanage because he thought the child would receive better care there than with Halpin, an alcoholic. Tacitly admitting that he had fathered an illegitimate son probably saved his political life. Deeply offended by the press for reporting this story, Cleveland vowed never to forgive the "dirty class that defiled themselves with filthy scandal."

Personal scandal continued to plague Cleveland. His marriage to an attractive but much younger woman, Frances Folsom, initially helped him with the press, but later, reporters accused him of beating her.[103] Although she repudiated the rumors, Cleveland's reputation suffered. Gail Collins speculates that the women's rights movement, then in its infancy, spread the wife-beating story to help their organizational efforts.

Cleveland lost his bid for reelection in 1888 despite receiving more popular votes than his opponent, Benjamin Harrison. Running on a low-tariff platform, Cleveland piled up large victory margins in the South, but lost every other section of the nation. Harrison easily won in the electoral college because his campaign, with its much broader national appeal, carried many more states. Four years later, Cleveland beat Harrison. During this campaign, Harrison's wife died, so Harrison quit campaigning. In a moral move with possible political benefit, Cleveland ended his own campaign, showing respect for Harrison and earning the public's respect for his action.

Sorely damaged by accounts of fathering an illegitimate child and beating his wife, Cleveland survived by directly addressing the issues. He did not deny fathering an illegitimate child, and his wife forcefully denied the charge of wife-beating. Integrity in the midst of moral adversity served him well.

Benjamin Harrison, 1889–1893

"Passive and uneventful" summarizes the Harrison presidency. Going along with Republican Party leaders, Benjamin Harrison supported a high tariff both in his campaign against Grover Cleveland in 1888 and later as president. Signing a bill implementing high tariffs, Harrison became part of House Speaker Thomas B. "Czar" Reed's "Billion Dollar Congress."[104] The high tariffs caused high prices, which allowed the Democrats to capture Congress at midterm. The Harrison administration welcomed six new states to the Union. Although he sought antilynching legislation, none was forthcoming. A follower rather than a leader, Harrison raises an interesting question: Is a president somehow immoral if he fails to fight for great causes and leaves no significant legacy?

POLITICAL MACHINES, BIG BUSINESS, AND PERSONAL CONVICTIONS, 1897–1921

As Civil War issues gradually declined, turn-of-the-century politics offered conflicts that pitted political machines, big business, and personal convictions against one another. Many moral issues arose as some presidents fought for their convictions against the interests of political machines and big business. Others depended on political machines for success and refused to challenge them; and some remained captives of big business.

William McKinley, 1897–1901

An examination of President William McKinley's time as chief executive shows the utmost moral purity in his personal life and some questionable moral stances in administrative policy. Mural Halstead, McKinley's friend for many years, described him as "a growing man through all his years, and as President, he was a marvel of executive capacity, personal industry, and so ready was he for great occasions that his command of opportunities was but slowly understood and is not yet recognized."[105] The common thread running through most accounts is that McKinley did his job without a need for congratulation.

Writing in 1916, Charles S. Olcott said, "McKinley's private life was so pure, his personal integrity so well known, and his political conduct so far above suspicion that not a word of reproach in any of these directions was uttered."[106] Halstead, whose encomium was published shortly after McKinley's assassination in 1901, said that his life was "illustrious indeed without a blemish or a flaw, nothing to avoid, explain or extenuate. His reputation is the white light of a cloudless sky, no shadow falling to dim the deeds of the day."[107] Contemporaneous accounts of McKinley's personal life cast him only in the most favorable of lights.

Yet some of McKinley's actions, or failures to act, as president reveal a certain vulnerability to political pressures. McKinley maintained a very close friendship with Senator Mark Hanna, who seemed to have a profound influence over decisions made in the administration. One indication of McKinley's dependence on Hanna came with the president's duty to make appointments. A majority of the patronage positions were filled by people chosen by Hanna.[108] The fourth assistant postmaster general wrote some years after McKinley's assassination that McKinley "gave Hanna's requests great consideration and had confidence in the clearness of his opinions, but in the end he always followed his own judgment."[109] This deference to Hanna with regard to patronage, while it does not demonstrate any morally reprehensible action on McKinley's part, does demonstrate his tendency to show favoritism to his friends and political allies.

Probably the most debated and important issue facing the McKinley administration was that of the burgeoning trusts in America. Under McKinley, America enjoyed "unexampled prosperity."[110] One of the major policies of the McKinley administration was to sponsor healthy economic growth. McKinley stated in 1901, "We have a vast and intricate business built up through years of toil and struggle, in which every part of the country has its stake, which will not permit of either neglect or undue selfishness. No narrow or sordid policy will subserve it."[111] With this unbridled expansion of the economy, big business seemed to grow out of hand. McKinley failed to take a tough stand either for or against the swelling monopolies. Although McKinley declined to align himself with either side, Hanna stated, "In the numerous discussions that I heard upon the Constitution and the Declaration of Independence during the last session I got sort of an idea that a man had a right to do what he pleased."[112] The leader of the political opposition, William Jennings Bryan, spoke out boldly against the trusts, stating that "the Democratic Party will continue its attack upon monopoly."[113] Bryan's outspoken opposition made McKinley's administration look like proponents of big business. Overall,

McKinley's administration did not make a concerted effort either to enforce or to inhibit the 1890 Sherman Antitrust Act.

The McKinley administration also faced criticism from the anti-imperialists of the late nineteenth century. The Philippines had been put into the control of the United States after the Spanish-American War, and the anti-imperialists saw this as a morally unsteady policy. The administration's move to restrict distribution of anti-imperialist literature perhaps offers more insight into its morality. For only a short time, the administration, not necessarily McKinley himself, ordered the postmaster general not to mail Edwin Atkinson's anti-imperialist pamphlets overseas.[114] The implications of this action for Americans' rights to free speech quickly ended the policy, but the fact that the administration took to this restrictive approach puts it in a bad light.

McKinley did focus part of his political agenda on black Americans, if only in a small and insubstantial way. In an attempt to attract black voters, he allowed black members of the military to attain higher ranks during the Spanish-American War than they had normally held before.[115] Although McKinley did very little to change the position of blacks in America, a black Republican defended him, saying that "we colored Americans, from a national point of view, are being better treated now and more fully recognized under the present Administration, both in civil office and in the Army than ever before in the history of this nation."[116]

McKinley's administration ended prematurely with the president's assassination by anarchist Leon Czolgosz. McKinley was the third president, and the second in only twenty years, to be assassinated. The moral pinnacle of McKinley's presidency may have been at the scene of the shooting. With a bullet deep in his stomach, McKinley told his secret service agents, "Don't hurt him," and he described his assassin as "some poor misguided fellow."[117] Lewis Gould tells how McKinley thought first of his wife and how she would take his death. He lived just over a week after the gunshot wound and died of a gangrene infection. In John Jay's eulogy of McKinley, he spoke of how McKinley "showed in his life how a citizen should live, and in his last hour taught us how a gentleman could die."[118]

The political issues that proved morally hazardous for McKinley were passed on to McKinley's fiery vice president, Theodore Roosevelt. Roosevelt took the reins to a country that had a strong economy and was a growing power in the world.

Theodore Roosevelt, 1901–1909

Theodore Roosevelt determined that only specific constitutional restrictions could limit his actions as president. Today his presidency stands as a landmark in the gradual growth of presidential power and expanded presidential agendas. His expansive definition of presidential power undergirded his personal ambition and public policy agenda. Absent a specific constitutional restriction, Roosevelt believed, he could lead without restraint. By extending the boundary lines for presidential action, Roosevelt paved the way for subsequent presidents to lead moral crusades. His ambitious personality and aggressive agenda created many controversies. Simply put, he dominated the news. His presidency set many important precedents for making the president the catalyst for governmental action.[119] On the personal level, Roosevelt had to protect his reputation against rumors of alcoholism.

Roosevelt changed the relationship between the president and the American people. Before Roosevelt, presidents did not take their policies straight to the American people. William Allen White stated that Roosevelt "used the front porch of the White House as a sounding board which sent his preachments and moral proclamations booming through the land."[120]

Roosevelt's ambition occasionally caused him to act unethically. When a Colombian dictator refused to allow the United States to build a canal through Panama, a Colombian possession, Roosevelt sponsored a Panamanian revolution.[121] His international imperialist policies sometimes made him look like an absolute monarch. For example, without receiving the approval of the Senate, he committed to possible involvement in the Russo–Japanese War.[122] Roosevelt enjoyed political power, and he constantly tried to increase his power.

On a lighthearted note, Roosevelt was not always truthful with the American people about his heritage. Besides Teddy, Roosevelt's other nickname was "Old Fifty-Seven Varieties." Roosevelt changed his family lineage depending on his audience. He claimed southern ancestry through his mother, northern ancestry through his father, and western ancestry by personal desire.[123]

Roosevelt's physique and behavior invited rumors of alcoholism. His "rolling gait, clenched teeth, choppy speech, and startling actions" made him appear less than sober.[124] In reality, Roosevelt did not even drink beer, nor did he smoke. To clear his name, he sued members of the press for libel. Roosevelt won the case because there was no evidence against him. Displaying compassion for his enemies, Roosevelt asked the jury to award "only nominal damages."[125]

After winning the case, Roosevelt said to the public, "I have achieved my purpose, and I am content." That quote symbolizes Roosevelt's career, which was characterized by his stopping at almost nothing to achieve his purpose.

William Howard Taft, 1909–1913

William Howard Taft rejected Roosevelt's expansion of presidential power, contending that the Constitution must specifically allow, not specifically deny, presidential action.[126] Just as Roosevelt's views established precedents for activist presidents, Taft's views expressed the philosophical underpinnings for passive presidents. Implicitly, Taft found Roosevelt's views illegal and, hence, immoral.[127] Although he did not dominate the news as Roosevelt had, Taft quietly achieved more than Roosevelt on one of the most significant moral issues of their presidencies, trust-busting. Acting against big-business corruption, Taft busted eighty trusts, twice as many as Roosevelt. Taft's acute sense of personal integrity and reserved personality probably contributed to his strict and limited view of presidential power. He hesitated to do anything that might reflect negatively on him. By contrast, Roosevelt thought that failure to act would bring reproach.

Finding the rough-and-tumble of politics uncomfortable, Taft said, "Politics when I am in it, makes me sick." He even turned down large campaign contributions, believing that they would corrupt him. His passivity also affected his administration. He took two years to fill his cabinet, and then he did not exercise control over its members.[128] As a personal moral example, Taft appears above reproach, but politically he lacked the dynamic leadership qualities we now deem crucial to successful presidencies. Perhaps Taft had too much integrity for effective presidential leadership.

Woodrow Wilson, 1913–1921

Although often described as moral, Woodrow Wilson and his presidency reveal serious shortcomings. Wilson's personal life contained troubling charges of marital infidelity, and his positions on several of today's moral issues present serious concerns. Few presidents rival Wilson in bringing morality to bear on public issues, but the appearance and substance of morality sometimes conflicted.

Woodrow Wilson, the son of a Presbyterian minister, had at least one questionable relationship with a woman other than his wife. His affair in 1907 with Mary Allen Peck of Bermuda tarnished his personal moral reputation.[129] After the Peck affair, he seemed happily married to his first wife until she died seventeen months into his first term. But only eight months later, he married Edith Galt, causing the press and the public to suspect that Wilson had an affair with her before his first wife's death. Allegations about Wilson's marital immorality produced more than a few choice comments. Alice Ross, for example, remarked: "Wilson always said his prayers before he jumped into bed with anyone."[130] During Wilson's deep depression after his first wife's death, his administration became chaotic, and he did not seem to care. Neglecting appointments and important business, he allowed his cabinet to make questionable decisions.

Wilson offered a superior moral agenda, but he neglected such moral issues as the treatment of blacks, children, and women. Wilson believed racial segregation was morally just in that it prevented trouble between blacks and whites.[131] He vetoed a bill to end child labor abuse, considering the bill a violation of the Constitution rather than seeing it as a morally just act to protect children.[132] Wilson also flip-flopped on women's suffrage. First, although favoring giving women the vote early in his political career, he hid behind the Democrat Party's opposition later in his career, choosing, as he said, to serve as a "representative of the party."[133] Second, claiming that women's suffrage was a states' rights issue, he later dodged it by leaving it to the states. After World War I, however, he supported a constitutional amendment granting women's suffrage. The Nineteenth Amendment was ratified in 1920.

For Wilson, World War I was a moral crusade, "A war to make the world safe for democracy." Following the war, he led another moral crusade for world peace, creating the League of Nations. Risking his own health, he finally failed in his fight to win Senate ratification of that treaty. As his administration waned, his health declined, and increasingly his wife became more prominent in making his decisions.

Wilson had a checkered sense of morality, fighting intently for some issues, overlooking others, and dodging still others. Like Theodore Roosevelt, he added to the scope of presidential power by looking upon the presidency as a place for aggressive moral action.

THE MORAL ROLLER COASTER IN THE ROARING TWENTIES

Appearance defied reality during the 1920s. On the surface, America appeared economically, politically, and socially healthy, but by the decade's end, one of the nation's greatest challenges brought momentous changes. The passive presidencies of Harding, Coolidge, and Hoover became the prelude to the modern norm of active and powerful presidencies.

Warren G. Harding, 1921–1923

Warren Harding confessed, "I am not fit for this office and should never have been here."[134] His life and administration littered history with sin and deception. Personal and public policy scandals highlighted his presidency. Even though he was not directly responsible for some of the scandals, such as the Teapot Dome and Veterans' Bureau affairs, no one attempts to remove them from his legacy. He personally set the example of immorality. Others merely followed in his wake.

Does an administration's moral reputation mirror a president's? Harding's history sounds a strong affirmative. Harding sacrificed the permanent on the altar of the immediate. He had extramarital affairs and enjoyed wild parties, refusing to give up his sin for his country. He sacrificed his opportunity for a permanent place in the annals of presidential greatness on the altar of immediate personal gratification. And he paid for it dearly. Even the scandal of his death, his worst scandal, was a final and fitting exclamation mark to a life of immorality.

Harding, like Ulysses Grant, made poor personnel decisions. His cabinet boiled over with corruption. Secretary of the Interior Albert Fall took center stage in the Teapot Dome scandal, receiving bribes for leases to drill oil on petroleum-rich public land.[135] Fall accepted $100,000 in a paper sack on one occasion and received extremely expensive cows for his ranch on another. Harding's response tells the story of his administrative shortcomings: "This isn't the first time that this rumor has come to me, but if

Albert Fall isn't an honest man, I'm not fit to be President of the United States."[136]

Harding's principal appointees in the Veterans' Bureau and the Office of Attorney General solidified his reputation in the presidential basement. Harding placed Charlie Forbes, a lover of the high life, in charge of the Veterans' Bureau. In that position, Forbes turned a handsome profit on kickbacks from the construction of hospitals, the sale of excess war materials, and inflated prices on new supplies. One line from Francis Russell's *Shadow of Blooming Grove* sums up Forbes's corruption: "One Chicago afternoon [while] Forbes, a bottle of Scotch on the table, was shooting craps . . . in the living room of their fifty-dollar-a-day suite at the Drake Hotel, Martiner (businessman) called Forbes into the bathroom and handed him ten five-hundred dollar bills."[137] Attorney General Harry Daugherty, who handled blackmail threats against Harding, went to trial for selling pardons, but he dodged conviction.[138]

Sexual immorality also hovered over Harding. His affairs began long before he reached the White House. Among them was an affair with Carrie Phillips, of whom one person said, "This woman has made herself useful to men."[139] Washington police records show that, on one night, a drunk Harding received cuts and bruises at the house of a regular lady friend."[140] After Harding found a more interesting mistress, Phillips blackmailed him into giving her relatives federal jobs. Harding even tried to appoint Phillips' husband, on whom she had been cheating, as ambassador to Japan. According to the *Washington Post,* Harding became the only president to succumb to payoffs on blackmail threats.[141]

Among Harding's many other mistresses, Susie Holder, once Florence Harding's best friend, allegedly had a daughter by Harding.[142] Harding also had an affair with his Senate aide, Grace Cross. Probably his best-known mistress, Nan Britton, wrote the first-ever memoirs of a presidential mistress.[143] Harding had an illegitimate son by Rosa Hoyde, and Augusta Cole terminated a pregnancy caused by Harding. He had a string of "New York" women in his entourage, and one committed suicide because Harding refused to marry her. Topping off the list, Harding soiled the reputation of the first Miss America by having an affair with her shortly after she won her crown in Atlantic City.[144]

Harding's sex scandals went beyond an unhealthy desire for women. Sometimes he had the law broken to protect himself. When a prostitute died of a head injury during a stag party in New York, the FBI buried her body in a potter's field that night to avoid scandal.[145]

During Harding's administration, Prohibition was the law, but not for Harding, who served alcohol in the Oval Office. Scandal surrounded Harding's chief bootlegger, Jess Smith. Although he didn't hold a government job, Smith rode in government cars and attended important meetings at the Justice Department. Before Harding's death, Smith committed suicide.

Illegal restrictions on freedom of the press also haunted Harding. The Secret Service raided the home of journalist William Eastabrook Chancellor, forcing him to burn papers that contained politically damaging stories about Harding.[146] Chancellor also published a book that contained stories about Harding, but the Secret Service confiscated all copies from libraries, bookstores, and other places.[147]

Why did the press fail to report such activities? Perhaps since Chancellor was a loner, he lacked the political and legal strength to press his case. Or perhaps the public had little, if any, interest in such issues, preferring instead to read stories about celebrities of the Roaring Twenties. Or perhaps Harding's big business supporters, who owned most of the major newspapers, did not want to damage him.

Looking at Harding's religious convictions helps to clarify his personal morality. Francis Russell concluded, "Religion was for Harding like the Constitution, something to be honored and let alone."[148] Further, Russell said that Harding "believed—in odd moments when he thought about it—in a God somewhere, an afterlife somehow in which one would not be judged too harshly for brass rails and poker games and the occasional midnight visits to the houses by the railroad station."[149]

No novelist could have written a more fitting close to Harding's life. His mysteriously complex death occurred during a fifteen-thousand-mile train trip to Alaska, when he got food poisoning from a tainted crab. The physicians on the trip were Joel Boone, Harding's official doctor, and his wife's doctor, "Doc" Sawyer. According to the *Washington Post,* Boone and Sawyer gave Harding purgatives to flush out the toxins. Then when Boone left the room and while Florence Harding remained, Sawyer gave Harding too many purgatives. Soon after, Harding died.

Florence Harding would not permit an autopsy of her husband's body, and she and others allegedly conspired to cover up who was in the room with the president when he died. She protected Sawyer, and upon returning to the White House, she burned documents piled in wooden crates. Mrs. Harding and "Doc" Sawyer appear very suspicious, and since the president had lived in infidelity for many years, she had a plausible motive for killing her husband. The story of Harding's death varies, depending on who tells it. The facts remain unclear, but true to his life, moral scandal clouded his death.

Ironically, one of the best cabinet secretaries ever to serve in any administration was a Harding appointee, Herbert Hoover, who served as secretary of commerce. Also during the Harding administration, the Budget and Accounting Act of 1921 made lasting reforms of the government's auditing and administration of finances. Thus, the dark cloud of Harding's administration had a thin silver lining.

Calvin Coolidge, 1923–1929

Harding was succeeded by his vice president, Calvin Coolidge, who could scarcely have been more different. Edward Connery Latham remarked that "Coolidge possessed an impeccable honesty, a refreshing serenity, a remarkable simplicity and humility, an incisive and homely wisdom."[150]

Coolidge quickly reformed the cabinet, proclaiming that "he would not sacrifice an innocent man or maintain in office an unfit one."[151] Compared to Harding, Coolidge had a rather dull personality, a faithful marriage, a warm heart, and always a sober mind.[152] Although scandal and corruption were not in his lexicon, Coolidge made some questionable economic decisions.

Coolidge's popularity soared during the economic growth of the golden twenties. He and his economic adviser, Andrew Mellon, encouraged the raging bull stock market, failing either to slow the market or to warn of possible problems. Regarding the market, Coolidge had a "habitual avoidance of unnecessary responsibility."[153] His approach to problems was often to do nothing, trusting that they would go away.

Stock market successes, however, did help the country. Coolidge and the Republican Congress paid off the national debt and decreased the income tax. To the dismay of some Americans, they eased the tax burden for the rich more than the common man.[154] Although stock market successes enhanced Coolidge's popularity in the 1920s, his failure to act cautiously and to warn of potential problems hurt his reputation in the long run.

William Allen White said Coolidge was like a puppet of the Chamber of Commerce: "In the booming stock market the President of the United States and the United States Chamber of Commerce were making one big noise in the same rain-barrel."[155] The U.S. Chamber of Commerce forcefully backed Coolidge throughout his presidency. In turn, he gave top priority to business interests. Coolidge asked for recognition of the Soviet Union without consulting with the Chamber of Commerce. When that organization announced its opposition, Coolidge reversed his decision. Other than his economic decisions and ties to business, Coolidge maintained a clean record free of scandal and corruption.

Herbert Hoover, 1929–1933

Coolidge and Hoover bore striking similarities, especially in their strong moral convictions. The economy, however, dealt them different hands. The economic powerhouse of the 1920s ran out of steam during Hoover's administration, putting Hoover in a moral bind. Should he adhere to his constitutional convictions or jettison them in the face of economic chaos? Choosing personal conviction over political convenience, he suffered overwhelming political defeat. He became a profile in moral courage. The flood of political animosity that engulfed Hoover politically also wiped out his reform agenda.

Like all presidents, Hoover had personal flaws. As a businessman in China in 1899, Hoover used Chinese laborers for one-twenty-fifth the cost of American workers.[156] Remarking on his time in China, Hoover stated: "The simply appalling and universal dishonesty of the Chinese working classes, the racial slowness, the low average of intelligence, gives them an efficiency far below workmen of England and America."[157]

As president, Hoover had enlightened ideas about race relations. Hoover believed that men should be "humane, reformist, and respectful."[158] He tried to reform the nation's treatment of blacks, inviting representatives of the Tuskegee Institute to the White House and increasing the number of blacks working in the federal government.

Hoover had many ideas for reform, but his goal of reforming big business backfired. He entered the Oval Office decrying the arrogance of big business and warning Americans about its unchecked power.[159] Hoover "wanted to lower federal income taxes on 'earned' as against 'unearned' income."[160] His proposal, intended to lower taxes for working people at the expense of investors in the stock market, did not help the delicate state of the economy. On October 24, 1929, the stock market crashed, and by November 14, stock market losses totaled over $30 billion.[161] In response to the stock market crash, Hoover reversed his stance toward big business.

Hoover's depression policies upset many Americans, but he remained steadfast in his moral view of government. Hoover supported aid to the hungry and unemployed, but he argued that support should come from local and state governments. Believing in the so-called trickle-down theory of economic prosperity, he wanted economic recovery to occur through rejuvenated businesses and not through government handouts, which he considered a Band-Aid approach to recovery.[162] Government handouts, he thought, would reduce personal responsibility and increase personal dependence on the government. He held conferences on the economic crisis and proposed $116 million in public works, but he also emphasized the dangers of federal relief. An enlarged national government in response to the economic crisis, he believed, would ultimately pose a threat to American liberty.

Sticking to his guns, Hoover vetoed public works projects offered by Congress and he "declared that to oppose any additional government expenditures was to perform a patriotic duty."[163] He actually recognized the same problems in the economy as Franklin Roosevelt did later, but Hoover tried to solve them differently. He asked for more stable banking with safeguards on credit and deposits.[164] Unlike Roosevelt, Hoover wanted to balance the budget with a higher sales tax. Hoover's poor public relations also cost him popularity with the voters. As Hoover's popularity decreased, people refused to listen to his reasoning. In a campaign speech, he claimed that the upcoming election would affect the welfare of generations of Americans to come, arguing that the Democrats' philosophy of government endangered American foundations of life.[165] By that point in the campaign, people would not believe Hoover's prophetic claims.

On other issues, Hoover pursued moral ideals. He ordered Attorney General William D. Mitchell to get Al Capone, regardless of the expense.[166] Hoover supported Prohibition in the early stages, but he later supported its reversal as president. He applied Quaker ideals to his foreign policy decisions regarding peace. The Kellogg–Briand Pact had the signatures of sixty-two nations that promised not to use war as an instrument of national policy. Unfortunately, his good intentions made no lasting impressions.

Hoover was a man of good moral intentions and solid moral convictions, but the public rejected the policies emanating from those intentions and convictions. The people wanted to move at a faster pace and in a different direction than Hoover's approach would allow.

CONCLUSION

The scarlet thread of scandal, woven into the fabric of all presidencies from Washington through Hoover, affected them in diverse ways. Time appears to have diminished the memory of moral scandal for some presidents. For a few, historical revisionism has either improved their legacies or cast a shadow over their records. Although some seem forever adversely affected by moral scandal, presidential giants like Washington and Lincoln appear always to rise above its clouds. Issues of personal morality dominated some presidential careers, while public policy morality dominated the careers of others. Religious faith deeply affected the personal moral behavior of some presidents, while it guided the public policy decisions for others. Finally, a morality cycle appears in some places. For example, after Grant and Harding came presidents with upright records. In many ways, the scarlet thread of scandal from Washington through Hoover foreshadowed what was to follow.

4

PRESIDENTIAL SCANDAL IN A GOLDEN AGE, 1932–1960

The intention of the eighteenth and nineteenth century law was to install and protect the principle of conflict; this [principle], if we begin to plan, we shall be changing once for all, and it will require the laying of rough, unholy hands on many a sacred precedent, doubtless calling on an enlarged and nationalized police power for enforcement.

— Rexford Guy Tugwell

No twenty-year period of American history challenged and changed America more than the period from 1932 to 1952. The Great Depression and World War II transformed America constitutionally, economically, internationally, politically, religiously, and socially.

Constitutionally, the Supreme Court redefined the Constitution to allow the national government an expanded role in American society, especially in the economy. Economically, the national government began to control the economic pulse and policies of the nation through such newly created agencies as the Securities and Exchange Commission and the Council of Economic Advisers. Internationally, America emerged as one of two major world powers. The United States advanced the Truman Doctrine and the Marshall Plan to establish economic and political recovery and stability in war-torn countries. American leadership engineered creation of the United Nations and the North Atlantic Treaty Organization to secure and sustain peace. Politically, Democrats replaced Republicans as the nation's majority party. President Franklin Roosevelt created a three-part coalition of political machines in northern cities, labor union bosses, and the all-white, one-party, Democratic South. This coalition dominated American politics until it began to crumble during the 1960s. Blacks and Jews, previously aligned with the

Republican Party, also became part of the Roosevelt coalition. Religiously, America's dominant mainline Protestant churches, such as Methodists, Presbyterians, and Episcopalians, set aside their historic conservative biblical doctrines in favor of liberal scriptural interpretations. Their newfound liberalism also prompted increased political participation. Roman Catholics and Jews emerged as political forces in the big cities and urban states. Socially, the widespread participation of blacks and women in World War II led to new roles for them in the postwar society and economy.

Presiding over these momentous changes were two Democratic presidents, Franklin D. Roosevelt and Harry S. Truman. Both undergirded their activist liberal agendas with distinct moral tones. They called their programs the New Deal and the Fair Deal, respectively, implying that earlier policies were morally deficient and inadequate. President Dwight D. Eisenhower, who inherited these massive changes in public policy, did not try to undo them. His administration served as a respite from the turbulent changes of the 1930s and 1940s.

MARKS OF THE GOLDEN AGE

The struggles of the Great Depression, the courage of the World War II generation, and the sense of community in the 1950s marked this era as a golden age in American life. The Great Depression tested the nation's optimism, leaving a renewed and vigorous cultural identity. Highlighting this era was "nothing less than belief in the efficacy of the American Dream, the core cultural myth that America's search for material and moral prosperity serves individual and collective destiny."[1]

As shown in popular culture, the Great Depression strengthened America's collective psyche. Hollywood's responses—movies like *Bringing Up Baby, It Happened One Night,* and *My Man Godfrey*—showed Americans' ability to laugh in spite of economic gloom and hard times.

Initially, Americans reacted to the depression with bitterness and foreboding, but as the depression progressed, the entire culture adopted this optimistic mind-set. The film director who did the most to illustrate this trend in the 1930s was undoubtedly Frank Capra. Movies such as *Meet John Doe* and *Mr. Smith Goes to Washington* did much to mirror the feelings of the common man. In *Mr. Smith Goes to Washington,* an idealistic young "Boy Ranger" leader (portrayed by Jimmy Stewart) is appointed to fill an open term in the U.S. Senate.

Stewart's character, representing the common man, has the traditional American values of honesty, reverence, loyalty, and a willingness to work hard. In Washington, however, he confronts a warped version of American culture: rich, powerful, and unscrupulous men dominating the system and using it to better themselves. As they unite to discredit and destroy him, he finally launches a doomed filibuster on the Senate floor. Finally, people begin to listen as he angrily preaches to the nation about traditional democratic and Christian values.

Stewart collapses, and a guilty senior senator confesses. His "vindication also renewed his ideal, the national values to sustain us all through difficult times."[2] The message from such movies was clear: The average American may lack financial wealth but not cultural wealth. By continuing to put his belief in traditional American values, he will eventually overcome any crisis.

This popular mind-set, strengthened by outside events, continued. The war in Europe offered Americans a moral dilemma. While the stakes were undoubtedly high, the justifications for entering the war were strong. Again, Hollywood mirrored this dilemma. *Casablanca* was released in 1942, at a time when many Americans were unsure and frightened about the war's prospects. It centers around Rick Blaine, an American in Morocco, at that time under the administration of the Vichy government of occupied France, who does not want to get involved in the conflict.

Rick has become disillusioned with the American dream, and he has determined to look out only for himself. "I stick my neck out for nobody," Rick insists. At the time, many Americans were thinking the same thing. When a Czech Resistance leader against fascism arrives in Casablanca, Rick has a chance to save him from the German authorities. However, Rick wants to stay uninvolved. He seems to represent the popular American view. While defending European democracy was indeed a noble task, the war would be very costly. Like Rick, many Americans wanted to stay out of it. In the end, of course, Rick does the right thing. He helps the Resistance leader to escape, and then he joins the Free French himself. Similarly, the attitudes of the American public began to change as 1943 approached. There was less complaint and foreboding. Instead, the nation committed itself to the war as a noble cause, and it accepted the personal sacrifices that accompanied such a cause. Did

Casablanca accurately mirror this trend? "President Roosevelt viewed the film on December 31, 1942, and soon thereafter severed relations with Vichy!"[3]

Thus, the popular American culture that emerged in the 1940s from these events is very easy to identify. There was a strong sense of right and wrong. Critics of the age have suggested that this was an extreme. Americans saw the world only in black and white. If this was true, it was largely because the nation had such a strong sense of national identity. It had weathered conflicts with great resolve and courage. The confidence of the average American was high, and Americans had a strong sense that they could do anything.

Frank Capra's postwar film *It's a Wonderful Life* mirrors these ideals in Jimmy Stewart's character, George Bailey. George is humble, religious, patriotic, and dutiful. He cares more for his neighbor than for himself and devotes his life to helping his town. In many ways, the nation's ability to overcome the two major emergencies led to these ideals. America's success seemed to justify its beliefs. The resulting confidence probably did serve to paint the world in black and white. The nation was so sure of itself that it could not contemplate the possibility of being wrong.[4]

This era may also be considered a golden age of American history because of its leadership. In ranking chief executives, presidential historians often look at a president's ability to mirror the times. Did the president represent and understand the feelings of the nation? It is interesting to note that many presidents have been considered out of step or out of touch during times of widespread uncertainty.

During this era, however, the nation's leaders were strong and understanding. They grasped the feelings of the common man, and they understood how to communicate with him. Franklin D. Roosevelt and Harry S. Truman had both experienced personal adversity, and both believed in the ultimate power of perseverance. Because of the severe tests of their times, their presidencies were far more influential than most. They were responsible for helping to shape the national feelings that emerged in the 1940s. And in the 1950s, Eisenhower, who had risen from the rural Plains town of Abilene, Kansas, to become a five-star general and commander of the European invasion during World II, had a charismatic attraction for the American people.

In an era that seemed strikingly moral and where issues appeared black and white, right and wrong, what type of morality did America's presidents have? Did they live by their morality? Was their morality primarily personal or did it focus on public policy? Was their morality a major influence in postwar America?

PRESIDENT FRANKLIN D. ROOSEVELT, 1933–1945

FDR: The Lion and the Fox?

Americans have seen more than their share of complex, enigmatic leaders. From Nixon to Clinton, the country has experienced leaders who are difficult to summarize quickly. That its presidents could be so quickly condensed and understood is an appropriate sign of the 1930s and 1940s. Franklin D. Roosevelt's character can easily be summed up in one word: confidence.

Not only did Roosevelt have great personal confidence, but also he was able to inspire confidence in others. During Roosevelt's life, his confidence helped him more than any other trait. It made him a model war leader, and it allowed him to comfort the nation during the depression. However, his confidence also hindered Roosevelt. He often made mistakes by overestimating his own abilities. He had a sense that whatever benefited him must be right. Thus, for better or worse, Franklin Roosevelt's morality cannot be understood without a thorough discussion of his confidence.

Doris Kearns Goodwin writes that "he seemed to develop what Sigmund Freud called the feeling of the conqueror, that confidence of success that often induces real success."[5] Almost everyone associated with him during his long presidency makes reference to it. "There's something that he's got," White House aide Harry Hopkins said. "It seems unreasonable at times, but he falls back on something that gives him complete assurance that everything is going to be all right."[6]

FDR's wife, Eleanor, spoke often of this characteristic. "I have never known a man who gave one a greater sense of security. I never heard him say there was a problem that he thought was impossible for human beings to solve."[7] Labor Secretary Frances Perkins said that "his capacity to inspire and encourage those around him to do tough, confused, and practically impossible jobs was without dispute."[8]

Roosevelt had a way of comforting those around him, a trait that was especially useful during the depression. Historian Garry Wills perceived that "people drew strength from the very cock of his head, the angle of his cigarette holder, the trademark grin that was a semaphore of hope."[9] Biographer Rexford Tugwell suggests, "Vitality, charm, a sense of confidence in the midst of spreading fear—these were what Franklin had to offer."[10]

White House counsel Sam Rosenman noted the demeanor of Roosevelt's military advisers after meeting with him. "I always remember their calm, determined, fighting faces; and I always felt certain that a great deal of that calm confidence and firm determination were reflections of the spirit of the man whom they had just left."[11] New York Times reporter Anne McCormick probably summed up Roosevelt's persona best. She stated that he was "more at ease in all circumstances, more at home in his position, than any leader of his time. His nerves are stronger, his temper cooler and more even. If he worries, he gives no sign of it."[12] "Armed with such an inner confidence," Tugwell insists, "he could not really be shaken by any criticism or attack."[13]

This remarkable confidence probably came from two distinct sources. One was undoubtedly related to his upbringing. The Roosevelts of New York were very prominent, and great things were expected of Franklin almost at once. Roosevelt's mother adored her only son and doted on him. She was careful to record and preserve almost everything the young boy did. She would label and store away items such as "his first pair of shoes" or "his first model ship." Roosevelt was never limited or held back by his parents. He was raised in a very loving atmosphere, and he remained the center of his mother's attention all of his life. Under such circumstances, it is no surprise that he came to see himself as a person of some importance. He believed that his opinions truly mattered.

His struggle with polio had an equally strong effect on Roosevelt's personality and probably did much to offset the potential bad effects of his mother's adoration. Roosevelt's battle with polio taught him the importance of strength and perseverance. It was a terrific and horrifying struggle. Roosevelt had always been healthy and athletic. He had never been faced with any serious or catastrophic injuries. The fight against polio was long and somewhat depressing, and he was changed in many ways. Perkins noted that "there had been a plowing up of his nature. The man emerged completely warm-hearted, with new humility of spirit and a firmer understanding of philosophical concepts."[14] The struggle tempered his arrogance, Doris Kearns Goodwin notes, and made him "less superficial, more focused, more complex."[15] After living a comfortable youth, Roosevelt suddenly understood the plight of the poor and underprivileged. He was able to comfort the nation during his presidency largely because he understood how it felt. He understood hopelessness and personal disgust, and he knew how to combat it.

Roosevelt once said, "At night when I lay my head on my pillow and I think of the things that have come before me in the day and the decisions that I have made, I say to myself—well, I have done the best I could, and turn over and go to sleep."[16] Such an iron constitution is certainly a good trait to have as a war leader, and it comes as no surprise that historians almost unanimously praise Franklin Roosevelt for his performance during the two great national emergencies of his administration.

Roosevelt's unquestioning belief in himself was a double-edged sword, however. It is often difficult to pin down his moral code, and his decisions sometimes seem contradictory. Many leaders, such as his successor, Harry Truman, held outside sources of morality as their guide. Roosevelt's guide to morality was himself, and this caused many problems. Perkins remarked that "there was always much that was hard to explain, many actions that seemed inconsistent, many things begun and then apparently abandoned. It was impossible to develop a recognizably simple personality from the known facts, one exactly typed and reduced to rule."[17] Unless one thought like Roosevelt, it would be impossible to find any such rule.

Roosevelt received much credit for his efforts to end the Great Depression. While the ultimate effects of his measures can be argued endlessly, many of his economic programs did increase national morale. The ones that seemed to have little or no effect Roosevelt generally ignored or undid. That was one of the advantages of Roosevelt's personal morality: since he was free from any strict moral code, he was able to be more flexible when searching for an answer. "He recognized the difficulties and often said that, while he did not know the answer, he was completely confident that there was an answer and that one had to try until one either found it for himself or got it from someone else," his wife once remarked.[18] If this meant that he had to borrow ideas with which he would have otherwise disagreed, he was free to do so. Roosevelt understood that people needed action. They could find comfort in the fact that a solution was being sought, and this trait gave him much free rein.

The lack of an external moral code has caused FDR to receive much criticism as well. His decision to seek a third term and his attempts to "pack" the Supreme Court caused many to argue that Roosevelt "sought to undermine the very pillars of the Republic."[19] While Roosevelt certainly had no such plans, he did not feel restrained by historical tradition in the government. He often acted without precedent, which has led some to praise him as a presidential innovator and others to denounce him as a tyrant. The truth seems to have been rooted in his morality. He truly believed in his own opinions and intuition, and he usually acted on them.

Roosevelt also had a strong desire to be liked. His reliance on a personal code allowed him wide latitude in this area. He was at times forced to go back on promises that he had made. During the 1932 campaign, he foolishly promised in Pittsburgh to cut government expenditures in order to balance the budget. Once in office, however, he was forced to leave the budget out of balance in order to fund relief programs. He logically defended his actions by stating that it would be foolish to stick to such a pledge when people were starving. Roosevelt's idea of a campaign promise did not mesh well with the nation's, however, and he was harshly criticized during the 1936 campaign. One adviser jokingly suggested that he deny ever having been in Pittsburgh.

Roosevelt's desire to be liked hurt him on a more personal level as well. His wife remarked, "Perhaps in the long run, fewer friends would have been lost by bluntness than by misunderstandings that arose from his charming, engaging ambiguity."[20] Roosevelt often gave people the impression that he agreed with them when he actually felt that they were wrong. Along the same lines, he often played his own advisers against each other, assigning the same task to several people. He seemed to enjoy having the power to deceive others. Harry Truman blamed it on "that growing ego of his, which probably wasn't too minuscule to start with."[21]

Roosevelt's reliance on a personal code of morality might well have been the source of both his greatest strength and his greatest weakness. This is not to suggest, however, that he ignored religion. On the contrary, Roosevelt's religious convictions were quite apparent. His concept of social justice seems to have been intertwined with Christianity. One biographer was moved to note that Roosevelt "saw no real conflict between Church and State. The higher aims of both coincided, and the two, while wholly separate in their functioning, can work hand in hand."[22] He "regarded the Scriptures as an incomparable source of wisdom and frequently turned to them in his writing and speaking."[23] Roosevelt knew that Americans often drew strength from religion, and his use of religious imagery in speeches was comforting to them.

FDR: Friend or Foe?

The history of political scandals in the United States certainly does much to bolster the claim that the love of money is the root of all evil. But through the long years of the Roosevelt administration there were no major scandals concerning money. This makes sense given the constant specter of the Great Depression. But the programs of the New Deal had a substantial effect on the nation for many years to come.

Rexford Tugwell, one of Roosevelt's economic advisers, says in his biography that the New Deal programs "seem to be characterized by more confusion and contradiction than progress toward consistent objectives."[24] There were shifts in foreign affairs from economic isolationism to collective security. At times, Roosevelt stressed a partnership with business; at others, he resorted to regulation. He at first advocated home relief for the unemployed and then insisted on work projects.

"Everything done in 1934, almost, seems to have been reversed in 1935," Tugwell says.[25] Roosevelt also met considerable opposition when he toyed with silver and gold as a means of adjusting prices. Inconsistent and contradictory policies gave Roosevelt's critics much ammunition. "They seem to show that most of the time he knew neither what he was doing nor why he was doing it. He could not possibly be right in so many instances when he was on both sides at once."[26]

Tugwell later suggests, however, a pattern of action that seems to fit nicely with Roosevelt's personality. He was not operating consistently under any sort of economic or social theory. He was interested only in results. If something did not work, he would throw it out and try something else. Garry Wills noted, "Those who wanted ideological consistency, or even policy coherence, were rightly exasperated with Roosevelt. He switched economic plans as often as he changed treatments for polio."[27]

Roosevelt's moral code stressed necessity, especially political necessity. At the same time, his understanding of common psychology taught him that people needed hope. They needed to see that something, anything, was being done. This attitude was part of the emerging social culture of the country, and Roosevelt seemed to grasp that. It was a "can do" attitude. It seemed to say, "We'll keeping trying until we succeed, and we will never give up." With a strong Democratic majority in Congress, Roosevelt had the opportunity to be extremely active in his first one hundred days, and he took advantage of it.

A Taft or a Coolidge might not have seized such an opportunity. And while the New Deal was largely ineffective and sometimes contradictory, it did have a strong political and psychological consequence. "He had enabled his countrymen to keep their heads while peoples all about them in the world were losing theirs."[28] In this sense, it is difficult to argue against the assertion that Roosevelt was a great leader in times of crisis. He had an enormous skill for comforting a panic-stricken people and for directing their energies. "Roosevelt seemed to offer something for everybody, but the gift of hope, precious beyond measure at that volatile moment, he offered equally to all."[29]

A great leader for the present, however, is not necessarily a great leader for the future. Roosevelt might have been well suited for times of emergency, but the ultimate effects of his New Deal programs were not necessarily wholly desirable. While FDR's primary concern was to combat the depression, he could not have overlooked the fact that he was ballooning the federal budget, although it is unlikely that he could have foreseen the great fiscal problems that his programs would eventually cause. (Roosevelt is wrongly blamed by many for budget problems that were provoked by Lyndon B. Johnson's Great Society.) In fairness, it must be noted that Roosevelt did disband many New Deal agencies when he felt that they had outlived their usefulness. By 1943, the Civilian Conservation Corps, the Works Progress Administration, and the National Youth Administration were gone.

The moral philosophy of Roosevelt's New Deal, however, eventually turned into an ideological position for the Democratic Party. While it certainly was not socialism, it did represent the idea that government existed to care for its people. This philosophy undoubtedly came from Roosevelt's own morality.

He seemed to have a genuine sympathy for the underprivileged, probably as a result of his own suffering. Roosevelt also invoked his religious convictions often. He frequently quoted from the Sermon on the Mount, his favorite Bible passage, and especially stressed the need for Americans to pitch in and help their neighbors. This certainly worked to mirror the emerging popular culture of the era.

In the long run, of course, Roosevelt has been greatly criticized because of this. Some contemporary presidential scholars have even ranked him as only "near great" or in some instances "average."[30] During the recent administrations, a backlash has occurred and the nation's large social programs have been reexamined. The original American ideas of small government and freedom from government have begun to reemerge, and this has worked to paint Roosevelt's acts in a darker light.

Two arguments in defense of Roosevelt point to his emphasis on achieving success. First, Roosevelt believed that pressing problems overrode the need to observe precedent and principle.[31] Second, during the depths of the Great Depression, communism and socialism had substantial appeal to many Americans. By offering new and expanded social welfare programs, Roosevelt impeded the popular appeal of those ideologies. Simply put, he defeated communism and socialism by borrowing from them. Again pragmatism trumped principle in Roosevelt's approach to crisis decision making. Critics argue that this public policy pragmatism began to diminish personal responsibility and to increase popular reliance and dependence on government, problems that were exacerbated in later administrations.

Two important aspects of Roosevelt's morality become apparent while examining his economic policies. First, he was willing to go against and tear down traditional American ideas or institutions. Again, his moral code did not come from an outer source; it came from within. Second, he was not deeply concerned with the lasting effects of his programs.

He truly believed in their moral goodness, partly because he had a sincere sympathy for the underprivileged. During World War I, President Wilson had thought in terms of abstract concepts and grand visions. Roosevelt thought in terms of people. This belief in a caregiver role for government became a strong ideology in America, and it can be tied to Roosevelt's own moral code.

Roosevelt's confidence and serene personality seems to have made the need for power—often a motivating force behind moral issues—less of an issue for him. He did enjoy exercising his power, however, and this often led to internal problems within his administration. In order to reign supreme in his world, Roosevelt often encouraged and instigated competition within his own ranks. He would appoint "people of clashing attitudes and temperaments to the competing positions."[32]

Few people were certain of where they stood with the president, and aide Raymond Moley even claimed that they "had the chilling fear that he regarded them as dispensable."[33] Such an administrative approach surely had its good points. Roosevelt seldom had problems with disloyal workers, and he was always at the reins of his organization. However, the constant competition was undoubtedly nerve-wracking. "The thing FDR prided himself the most about was 'I have a happy ship,'" said Treasury Secretary Henry Morgenthau. "But he never had a happy ship."[34] This made working under Roosevelt difficult, and his methods for ensuring power probably hindered his administrative abilities.

The story of Roosevelt's life contains few blatant examples of immorality. In most cases, his decisions must be viewed in terms of political ideology. However, not even Franklin Roosevelt was immune from the temptation of sex. His extramarital affair with Lucy Mercer is fairly well documented, and it is one of the few clear, major misdeeds of Roosevelt's life.

Some might argue that this had little effect on his administration. Mercer had been hired as FDR's social secretary in 1913 (by his wife, ironically), while he served as assistant secretary of the navy. The affair effectively ended in 1918 after Eleanor learned of it. She threatened to leave him if he did not promise to stop seeing Mercer, and he agreed to her terms. However, this did not end the effects of his extramarital actions. The revelation changed Eleanor, who became far more independent and relied less on her husband.

During his presidency, Roosevelt broke his promise to his wife and began to see Mercer again. These meetings always happened while Eleanor was out of town, so that they could be kept from her. In fact, his family and his subordinates went to great lengths to hide the relationship from his wife. Biographer Joseph Alsop wrote that he even shared diplomatic and military secrets with Mercer.[35]

Mercer was with the president in Warm Springs, Georgia, when he died, a fact that caused Eleanor a great deal of pain. This illustrates two points that paint Roosevelt in a rather poor moral light. His initial association with Mercer was clearly wrong, and Roosevelt promised his wife that he would stop. But he broke this promise, compounding his moral mistake. Second, Roosevelt enlisted the aid of his associates in a coverup, an activity of which few Americans would have approved. FDR's reported sharing of national secrets with Mercer is also reprehensible.

Politicians are often hurt by what is referred to as the "credibility gap," and Roosevelt was no exception. Several examples have already been cited, most notably the contradictory aspects of the New Deal. Roosevelt was also hurt politically by his 1932 campaign promise in Pittsburgh to balance the budget. In that campaign, he charged—ironically, in light of later events—that Hoover's was "the greatest spending Administration in peace times in all our history."[36]

He also assured the nation in 1940 that "this country is not going to war."[37] Many overlook this fact in the face of Pearl Harbor, reasoning that he had no choice after the attack. However, Roosevelt had already begun to mobilize and prepare for war. This could be considered wise and prudent on his part, especially given what eventually occurred. However, it did contradict his promise, thereby raising the specter of a credibility gap.

The administrations of the 1930s and 1940s had far fewer moral issues than later administrations. Civil rights, homosexuality, and abortion hardly made a blip on Roosevelt's public policy radar screen. This meshed with the popular culture of the day, which stressed togetherness and getting along. The only clear public policy moral issue that Roosevelt faced was one that he truly brought on himself: his attempt to pack the Supreme Court.

The Supreme Court was the only branch of government that Roosevelt did not control. The Court had struck down many of his early New Deal programs, angering Roosevelt. His attempted reorganization of the Court was a challenge to the Constitution. In 1937, Roosevelt had Senator Joseph Robinson sponsor a plan in the Senate to restructure the Court. Under the new structure, a president would have the power to appoint one new justice, up to a maximum of six, for every sitting justice seventy years of age or older with at least ten years of service. Although Roosevelt attempted to paint this new idea as a progressive plan, his real intention was quite obviously to pack the Court in his favor. This era in American history cherished the past, and the idea of tampering with an institution as old as the Court was not received well politically.

Roosevelt had just emerged from a landslide reelection, and his party had retained a majority in Congress. For these reasons, Roosevelt probably felt that his mandate would carry the day. Any other president might not have attempted such a bold undertaking, but FDR's unusual confidence can probably account for this moral decision. After Roosevelt lost the fight, Rexford Tugwell remarked that "it took him an unconscionable time to discover his weakness. This must be charged mostly to overconfidence."[38]

There were other issues that FDR advocated as well, but none had such clear moral implications. His Good Neighbor Policy toward Latin America was important as a means of creating a united Western Hemisphere during the coming war. The title of the policy played especially well in the popular culture of the day. The recognition of the Soviet Union also occurred on his watch. The Soviet policy led to extreme charges, but little came of them.

Columnist Westbrook Pegler insisted: "Roosevelt made many decisions in favor of Soviet Russia, beginning with the recognition of the Soviet Government. Thereafter he permitted the whole bureaucracy to be infested with spies."[39] In Roosevelt's defense, Stalin's regime was the legitimate government of Russia, and refusing to acknowledge that fact, especially with Russia looming as a possible ally, would have done little for the country.

Neither friend nor foe could scarcely doubt his sincerity, however. He did what he thought best for the country. His social programs may have caused the nation problems down the road, but he instituted them with the idea of helping people. He wanted to pack the Court to win approval for policies he thought right for the country. Setting aside precedents and principles enabled him to experiment with policies until he found something that worked.

Roosevelt's supreme self-confidence showed itself one last time. His failing health led many party leaders to think Roosevelt would not finish his fourth term. Roosevelt, however, did little either to choose carefully or to prepare his successor, Senator Harry S. Truman of Missouri. A cloud of invincibility concealed his mortality. Roosevelt "had been President for so long and through such trying, stirring times that it seemed to many Americans, including the junior Senator from Missouri, that he virtually was the presidency himself."[40]

In choosing his vice presidential running mate, Roosevelt passed over the well-prepared James F. Byrnes for the little-known and inexperienced Truman. Byrnes had served in the U.S. House of Representatives and the U.S. Senate, on the U.S. Supreme Court, as secretary of state, and as the senior White House adviser to Roosevelt. Truman, the product of a political machine, had served only in the U.S. Senate.

Roosevelt, who knew that he was in very poor health, seemed to have trouble with the idea that someone else might lead his country. David McCullough called FDR "larger than life, even in a wheelchair," while

Truman was the "little man from Missouri."[41] Under these circumstances Harry Truman became president in 1945.

HARRY S. TRUMAN, 1945–1953

Emerging from the Shadow

In the shadow of Roosevelt, Truman seemed small. He offered nothing remarkable. He lacked Roosevelt's education and wealth. For twelve years, the country had leaned on FDR for comfort and support. Now, it watched as a small, average-looking man from Missouri replaced the larger-than-life Roosevelt. David McCullough writes, "To many, it was not just that the greatest of men had fallen, but that the least of men—or at any rate the least likely of men—had assumed his place."[42]

From this doubtful start in 1945, Harry S. Truman has gradually risen in stature. Today, many rank him among the better presidents.[43] Why? Undoubtedly, biographies play a part as they capture Truman's rise from obscurity and his decisive crisis decisions. Truman came out of Roosevelt's shadow by making some of the most momentous military and foreign policy decisions in the nation's history. Also in the annals of presidential elections, none rivals Truman's come-from-behind victory over the favored Thomas E. Dewey in 1948. Now a part of presidential election folklore is the picture of Truman holding the *Chicago Tribune* with its front-page story headlined, "Dewey Wins."

While not as dramatic a story as Lincoln's rise to stardom from a log cabin, Truman's story fits in that mold. Truman had more than three strikes against him. He was an unknown, religious, average-looking, non-college-educated product of a political machine. Painted on this canvass of adversity, however, is a story of political success.

"To Err Is Truman"

Truman's morality and modesty appear too good to be true. Compared with many other presidents, Truman demonstrated the values of hard work, perseverance, honesty, and kindness. When someone suggested that Secretary of State George Marshall might make a better president, "Truman's response was that yes, of course, Marshall would make a better president."[44] Such modesty is not the norm among presidents and politicians.

What defines Truman? While he lacked Roosevelt's brand of self-confidence, Truman had confidence of another sort. McCullough says that Truman "knew himself and understood himself and liked himself. I don't mean vanity or conceit. I'm talking about self-respect, self-understanding. To an exceptional degree, power never went to his head."[45] He was neither supremely self-confident nor arrogant.

Also unlike Roosevelt, Truman's self-confidence did not dictate his morality. His religious convictions tied together belief and action. He said: "I am by religion like everyone else. I think there's more in acting than in talking."[46] His religious beliefs set boundary lines for him.

When Truman was twelve years old, he read the Bible twice. In his memoir *Mr. Citizen,* he wrote that, "The Old Testament and the New will give you a way of life that will cause you to live happily."[47] While Roosevelt trusted his own morality in government, Truman said that "the fundamental basis of all government is in this Book right here, and started with Moses on the Mount."[48] During his presidency, Truman would regularly compose short prayers at his desk. Roosevelt was a wealthy, Harvard-educated leader, but Truman, a child of Middle America, held religious beliefs and convictions that mirrored those of the nation's majority.

Truman's brand of self-confidence surfaced in his writings. Roosevelt never opened himself up to the country as Truman did: "In private correspondence, Truman could be extremely revealing, whereas Roosevelt never dropped the mask, never poured his heart out on paper as did Truman in hundreds of letters and notes to himself, even after it was clear that he was to be a figure in history."[49]

In short, Truman knew who he was, and he believed that he had nothing to hide. He has been called unremarkable by critics, partly because he did not always hold back his fears in his writings. Other important distinctions must be made in order to understand Truman's character. While Truman lacked Roosevelt's Harvard education, he had great intellectual curiosity. He read widely and even studied Cicero in the original Latin.[50]

Truman connected with the average American. Unlike Roosevelt, Truman had fought on the front lines in World War I. Instead of attending college, Truman tried his hand at farming and then at business. Truman accepted who he was, and he made no efforts to portray himself as anything else. He acted according to his personal moral and religious convictions, making difficult decisions and accepting their consequences. His character was transparent.

The idea of a president with no sexual skeletons in his closet has become something of a novelty, but absolutely no such scandals are associated with Truman's presidency. What is more, Truman's loyalty to his future wife was documented long before they were even married. One of his friends during World War I wrote, "I never saw him do anything out of the way that would be questionable in the way of a moral situation. He was clean all the way through. I always admired him for that quality and you know when a man's in the Army, why his morals get a pretty good test."[51] Throughout his presidency, Truman remained very close to his wife. While he was in Europe negotiating the end of the World War II, he sent her twenty-two letters in one month![52]

Truman sometimes let his loyalty cost him politically. When his workers got caught up in scandals, Truman "angrily regarded attacks on any of his subordinates as attacks upon himself."[53] "One problem with President Truman," Secretary of the Interior Harold Ickes suggested, "is that he becomes defiant when his friends are criticized."[54]

In trying times, Roosevelt often abandoned one line of thought for another, more promising one; Truman, never: He always stood firm in his beliefs, accepting who he was, and never questioned his reasoning. When he saw the need for a decision, he made it without considering the political implications. Sometimes this approach hurt him in the short run by making him appear stubborn or foolish, but it also made him appear courageous. Truman would have accepted neither judgment. He simply did what he thought right.

Truman's moral dimensions mirrored a golden age that painted morality in vivid shades of black and white, right and wrong.

"In All This Long Career I Had Certain Rules Which I Followed"

Moral questions sometimes trace their roots to money, and so it was with Truman. Some of the most morally questionable events of the Truman administration concerned the financial dealings of Truman's underlings. During a Senate investigation of the Reconstruction Finance Corporation (RFC), charges were made that Donald Dawson, an administrative assistant to Truman, had influenced the RFC to give loans to favored organizations. While these charges never implicated Truman, he jumped into the fray in typical style by defending his subordinates. He called the report "asinine,"[55] which did little to create sympathy for his position.

Other allegations were made during his administration. Many of Truman's friends were accused of influence peddling. In return for small gifts to the White House, the friends granted donors larger favors. Again, this did not reach Truman personally, but he assumed responsibility for the actions of his administration. Little came of the scandals, which "often involved stupidity as much as corruption in the usual sense."[56] Nonetheless, Truman allowed the issues to stick to him when they otherwise might not have.

The "Truman scandals" reveal several aspects of Truman's moral code. Having been raised with the idea that friends looked out for each other, he was loyal, sometimes blindly so, to his friends and associates. At times during his administration, this had the effect of causing others to stick by him in difficult times; loyalty was also an important trait to Americans during the 1940s and 1950s.

Truman's handling of the issues was not always smooth. His calling the report "asinine" and his many disparaging remarks about the media did little to boost his national image. At these times, he seemed less like a kindly next-door neighbor and more like a grumpy old man.

None of the other money issues that the Truman administration dealt with was as pointedly moral as the scandals, but they do reveal something of his morality. The Marshall Plan was approved in 1948. The plan paid about $13 billion to European nations for reconstruction projects. Truman's main aim in the Marshall Plan was to reinforce Europe against the threat of Soviet Russia. At the same time, however, he seemed to comprehend the lessons of World War I. His understanding of history was often praised, and he was determined to prevent further conflict.

Truman's domestic program, the Fair Deal, increased the minimum wage, extended Social Security coverage, and instituted an urban renewal program. Through these actions, Truman clearly painted himself in the social tradition of Roosevelt. The argument can be made, therefore, that he stood against the "small government" of the Founders. A failed aspect of the Fair Deal would have created a national health insurance plan, which only bolsters this argument. Truman's main concern was helping people, and few doubt his sincerity. Nonetheless, it is clear that Truman had no ideological fear of a powerful government.

A discussion of power as a motivating force behind immorality must begin at the start of Truman's political career. Truman was the product of

Tom Pendergast's political machine, and this unsavory association followed him throughout his career. Although Truman's diaries show that he was not happy about some of the actions machine politics required of him early in his career, he did not dislike Pendergast. True to form, he was always fiercely loyal to his old patron. When Pendergast died, Truman commandeered an Air Force bomber in order to attend the funeral. "You don't forget a friend," he insisted.[57] From what is known of Truman's association with the machine, there is no evidence that he was ever involved in blatantly illegal activities. Throughout his career no trace of corruption was ever found on his record either by opposing candidates or by the eventual FBI investigation of Pendergast.

Truman, unlike some political leaders, was not tempted to immorality by a need for power. His modesty has been well documented. According to one famous story, just after a shaken Truman had been sworn in, Speaker of the House Sam Rayburn advised him that "the special interests and sycophants will stand in the rain a week to see you and will treat you like a king. They'll come sliding in and tell you you're the greatest man alive—but you know and I know you ain't."[58]

Truman never seemed to forget this advice. He accepted his limitations. He knew, for example, that he was an average public speaker and that he lacked Roosevelt's ability to sway crowds with his words. The most critical analysis of Truman's public speaking ability comes, surprisingly, from his daughter, Margaret.[59] Despite Truman's self-acceptance, however, he was sometimes forced into action because of his leadership style.

Unlike Roosevelt, Truman was a manager. He involved himself closely in the operations of his administration, and he expected his subordinates to obey him. McCullough writes at length about Truman's sense of history. "If [a president] is blasted by the press, if his polls are plummeting as Truman's did during the Korean War, these are not his first concerns. What matters—or ought to matter—is what's best for the country and the world in the long run."[60]

In this way, Truman had a good understanding of the importance of a strong chief executive. He undoubtedly wanted to avoid leaving the office weaker than he found it. He generally responded to direct assaults on his authority from within his administration. This illustrates two aspects of his character and morality: his concern with the effects of his actions, something Roosevelt sometimes ignored; and his ability to act decisively on an unpopular issue. The best example, of course, is his resolution to fire General Douglas MacArthur.

"He [MacArthur] wouldn't respect the authority of the president," insists Merle Miller in *Plain Speaking*.[61] This was more or less the heart of the problem. As the Korean War progressed, MacArthur became more and more frustrated with the war's conduct. He wanted to press for absolute victory, not merely containment. "We must win," the general insisted. "There is no substitute for victory."[62]

MacArthur's public statements on the war constituted a basic challenge to Truman, and the Joint Chiefs of Staff agreed that Truman would be justified in dismissing MacArthur. While Truman was still mulling over this decision, word of the general's possible firing was leaked to the press, and the White House reacted quickly. Without first informing MacArthur, the White House announced in a press conference that the general was to be relieved of his command.

Biographer William Pemberton wrote that "near hysteria seemed to grip many Americans. Republican leaders discussed the possibility of impeaching Truman. Senator Joseph McCarthy charged that Truman was drunk when he made the decision."[63] The moral implications of Truman's action should be examined on several levels. It must be stressed that the decision wounded him severely. His administration never recovered politically. "Sixty-nine percent of people polled supported MacArthur."[64]

Truman undoubtedly knew that the reaction would be severe, and yet he made the decision that he felt was right. MacArthur was, after all, a national hero. Senator William Jenner was even moved to suggest that the executive branch was controlled by the Soviets. Truman accepted all of this. He accepted it because he knew that he had done what he thought was best, and he accepted it because he felt that no future president should have to fight for control of the military. These are two aspects that FDR might not have considered.

On the other hand, Truman's quick temper probably prevented him from handling the firing well. Most agree that MacArthur should have been notified before the announcement, a move that certainly would have softened the blow. In this instance, Truman's habit of sticking by his subordinates seems to have paid huge dividends. His entire military staff, including General Dwight Eisenhower, who was then NATO commander, stood behind him. This helped legitimize his action to the nation.

Truman had another major power decision to make in 1952. An

impending strike in the steel industry prompted Truman to order the federal seizure of the mills. With the Korean War roaring in the background, the country could not afford a steel strike, and Truman acted, never doubting that he was doing the right thing. Two months later, the Supreme Court ruled that he had acted unconstitutionally, and it negated the order. The broader implications of this "defeat" were not as important as those of the MacArthur situation, but the decision demonstrates yet again that Truman was willing to act on his beliefs without compromise. McCullough writes, "We were at war and a prolonged shutdown of production of steel threatened the very lives of our fighting forces in Korea."[65] Truman saw his actions as merely an attempt to save lives.

Of course, Truman is remembered mainly for his decision on the biggest "power" issue of all time, the use of nuclear weapons. Rows of books have been written on this subject, and Truman's actions have been endlessly questioned. Truman was, without question, a pragmatist. The country had been through a long, bloody conflict. He had the means necessary to end the war. Tens of thousands of American soldiers were dying at each island battle in the South Pacific, and the Japanese were certain to fight even more ferociously when the war reached their homeland.

The United States was already sending bombing raids against Japan that were taking 20,000 to 40,000 Japanese lives at a blow. One raid against Tokyo on March 10, 1945, was estimated to have killed as many as 100,000 Japanese. "When Robert Oppenheimer, director of the project that developed the bomb, was asked how many casualties might result from the use of the bomb, presuming it worked, he said perhaps as many as 20,000."[66] While the moral implications of Truman's decision to use the atomic bomb may be debated forever, it must be remembered that his advisers had no idea what they were dealing with.

McCullough writes, "The President—the commander-in-chief—gave the order. The war ended."[67] George Elsey is less diplomatic: "It's all well and good to come along later and say the bomb was a horrible thing. The whole . . . war was a horrible thing."[68] At any rate, it is somewhat difficult to judge Truman morally under such circumstances. He ordered the deaths of countless Japanese, but he was in a position to do little else. His only options included the choice of how to kill them and how many American lives to throw away in the process.

Truman's own response fits well into the model of acceptance: "The final decision of where and when to use the atomic bomb was up to me.

Let there be no mistake about it. I regarded the bomb as a military weapon and never had any doubt that it should be used."[69] Truman took the brunt of the criticism by taking full responsibility, as usual. He also never questioned his decision. He had done it, and that was that. "In years to come, Truman often said that having made the decision about the bomb, he went to bed and slept soundly."[70]

If Truman is to be held accountable for the use of nuclear weapons, it makes more sense to evaluate him after the full horror of the device became known. The second atomic attack is harder to defend, and it seems that the indescribable danger of the weapon must have become apparent to Truman. One of his main quarrels with MacArthur during the Korean War concerned Truman's refusal to use nuclear weapons. MacArthur was convinced that Truman did not really want to win the war.

Truman was instrumental in ensuring that control of the nation's atomic devices stayed in civilian hands. The entire nuclear question is probably a case of technology outrunning human morality. Truman was perhaps faced with a greater moral question than he initially realized. His actions with regard to this issue reveal much of his moral character, however.

The Truman administration handled several other issues that had moral implications. In March 1947, Truman issued his famous Truman Doctrine. "I believe that it must be the policy of the United States to support free peoples who are resisting attempted subjugation by armed minorities or by outside pressures."[71] This led, of course, to the policy of containment, and it helped kick off the Cold War. In a more immediate sense, it obliged the U.S. to intervene in Korea. For Truman, the moral motivations for this probably were related to loyalty. America's allies in Europe were fearful of Soviet threats. An "iron curtain," Churchill said, was "descending over Europe."[72]

The paranoia created by communism reached Washington in 1946, and Truman created the Temporary Commission on Employee Loyalty. Of Truman's loyalty oath program, McCullough writes, "It was uncalled for, expensive, it contributed substantially to the mounting bureaucracy of Washington and damaged the reputations and lives of numbers of people who should never have had any such thing happen to them."[73] Truman initiated the program as a political move. The idea was to head off the rising right-wing cry against Communists, but it failed. Truman later remarked that acting in the cause of "good politics" was against his nature.

Truman did more to promote civil rights for blacks than any president since Lincoln. "He created the epoch-making Commission on Civil Rights" and "ordered the desegregation of the armed services and the federal Civil Service."[74] His stand was not popular all over the country, but Truman accepted the criticism that accompanied his decision. This was before Martin Luther King Jr. and the march on Washington, and it was quite a bold stand.

Finally, the United States recognized the creation of Israel in 1948, just after it had been proclaimed a state. Truman's decision on this matter was far more complicated than it first appears, and it emphasizes his two most important character traits. Secretary of State Marshall was against immediate recognition because he was concerned about Middle Eastern oil supplies. Marshall was the most respected member of Truman's cabinet, and Truman thought very highly of him. McCullough writes, "If Truman were to decide against him and Marshall were then to resign, it would almost certainly mean defeat for Truman in November."[75] But Truman always acted on his beliefs, and he accepted the consequences. He had long been a proponent of a Jewish state, and he recognized Israel at once. In yet another show of loyalty appreciated, Marshall stood by him.

The Truman presidency will always be remembered for the great comeback election win in 1948. It probably did more to show the sort of man that Harry Truman was than anything else. He fought until the very end. He worked hard and never gave up. It is difficult to come away from a study of Harry Truman without liking him immensely. Of modern presidents, Truman might be considered the most moral.

As time goes by, his stock will probably continue to rise. Unlike Roosevelt, with his extramarital affair, inconsistent policies, and tendency to play subordinates against each other, Truman provides almost no reason to doubt him morally. He accepted who he was and what he stood for. He was able to act above the realm of politics, a rare trait today. For this reason, Americans have little doubt that they know the man, and that they understand him.

THE "FEEL GOOD" ERA OF THE FIFTIES

The decade of the 1950s ushered in peace and prosperity. The American culture centered around the family and community. The "feel-good innocence" of the era reflects the post–World War II optimism thriving in

America. People respected their elders, and the nation collectively held strong moral beliefs.

Music in the 1950s captured the upbeat mood. The early 1950s produced light melodies, sweet lyrics, and wholesome, innocent singers. Most of the songs produced were "feel-good" tunes genuinely reflecting the mood of the post–World War II America. Artists like Pat Boone, Rosemary Clooney, and Perry Como dominated pop charts.

This sweetness bored the new independent life form, known as teenagers. They were looking for something more exciting. They discovered this vitality and irrepressible energy in rock and roll. The mid-1950s gave rise to influential singers such as Fats Domino ("Ain't That a Shame"), the Penguins ("Earth Angel"), Chuck Berry ("Maybellene"), and Bill Haley and the Comets ("Rock around the Clock"). In 1956, teen idol Elvis Presley, "the King," became popular with such hits as "Hound Dog," "Don't Be Cruel," and "Heartbreak Hotel." During this decade, Disneyland opened in Anaheim, California, in 1955; Grace Kelly of Philadelphia married Prince Rainier III of Monaco in 1956; and that same year American League's Most Valuable Player, Mickey Mantle of the New York Yankees, led in home runs, runs batted in, and batting average.

The fifties also saw the spread of television, although it was much less pervasive than today. People watched television mostly in the afternoons and evenings. It was black-and-white, and there were no remote controls.

Situation comedy was born in the 1950s; *I Love Lucy* and *The Honeymooners* made the nation laugh. There were *The Adventures of Superman* and, from the very end of the decade (October 2, 1959) into the mid-1960s, the original run of *The Twilight Zone* for the science-fiction crowd;. *Howdy Doody Time, Lassie,* and Walt Disney's *Mickey Mouse Club* for the children; and quiz shows and *American Bandstand* for teenagers. Many of these shows ran well into the subsequent decade, or even longer, and can still be seen in syndication today.

DWIGHT D. EISENHOWER, 1953–1961

"Gentle in Manner, Strong in Deed"

The thirty-fourth president of the United States, Dwight David Eisenhower, served from 1953 to 1961. Many attributed the peace of the 1950s to Eisenhower, the glorified and well-respected war hero who was gentle of character and kind of heart.

Eisenhower's average approval rating was a remarkable 64 percent.[76] In spite of Eisenhower's impressive ability to maintain the support of the American people, for roughly the decade and a half after he left the White House, most scholars and other writers on the presidency judged him to have been a lackluster leader. For example, in 1962, Arthur Schlesinger Sr. asked seventy-five leading authorities on the American presidency to rank the chief executives in order of greatness. Eisenhower placed twenty-first, tied with Chester Arthur. "The scholars' views of Eisenhower and his leadership fundamentally echoed the 1950s partisan rhetoric of Liberal Democrats, who viewed Eisenhower as bland, good-natured, and well intentioned, but politically inept and passive. He seemed to hold a minimalist view of the leadership of the Chief Executive."[77]

By the mid 1970s, a reappraisal of Eisenhower and his leadership had begun. "Interest in re-examining Eisenhower's presidency was spurred in part by the difficulties encountered by his successors and in part by retrospective assessments of the events that occurred while he was in office."[78]

The revisionist view of Eisenhower describes him, not as a passive president, but as an unusual activist whose activism, "which was grounded in a consciously articulated view of how to exercise leadership, took a distinctive and unconventional form."[79] According to Fred I. Greenstein, author of *The Hidden-Hand Presidency:*

> Eisenhower went to great lengths to conceal the political side of his leadership. He did this so well and played the part of nonpolitical chief of state so convincingly that until recently most writers on the presidency viewed him through the lens of his 1950s liberal critics as an aging hero who reigned more than he ruled and lacked the energy, motivation and political know-how to have a significant impact on events.[80]

Stephen E. Ambrose writes that Eisenhower

> was an inspiring and effective leader, indeed a model of leadership. The elements of his leadership were varied, deliberate and learned. He exuded simplicity. He deliberately projected an image of the folksy farm boy from Kansas. But in fact he was capable of a detached, informed and exhaustive examination of problems and personalities, based on wide and sophisticated knowledge and deep study. He projected a posture of being above politics, but he studied and

understood and acted on political problems and considerations more rigorously than most lifelong politicians ever could.[81]

Eisenhower's character had a notable influence on his leadership style. Eisenhower channeled both the public vagueness and the private precision into his style of leadership. His image, to some, was that of a solid man full of common sense. He portrayed himself as a reassuring figure living up to his own premise that, "as the visible symbol of the nation, the president should exhibit a respectable image of American life before the world."[82]

Eisenhower's public persona often made him appear like a "mediocre, fumbling, ignorant boob."[83] This facade was in fact a valuable political strategy to keep the calculating Eisenhower from appearing too Machiavellian. According to Greenstein:

> the intellectual thinness and syntactical flaws in press conference texts, Eisenhower would later write, resulted from caution. With press conferences open to quotation and broadcast, "an inadvertent misstatement in public would be a calamity." But he continued, realizing that "it is far better to stumble or speak guardedly than to move ahead smoothly and risk imperilling the country," by consistently focusing on ideas rather than on phrasing, he "was able to avoid causing the nation a serious setback through anything I said in many hours, over eight years of intensive questioning."[84]

To work with Congress, Eisenhower used a nonconfrontational leadership style and informal negotiations. He believed that this was the best method for getting results. Eisenhower's leadership "shows how he could manipulate situations to his own ends while still maintaining the personal image of a neutral spokesman for the national interest."[85] He followed several principles in carrying out his leadership strategy.

First, he frequently exercised political influence through intermediaries rather than directly or otherwise concealed his part in the leadership in order to downplay the political side of his role. Second, Eisenhower used language masterfully. In his private communications with close associates his language was a model of analytical clarity and contained informed, realistic accounts of his political strategies.[86] But in press conferences he often was evasive or professed ignorance of matters that were best not discussed, in a homely, idiomatic way that enhanced public affection for, and confidence in, him. And in his public addresses, he worked with his speech writers seeking to find language that was dignified yet, as he once put it, simple enough "to sound good to the fellow digging a ditch in Kansas."[87] Third, Eisenhower took pains never to criticize an adversary by name, for it would demean his own role and arouse underdog sympathies for the opponent. By refusing to "engage in personalities" he acted on the premise that impugning the motives of others engenders ill feeling that undermines the basic leadership task of welding political cooperation.[88] Fourth, he refused to discuss personality in the public realm, for much of his private reasoning and discourse involved sizing up what he called the "personal equation" of other political actors. He did this in order to use aides where they would be most effective and anticipate how best to exercise influence. "His preoccupation with personality analysis helped him to keep the political side of his leadership inconspicuous."[89] Fifth, Eisenhower was a vocal advocate of delegation of authority, varying the degree of authority given to those associates he sensed had the capacity to get the job done according to his own desires. This tactic was beneficial in two ways. It gave the associates credit for popular administration policies, and it protected Eisenhower from controversy, allowing them to take blame for unpopular policies. All of these tactics that Eisenhower incorporated into his presidency fit his times. Today, we expect a lot more of presidents and demand that they actively show the American public what they are doing.

The use of the "hidden hand" served Eisenhower well. "A president who seeks influence and cultivates a reputation for not intervening in day-to-day policy-making will necessarily hide his hand more often than one who seeks recognition as an effective political operator."[90]

The tranquility of the 1950s enabled Eisenhower to avoid "engaging in personalities" and to come across as the "good boy." Today a president would look like a wimp or like he was hiding something. Eisenhower's personality was a major contributing factor to his success. In 1946, the *New York Times* wrote that "one reason for General Eisenhower's steadily mounting prestige is his common sense approach to difficult and intricate problems. A second is his ability to express the problem clearly. A third is his always evident sincerity."[91]

Eisenhower had self-confidence, "based on the knowledge that he knew more, studied more, understood more, and thought things through more objectively. When he gave an order he believed in it."[92] Ambrose writes that:

Eisenhower's magnetic appeal to millions of his fellow citizens seemed to come about as a natural and effortless result of his sunny disposition. But he worked at his apparent artlessness. That big grin and bouncy step often masked depression, doubt, or utter weariness, for he believed it was the critical duty of a leader to always exude optimism. He made it a habit to save all his doubts for his pillow.[93]

Eisenhower gained the country's respect because he worked to attain it. According to Ambrose, Eisenhower's rule was

Never question another man's motives. His wisdom, yes, but not his motives. He also tried to always assume the best about others, until shown otherwise. He could do so consistently, even in a world full of high-powered men whose motives were often self-serving or base, because of his most outstanding personal characteristic: he was a man full of love, for life and for people.[94]

Eisenhower's times and his personal character have a direct effect on one another. The times played a role in molding his character. Passivity, tranquility, and respect for others characterized both this period and Eisenhower, who possessed the virtues of honesty, integrity, and religious devotion. Similarly, both the era of Eisenhower's leadership and his character helped to shape the moral issues of his presidency and how he reacted to them.

Mirror of the Nation's Morality

The major moral issues that arose during Eisenhower's presidency were the allegations of the love affair with Kay Summersby, the ending of the Korean War, the U-2 spy-plane incident, the Cold War and the Eisenhower Doctrine, the fall of Senator Joseph McCarthy, and racial integration. Each was a product of the times, except for the alleged affair, and that occurred long before he became president. How did he handle these moral issues?

Kay Summersby in May 1942 was a twenty-four-year-old native of Ireland who was assigned to drive Generals Eisenhower and Mark Clark during their ten-day visit to London. When Eisenhower assumed command of the European theater of operation in London the next month, he requested that Summersby become his personal driver. After her fiancé, Colonel Richard Arnold, lost his life in North Africa, she joined the Women's Army Corps and became a captain. Thereafter she received promotions from driver to personal secretary and finally to military aide to General Eisenhower. Summersby in her wartime memoir, *Eisenhower Was My Boss* (1948), did not mention having an affair with him, but in *Past Forgetting: My Love Affair with Dwight David Eisenhower* (1975), written while she was dying of cancer, she asserted they had fallen in love during the war.[95]

In *Plain Speaking,* Merle Miller quoted Truman as saying "that he had seen and destroyed correspondence between Eisenhower and General George C. Marshall, in which Eisenhower announced his intention to divorce his wife and marry Summersby. Marshall blistered Eisenhower, telling him that as his superior officer he would, according to Truman, 'bust him out of the Army and make his life miserable thereafter.'"[96] The Eisenhower family denied that Eisenhower ever contemplated divorce. After leaving Europe at the war's end, he never saw Summersby again.

The second major moral issue that Eisenhower faced was the Korean War. In December 1952, after the election and before his inauguration, he went to Korea to revive the stalled peace talks. The P'anmunjom armistice, signed in July 1953, ended the conflict by separating the two Koreas with a demilitarized zone at the thirty-eighth parallel, roughly the same border that existed before the war. The war and its settlement highlighted the United Nations' role in resisting aggression and conducting modern warfare without resort to nuclear weapons.[97] Eisenhower earned credit for ending the war, which had cost 150,000 American casualties, including some 34,000 killed in action, and helping to launch an era of tranquility.

The third moral issue that Eisenhower encountered as president was the Cold War. His administration undertook a nuclear missile buildup and adopted the strategy of the threat of massive retaliation as a deterrent. The Soviets spoke of "peaceful coexistence" with the West, but gave no sign of lifting the Iron Curtain. They kept pressure on Berlin and crushed the Hungarian revolt of 1956. In 1954, the Southeast Asia Treaty Organization provided that the United States would agree to come to the aid of Pakistan, the Philippines, and Thailand in the event of Communist aggression.[98]

The French asked for American air support during their last stand against the Vietnamese at Dien Bien Phu in 1954, but Eisenhower refused. Although he decided that it would not benefit the United States, he expressed concern about the consequences of a communist takeover there, saying: "You have a row of dominoes set up, and you knock over the first one, and what will happen to the last one is the certainty that it will go over very quickly. So you have a beginning of a disintegration that would have the most profound influences."[99] What Eisenhower chose to do was provide aid and U.S. military advisers to the Diem regime in South Vietnam.

To prevent the Soviet Union from filling the power vacuum left in the Middle East following the Suez crisis of 1956–1957, the president announced the Eisenhower Doctrine, which "asserted the United States' right to aid any country in the area threatened by Communist aggression or subversion."[100] Using this doctrine in 1958, Eisenhower dispatched Marines to Lebanon to shore up the pro-Western government in Beirut.

Less than two weeks before an East-West summit meeting in Paris in 1960, the Soviet Union released news that it had shot down an American U-2 spy plane deep within its air space. Eisenhower had commanded a U-2 spy plane to make a final surveillance flight over an area of the Soviet Union that he considered inadequately examined for possible nuclear and missile sites.[101] When the U-2 failed to return, the United States released a cover story that a plane on a meteorological expedition was lost and might have strayed over Soviet Air space. Eisenhower had intended the self-destruction of spy planes hit by enemy fire.[102] In this situation, the Soviet Union recovered the plane, film, and pilot, Francis Gary Powers, who admitted his mission. Before the Soviet Union's announcement of the capture, Eisenhower had personally denied that such flights occurred. He immediately reversed himself, acknowledging "that flights had taken place for five years under his direction and that they were necessary to provide the West with reliable information about Soviet military capabilities and intentions."[103] The U-2 incident strained Soviet-American relations as Eisenhower prepared to turn over the government to his successor, John F. Kennedy. A Soviet court convicted Powers of espionage and in 1962 exchanged him for Soviet spy Colonel Rudolf Abel.

The fourth moral issue that surfaced under Eisenhower was McCarthyism. In the 1950s, Senator Joseph McCarthy won instant notoriety when he claimed that he had a list of Communists who were working on the State Department payroll and subverting the nation. During this era when there was a "preoccupation with internal subversion and with such international events as the Communist victory in China, the very extravagance of his rhetoric—made more newsworthy because President Truman was goaded into replying to him—earned the Wisconsin Republican substantial media attention."[104]

Eisenhower reacted to McCarthy by not reacting at all. "The best treatment for McCarthy is to ignore him. That is one thing he cannot stand and if we continue this sort of silent treatment, he will blow his top, and still sink lower in political importance."[105] Eisenhower, hidden-handedly, sought to check some of McCarthy's assaults on the loyalty of public servants. He enlisted the highly respected U.S. senator Robert A. Taft (R-Ohio) to refute McCarthy's claim that Charles Bohlen, a career foreign service officer, was not sufficiently trustworthy to serve as ambassador to the Soviet Union. Eisenhower also acted to remedy failures in the government's procedures for screening employees.

Although McCarthy would not cease his assaults, Eisenhower would not give in to demands that he reply to McCarthy. However, he took indirect action by periodically criticizing the kinds of tactics McCarthy used, leaving it to the press to infer what he intended.[106] Eisenhower also worked behind the scenes to encourage the Senate itself to conduct hearings on McCarthy's actions. Hoping to give McCarthy enough rope to hang himself was Eisenhower's strategy, and it worked. Finally during the televised Army-McCarthy hearings, McCarthy's colleagues began to ostracize him.

Because Eisenhower's contribution to McCarthy's demise was largely indirect and behind the scenes, his seeming inaction helped reinforce the impression of his political passivity. However, he did not want to risk making McCarthy publicly popular by attacking him, so he chose to work covertly to cause him to fizzle out. This decision stemmed from his private sense of morality; he did not play name-calling games.

Critics believe that Eisenhower allowed McCarthy to hurt many lives and damage many careers.[107] Clinton Rossiter indicted Eisenhower for failing to face up to "the blunt truth that Congress is now completely unable—technically, politically, spiritually—to give the American people the kind of leadership essential to survive. . . . His experiment in cooperation has failed miserably. He must reassert the legitimate prerogatives of the Presidential office."[108]

When Arkansas governor Orval Faubus resisted the integration of Little Rock's Central High School in 1957, Eisenhower mobilized the National Guard to achieve that end. He had worked behind the scenes with Faubus to secure his cooperation, but Faubus reneged on his pledge.

Critics claim that Eisenhower acted only when he had to and that he did not demonstrate strong moral leadership in the racial issue. His defenders argue that he did what he could under difficult circumstances and that his decision worked. Moreover, they contend that the time was not yet ripe for a bolder approach.

Eisenhower: The Man and His Character

Overall, Eisenhower handled very few moral issues during his presidency. He presided over eight years of prosperity, marred by two minor recessions. The nation enjoyed domestic peace and tranquility, at least as measured against the 1960s.

Eisenhower did offer major alterations to New Deal and Fair Deal programs. The number of people covered by Social Security doubled, and benefits went up. Expenditures for public works were greater than they had been under Roosevelt or Truman. The interstate highway system and St. Lawrence Seaway were larger than anything the New Deal or the Fair Deal had attempted. Eisenhower put a Republican stamp of approval on twenty years of Democratic legislation, which was a major step towards bringing the two parties closer together.

He also made peace in Korea five months after taking office, and he reduced the cost of the arms race. Of his administration Eisenhower said: "The United States never lost a soldier or a foot of ground in my administration. We kept the peace. People asked me how it happened—by God, it didn't just happen, I'll tell you that."[109]

PRESIDENTIAL MORALITY IN A GOLDEN AGE

Compared to recent administrations, the twenty-eight years of Roosevelt, Truman, and Eisenhower administrations spawned very few personal moral issues. Historians and political scientists, while not always agreeing with these presidents, rarely doubt their sincerity. Their personal character and good intentions largely covered their moral flaws. They benefited from several factors: a less than antagonistic press, a sense of purpose from the Cold War, a popular culture that created a sense of national unity, and a strong and harmonious religious tradition. Later, as these conditions broke down, moral scandals erupted more frequently. Roosevelt, Truman, and Eisenhower fit and reinforced the popular culture of their era.

Public policy morality emerged in full bloom during the Roosevelt administration. Focusing not on the personal morality of a president but on his public policy decisions, this type of morality creates heated debates. Roosevelt's New Deal and Truman's Fair Deal won the support of people who wanted an activist liberal agenda. Eisenhower's more conservative agenda received their rebuke. Liberals believe liberal public policies are moral, while conservatives believe the opposite. As ideological divisions intensified between the 1960s and 1990s, disputes about public-policy morality increased.

5

TARNISHING THE GOLDEN AGE, 1961–1975

A full generation later the images of the decade are still vivid: civil rights protest marches and sit-ins at lunch counters; the "youth revolution" and the "generation gap"; *Hair* and the sexual revolution; drugs and "hippies"; huge marches in Washington protesting the Vietnamese War; young men running off to Canada or Scandinavia to avoid the draft; a president forced to give up his quest for reelection.

—Richard G. Hutchinson, *God in the White House*

A moral smog, descending on the nation during the 1960s and early 1970s, permanently darkened the golden age of the 1930s through the 1950s. As the 1960s progressed, the smog thickened, eclipsing the light of moral certainty. Events from President John F. Kennedy's assassination in 1963 to the assassinations of Martin Luther King Jr. and Robert F. Kennedy in 1968 sent the nation reeling. The civil rights movement became violent, as many blacks turned from King's nonviolent resistance to the aggressive Black Power movement of Eldridge Cleaver, H. Rap Brown, and Huey Newton. After King's assassination, large sections of cities exploded in riots and mass destruction. The Vietnam War produced public protests, young men avoiding the draft and refusing to serve the country, and flag burnings. Some Americans, led by the Weathermen, even advocated violent revolution.

Cynicism swept the nation. In just four years, from 1964 to 1968, popular trust in the federal government to do the right thing dropped from 73 percent to 60 percent. When the Watergate scandal broke in the early 1970s, trust tumbled even lower.[1]

Suddenly nothing was the same; everything careened off in new directions. The massive social change begun in that era is still not fully sorted out thirty years later. Richard G. Hutcheson says: "The 'sixties' will probably long be the symbolic designation for an era in which American society seemed to have turned itself upside down."[2]

"Do your own thing" and "Have it your way" undermined the foundations of family, community, and traditional religious faith and practices. The "me generation" turned to the self-fulfillment ethic, a direct challenge to the traditional underpinnings of American society: "Self-actualization had become the highest value system replacing for many people the older religious values of self-sacrifice. Also, the much heralded sexual revolution ushered in in the 60's with great fanfare was perhaps the ultimate expression of the self-fulfillment ethic."[3] According to historian John F. Wilson, the sixties "marked a stark repudiation of that spiritual ethic which had persisted throughout the life of the nation."[4] As society emphasized self-gratification, the secular triumphed over the sacred. Nothing seemed out of bounds. Decorum and standards lost their meaning. Four-letter words, once strictly forbidden in public, became common parlance.

These changes were mirrored in the popular culture. Britain's musical invasion of America and America's military invasion of Vietnam permanently altered the American landscape during the 1960s and 1970s. Today every American institution bears the marks of those invasions.

The early 1960s epitomized John F. Kennedy's campaign slogan, "Let's get America moving again." People, tiring of the 1950s' passivity, looked for thrills and excitement. Family musicals became less common, and gone were such popular television programs as *Father Knows Best*. The individualistic, self-fulfillment ethic began to reign.

In popular music, tunes from 1955 to 1964 are pretty much alike: light, airy, cheerful, optimistic, and supportive of tradition. Then from 1964 to 1974, light rock and roll gave way to hard rock. Gradually, Motown music with the Four Tops, the Temptations, and the Marvelettes faded away. Britain's Beatles began the invasion of America with countercultural style, and music with serious social messages followed. Tunes took on a hard, sharp-cutting edge, challenging authority and undermining traditional political, religious, and social institutions.

Music in the late 1960s and early 1970s reflected the nation's moral mood. Bob Dylan, The Band, Van Morrison, Jimi Hendrix, and Janis Joplin brought diverse dynamics, including psychedelic music, to center stage. The beat and mood of the music and the crowds it gathered reflected a nation in moral disarray. Only a decade removed from 1950s' tranquility, a huge crowd of youths met for what was billed as "3 days of peace and music" at the world's largest rock and roll show, known as Woodstock. This "Music and Art Fair" in August 1969 drew more than 450,000 people to a pasture in Sullivan County, New York. For four days—the acts ran over into the morning of the fourth day—the site became a countercultural mini-station in which minds were open, drugs were all but legal and love was "free." American culture reeled from the hit and the high of psychedelic art and music.

Pop art, perhaps epitomized by artist Andy Warhol, emerged with images and ideas antithetical to American tradition. Warhol and the pop art industry undressed the sacred and the sensitive. and they also advanced the commercialization of art, such as Warhol's Campbell's Tomato Soup can pictures.

Movies, too, reflected the changing culture. During the 1950s, Hollywood was glamorous—the place you could become whatever you wanted, at least in your dreams—and wholesome, lifting spirits and reinforcing cultural standards. The movies of the 1950s usually portrayed the same hopeful message, almost always upbeat and simple. Beginning in the 1960s and 1970s, such movies as *The Graduate* illustrated Hollywood's fall from idealism. Instead of portraying America optimistically, movies took on a pessimistic cutting edge, offering disturbing truths about society.

This social turbulence and moral controversy marked the presidencies of John F. Kennedy, Lyndon B. Johnson, and Richard M. Nixon. Kennedy's presidency rumbled like a volcano about to erupt, while the Johnson and Nixon presidencies were like volcanic eruptions.

JOHN F. KENNEDY, 1961–1963

Camelot or the Dark Side of Camelot?

Twenty years after John F. Kennedy's assassination, a public opinion poll rated him best overall among the nine presidents since Herbert Hoover. Kennedy "most inspired confidence in the White House," according to 40 percent of those surveyed; Roosevelt ranked a distant second at 23 percent. As the "most appealing personality," 60 percent chose Kennedy, leaving Roosevelt trailing far behind at 11 percent.[5]

Kennedy exuded the aura of a relaxed, handsome, good-humored, and gracious man. According to Thomas C. Reeves, this image was no accident, because "the Kennedys were the greatest masters of myth and illusion American politics had ever known."[6] Magnetic appeal and romantic attraction veiled the Kennedy image. His death was the loss of a vision of youth, energy, glamour, and extreme wealth. His tale became the tale of Camelot. Who was the true John F. Kennedy?

President John Fitzgerald Kennedy exemplified his era. Brazen and courageous, Kennedy "did not think that the rules applied to him and he did whatever he could get away with, including getting into the U.S. Navy without a physical examination."[7] Knowing that military service was a critical condition for winning the presidency, Kennedy enlisted in the U.S. Navy during World War II, dodging the physical examination to keep military authorities in the dark about his serious physical ailments, Addison's disease (a withering of the adrenal glands) and a degenerative back problem.

Achieving the status of commander of PT-109, a position someone in his frail health should never have held, he placed his own ambition above the welfare of the troops he commanded. However, when a Japanese destroyer ran down PT-109, "the lieutenant who never should have been there swam six miles holding the belt, in his teeth, of a badly burned man named Pappy McNulty, and saved his life—and then went back into the dark Pacific to try to save others. He lost his boat, but saved most of his crew."[8] Kennedy valued courage above all things.

Richard Reeves writes that Kennedy

> was a soaring cultural figure. . . . And the most significant thing about John Kennedy, transcending politics, was this: he did not wait his turn. And now, no one does. Part of that was he thought he would die young —and he had to make his move the first chance he got. He went after the presidency out of turn and essentially destroyed the old system of selecting presidents. The only way he could get the job was by creating a new system in which the press was more important than the old-fashioned political titans. . . .
>
> He used the primaries, which basically had been showcases before that, to win the press and the nomination before the party itself convened.[9]

At the Democratic Party's 1960 convention in Los Angeles, presidential aspirants, longtime party stalwarts, and powerful senior senators Lyndon B. Johnson and Hubert H. Humphrey were no match for Kennedy's carefully cultivated image and well-financed and superbly organized campaign.

Kennedy's inaugural sharply distinguished him from his predecessor, Dwight D. Eisenhower.

Eisenhower was the oldest man to occupy the presidency until that time; Kennedy, at forty-three, was the youngest person ever elected president. Eisenhower was the last president to be born in the nineteenth century; Kennedy was the first born in the twentieth. Eisenhower had been the great World War II commander, and Kennedy, a mere junior officer. Eisenhower had grandchildren; Kennedy had a three-year-old daughter and son who was born between election and inauguration. Eisenhower had taken care not to endanger his personal popularity by taking on divisive causes and had practiced a kind of indirect leadership, so indirect as often to be undetectable; Kennedy advocated that the president be at the center of the action.[10]

Like Eisenhower, however, Kennedy brought strong self-confidence to the presidency, although he expressed it differently. According to Reeves, Kennedy did not question his actions and "was at the center of all he surveyed. He enjoyed using people and setting them against each other for his own amusement. He lived his life as a race against boredom. He used people around him as pimps and worse," but even with this, he "brought out the best in the American people."[11]

Personal gratification, not personal morality, loomed large in Kennedy's decision making. The pursuit of political power and, above all, commitment to victory, created a cause-and-effect relationship. Kennedy's father, Joe Senior, instructed his children not to tolerate anything short of winning. His sister Eunice once observed that "Jack hates to lose. He learned how to play golf and he hates to lose at that. He hates to lose at anything. That's the only thing Jack really gets emotional about—when he loses. Sometimes, he even gets cross."[12]

Kennedy's father defined his son's principal aims, gaining public success and prestige. Morality was secondary; doing and saying what wins votes was primary. Martin Marty, associate editor of *Christian Century,* deemed Kennedy "spiritually rootless."[13]

When character became an important issue in the 1960 campaign, Kennedy pledged to "restore an atmosphere of moral leadership in the White House."[14] He told Americans that the next president "must set the moral tone—and I refer not to his language but to his actions."[15]

Kennedy was described as audacious, intense, impatient, even brusque.

"He was a man who was going to get what he wanted. He was a stunning figure." [16]

Internal Moral Gyroscope: Present or Lacking?

According to Seymour Hersh, author of *The Dark Side of Camelot*, "Kennedy's private life and personal obsessions—his character—affected the affairs of the nation and its foreign policy far more than has ever been known."[17] Arguing that the Kennedy image overwhelmed reality, Hersh cites evidence to show that personal weaknesses limited his ability to carry out his duties as president; questionable moral decisions affected both his personal life and public policies; and private aspirations and desires subverted his responsibilities to the American people and damaged the presidency itself.

Kennedy won by a razor-thin margin of 49.7 percent to 49.5 percent against Richard M. Nixon. Kennedy's campaign left behind a residue of doubts and questions, especially in Texas and Illinois. In Texas, where tens of thousands of ballots disappeared, results from two precincts stained Kennedy's victory: One precinct received 86 ballots but reported 147 votes for Kennedy and 24 for Nixon; and a second submitted 458 votes for Nixon and 350 for Kennedy but voided 182 ballots at the "discretion of the judges."[18] In Illinois, allegations of fraud occurred especially in precincts controlled by Democrats in Chicago. Investigations and resulting convictions revealed that one precinct counted 100 votes for Kennedy before the polls opened; seventy-one voters used false names to cast their ballots, thirty-four voted twice, and one voted three times; and residents of Chicago's flophouses used the names of absent or dead people to vote.[19]

Mafia ties also figure in Hersh's account of Kennedy's moral foibles. He presents evidence, including FBI wiretaps, to show that Kennedy met with Sam Giancana, the Chicago "godfather," on April 12, 1960; large Mafia donations helped pay off key West Virginia election officials in Kennedy's critical primary win over Hubert Humphrey; and Paul D'Amato, a Giancana henchman, "distributed more than fifty thousand dollars to local sheriffs to get out the vote for Kennedy—by any means possible" in West Virginia.[20]

Not unlike the era of his presidency, Kennedy followed an individualistic, pleasure-seeking self-fulfillment ethic. According to Hersh, Kennedy lived for the moment: "I never met anybody who felt that the minute was as important as it was [for Kennedy]. He had to live for today."[21] For Kennedy that meant indulgence in many extramarital affairs.

Until recently, the mystique of the Camelot myth concealed Kennedy's blatantly immoral involvement with women. One of Kennedy's reported trysts took place with Judith Campbell, who was introduced to him by a family friend, Frank Sinatra, in 1960. Her past apparently included romantic links to Mafia boss Sam Giancana. She reportedly served as a liaison between Giancana and Kennedy. Kennedy ostensibly carried on this affair during his presidency and while his wife, Jackie, was expecting the birth of their second child.

Campbell, however, was only one of many women in Kennedy's extramarital life. These affairs presented troubling timing problems for Kennedy. Traphes Bryant, a veteran White House employee, wrote in his diary:

> There was a conspiracy of silence to protect his secrets from Jacqueline and to keep her from finding out. The newspapers would tell how First Lady Jacqueline was off on another trip, but what they didn't report was how anxious the President sometimes was to see her go. And what consternation there sometimes was when she returned unexpectedly.[22]

An affair with Hollywood idol Marilyn Monroe became Kennedy's best known and most dangerous. "Longtime friends and associates of Monroe and Kennedy acknowledged that the two stars, who both enjoyed living on the edge, shared a powerful, and high-risk, attraction to each other."[23] Monroe's emotional instability and knowledge of Kennedy's underworld connections posed potentially serious problems. Monroe's loose lips apparently revealed what Kennedy concealed.

James Bacon, who covered Hollywood for the Associated Press, said in *The Dark Side of Camelot* that Monroe, whom he befriended early in her career, gave him a firsthand account of her relationship with Kennedy as early as the 1960 presidential campaign. Bacon concluded: "I think Marilyn was in love with JFK."[24] When asked by Hersh why he never filed a story about the affair, Bacon responded: "Before Watergate, reporters just didn't go into that sort of thing. I'd have to have been under the bed in order to put it on the wire for the AP. There was no pact. It was just a matter of judgment on the part of the reporters."[25]

Today's press, which exposes rather than hides moral peccadillos, makes life more difficult for presidents. Today's journalistic standards would have made Kennedy's extramarital adventures lead stories and front-page headlines. The press is now more adversarial in its relationships with presidents.

Yet another moral question arises from Kennedy's physical condition. Kennedy, who, as was noted earlier, suffered from Addison's disease and a degenerative back condition, lived in constant pain. To alleviate his pain, Kennedy recruited Dr. Max Jacobson, who later became better known as "Dr. Feel Good." He earned this nickname by injecting amphetamines laced with steroids and animal cells into his patients. Kennedy, who used Jacobson's services from one to three times a week, "had developed a strong dependence on amphetamines by the summer of 1961."[26] If used over long periods of time, amphetamines can alter a person's decision-making faculties, producing paranoia, schizophrenia, memory loss, hallucinations, and dependency. Kennedy's use of these drugs jeopardized the nation.

Kennedy's civil rights image also disguises reality. Civil rights did not top his agenda; he was a Johnny-come-lately to the issue. According to Bruce Miroff, author of *Pragmatic Illusions,* Kennedy's self-fulfillment ethic governed his interest in the subject: "Civil rights was granted full attention only when it imposed itself on the Kennedy Administration."[27]

Public protests and marches activated his interest. In 1962, when Governor George Wallace stood defiantly in the schoolhouse door at the University of Alabama, Kennedy finally began to focus on the problem. Other significant events also refined his focus. Freedom Riders challenged southern segregation, and violence erupted in April 1963 when civil rights activists, led by the Reverend Martin Luther King Jr., protested segregation in Birmingham, Alabama. In August 1963, King and others led two hundred thousand demonstrators in a Freedom March on Washington.

Kennedy's public policy leadership on civil rights followed events and the leadership of others. In November 1962, for example, he ordered an end to discrimination in federal housing programs and created the President's Committee on Equal Employment Opportunity. He also began to increase the appointment of blacks to executive branch positions and to enhance the attorney general's authority to sue segregated school systems.[28]

In a June 1963 television address, Kennedy challenged Americans "to live up to American ideals and abide by the Golden Rule." The president said:

If an American, because his skin is dark, cannot eat lunch in a restaurant open to the public, if he cannot send his children to the best public school available, if he cannot vote for the public officials who represent him, if in short, he cannot enjoy the full and free life which all of us want, then who among us would be content to have the color of his skin changed and stand in his place? Who among us would then be content with the counsels of patience and delay? . . . We preach freedom around the world, and we mean it, and we cherish our freedom here at home; but are we to say to the world and, much more importantly, to each other that this is a land of the free except for the Negroes; that we have no class or caste system, no ghettos, no master race except with respect to Negroes?[29]

On the international scene, Kennedy faced several moral dilemmas caused by the apparent advance of communism, the Soviet Union's lead in space exploration, and America's vulnerability to nuclear attack. Cuba provided his first moral test. Kennedy suffered a humiliating defeat during the abortive invasion of Cuba known as Bay of Pigs. On April 17, 1961, 1,500 Cuban exiles, trained and armed by the U.S. Central Intelligence Agency (CIA), invaded Cuba at Cochinos Bay, or the Bay of Pigs.

Their mission was to establish a beachhead and spark a popular uprising that would topple the Communist regime of Fidel Castro. The invaders were led to believe that the U.S. forces would follow in support if they met overwhelming resistance. The support never came.

Castro's tanks and soldiers pinned them to the sea. After three days of fighting, the United States paid Cuba $53 million in food and medical supplies for their release in 1962. The invasion had been planned by the Eisenhower administration, but President Kennedy approved its execution and accepted full responsibility for its failure.[30]

Upset by his personal defeat, Kennedy reacted by approving Operation Mongoose, a secret plan to overthrow the Cuban government that would cost $50 million per year.[31] In another plot, the CIA recruited Mafia leaders John Roselli, Sam Giancana, and Santos Trafficante to assassinate Castro for a $150,000 bounty and "the possibility of restoring the extremely lucrative gambling, drug, and prostitution operations they had enjoyed under Batista."[32] The Bay of Pigs and its aftermath reveal a president willing to compromise moral principles to win.

In October 1962, the CIA learned that the Soviet Union was constructing offensive nuclear missile bases in Cuba. Housing missiles capable of striking the eastern two-thirds of the United States and much of Latin America, the bases posed a serious threat. The Soviet Union claimed that the weapons were defensive, but aerial photographs proved otherwise. On October 22, Kennedy

> condemned the Soviet Union for lying about the nature of the buildup and ordered a quarantine of Cuba, in which, he said, "All ships of any kind bound for Cuba from whatever nation or port will, if found to contain cargoes of offensive weapons, be turned back." He then warned Moscow, "It shall be the policy of this nation to regard any nuclear missile launched from Cuba against any nation in the Western Hemisphere as an attack by the Soviet Union on the United States." . . . He also called for the "prompt dismantling and withdrawal of all offensive weapons in Cuba." Tense days followed as Soviet ships steamed toward the American blockade. Finally, in an exchange of notes . . . Soviet premier Nikita Khrushchev agreed to dismantle the missile sites and return the weapons to the Soviet Union in exchange for a U.S. pledge not to invade Cuba. By the end of 1962, American intelligence confirmed their removal. [33]

This tense "eyeball-to-eyeball" experience with the Soviet Union "impelled Kennedy to take new initiatives in seeking an end to the Cold War."[34] In June 1963, Kennedy gave one of his most important speeches. Speaking at American University, he marked the beginning of a new policy for communism: détente. "Kennedy called for a reexamination of American attitudes toward the Soviet Union and said that both sides in the Cold War had 'a mutually deep interest in a just and genuine peace and in halting the arms race.'"[35] Reacting to events, Kennedy displayed a determination to succeed that enabled him to turn moral liabilities into assets.

Three conclusions stand out about John F. Kennedy's presidential morality. First, he reflected the moral tenor of his times. Second, he risked the national interest on the altar of his personal desires. Third, he raised public awareness of some moral issues after other leaders and events aroused his attention.

LYNDON B. JOHNSON, 1963–1969

Fate Is Character

Did inner demons possess Johnson, as biographer Robert Dallek conjectures? Although that question oversteps the boundary lines of this discussion, it does point to Johnson's complexity. He is a mysterious man.

Fate is character, the ancient Greeks said. Lyndon Johnson's political career is a good case in point. He was as outsized and memorable a figure as any to sit in the White House. He has been described as a human dynamo, a whirlwind, a tornado in pants, a cross between a character Mark Twain and William Faulkner could have invented, a Jekyll and Hyde, a magnificent, inspiring leader one minute and an insufferable bastard the next. He was Winston Churchill's puzzle inside a riddle wrapped in an enigma.[36]

Dallek says:

From early in his childhood [Johnson] manifested character traits that shaped his behavior throughout his life. As a boy and a man he suffered from a sense of emptiness; he couldn't stand to be alone; he needed constant companionship, attention, affection, and approval. He had insatiable appetites for work, women, food, drink, conversation and material possessions. They were all in the service of filling himself up—of giving himself a sort of validity or sense of self-worth.[37]

According to Dallek, "Johnson's neediness translated into a number of traits that had a large impact on his political actions. He had a compulsion to be the best, to outdo everybody, to eclipse all his predecessors in the White House and become the greatest President in American history."[38] Lacking inner self-confidence, he compensated by attaching himself to grand goals. "By all accounts Johnson was a complex personality, fiercely competitive, always in a rush, a man who relished power, a master manipulator who harnessed his finely tuned political instincts to achieve lofty goals."[39]

A Tumultuous Presidency: LBJ Holds the Reins

Lyndon Johnson's perplexing personality directly affected his presidential decision-making. He craved power and attention. He told Doris Kearns Goodwin, "I wanted power to give things to people—all sorts of things to all sorts of people, especially the poor and the blacks."[40] Johnson saw the presidency as the fulcrum of power and the center of attention.

In a State of the Union address, Johnson announced an "'all-out war on human poverty and unemployment in the United States.' This 'unconditional war on poverty' was not to be 'short or easy' but an all-out campaign in which 'we shall not rest until that war is won.' The aim was 'not only to relieve the symptom of poverty, but to cure it and, above all, to prevent it.'"[41] His "war on poverty" policy revealed two interlocking beliefs: that the power of the presidency can cure large-scale social ills through great social policies and that it could bring attention and praise to himself.

The War on Poverty was the centerpiece of Johnson's utopian vision of a Great Society, which he said "rests on abundance and liberty for all. It demands an end to poverty and racial injustice."[42] Johnson believed that changing conditions and attitudes in America made the Great Society not just his utopian vision but also the inevitable direction of the nation.[43] He wanted to build the Great Society in three places—the cities, the countryside, and the classroom—through ambitious poverty, health care, education, and civil rights programs. Johnson's War on Poverty had three major objectives:

1. To lift approximately thirty-five million people out of poverty.

2. To create many new government programs: Job Corps to provide vocational training for disadvantaged youth aged sixteen to twenty-one; Volunteers in Service to America (VISTA) to enlist volunteers to work and teach in ghettos; Work-Study to enable students of low-income families to work their way through college; Work Experience to furnish child day-care and other services to poor heads of household; Head Start to instruct disadvantaged preschoolers; Upward Bound to tutor disadvantaged high school students; Foster Grandparents to allow elderly volunteers to befriend institutionalized children; and Legal Aid to provide legal services the poor.[44]

3. To morally arouse, mobilize, and harness Americans to achieve Johnson's vision.[45] To Johnson, his vision was a "movement of conscience—a national act of expiation, of humbling and prostrating ourselves before our Creator."[46]

Johnson's vast vision did not stop there. It also embraced Medicare, funded through Social Security, to provide hospital medical insurance for those sixty-five years of age or older; and Medicaid to provide hospital and medical benefits for the poor of any age.

Lyndon Johnson's landslide victory in 1964, made possible by Kennedy's assassination and the Republican Party's inept campaign, produced large Democratic majorities in Congress. He could then easily translate his moral vision into legislative victories. No other president, save Franklin Roosevelt, rivals Johnson's legislative success.[47]

Civil rights also marked Johnson's efforts to leave a moral mark on America. He envisioned "an America that knows no North or South, no East or West—an America undivided by creed or color, untorn by suspicion or strife."[48] After Kennedy's assassination, Johnson pledged to use every ounce of his strength to push for civil rights legislation to gain justice for every black American.[49] His landmark achievements included passage of the Civil Rights Act of 1964, which barred discrimination in employment and in services provided by hotels, restaurants, and other public facilities and authorized the attorney general to initiate desegregation suits; the Voting Rights Act of 1965—his proudest achievement—which outlawed legal barriers to minority voting and authorized the federal government to promote voter registration; and the Civil Rights Act of 1968, which barred discrimination in the sale and rental of housing and strengthened penalties for civil rights violations.[50]

Except for civil rights, Johnson's vision was long on promise and short on performance. His Great Society initiatives produced questionable results, but his civil rights policies transformed American society and politics, especially in the South. The public, however, remained unconvinced of the value and effectiveness of Johnson's programs. His immense vision overextended its reach, producing a credibility gap, according to Dallek:

> Johnson's rhetoric about curing poverty, building a Great Society, and ending racial strife undermined his credibility with the public and ability to govern and lead. His excessive claims for what his poverty fight could achieve not only undermined his believability but also made for public cynicism about the value of big social engineering programs under the control of government bureaucrats spending large amounts of money with limited results.
>
> The public had a similar response to Johnson's exaggerated accounts of what the Great Society and civil rights legislation were achieving.[51]

This growing credibility gap injured Johnson, ultimately contributing to his withdrawal from the 1968 presidential race. Strained relationships with the press also widened the gap. Johnson scorned the press because reporters refused to report stories favorable to him. To get them to report what he wanted, Johnson flooded the press with deceptive reports concerning his staff appointments, daily routine, travel plans, and medical reports.[52] Deception and misrepresentation led to distrust: "Johnson's swings from extreme to extreme and his persistent exaggeration of events slowly chipped away at the reliability of the White House word."[53]

Johnson especially exacerbated the credibility gap in foreign affairs. When he deployed twenty-four thousand troops to the Dominican Republic during a time of unrest, the press asked why he sent so many troops to such a small country. To protect two thousand Americans was the first answer. Later, however, Johnson gave a second answer: to prevent a Communist takeover.

Johnson's handling of the Vietnam War also widened the gap. American military participation in Vietnam began almost unnoticed under President Kennedy, who sent sixteen thousand military advisers to assist South Vietnamese "defenders of democracy."[54] This military commitment became a ticking time bomb. The danger of deeper involvement grew as the corruption and incompetence of the South Vietnamese government of Ngo Dinh Diem began to cause widespread unrest.[55]

In July of 1965, Johnson faced a moral dilemma. Should he escalate American participation in Vietnam? In the heat of the 1964 presidential campaign, he had opposed increased involvement, saying he would not send American "boys" to fight in Vietnam. But a year later he broke his promise. At a news conference on April 27, 1965, he said:

> Defeat in South Vietnam would deliver a friendly nation to terror and repression. It would encourage and spur on those who seek to conquer all free nations that are within their reach. If North Vietnam succeeded in taking over South Vietnam, our own welfare, our own freedom would be in danger. This is the clearest lesson of our time. From Munich until today we have learned that to yield to aggression brings only greater threats and brings even more destructive war. This is the same battle which we have fought for a generation.[56]

As a result of Johnson's reversal, America gradually became engulfed in moral controversy, social unrest, and violence.[57] The American military presence escalated from 33,500 soldiers in April 1965 to 180,000 in December 1965, to 400,000 in December 1966, to 470,000 in December 1967, and finally to a peak of 550,000 in 1968.[58]

American involvement in the Vietnam War slowly changed the public's perception of President Johnson. Once considered a political magician in control of events, he came to be viewed as a political pawn moved by circumstances and forces beyond his control.[59] Johnson's ill-tempered and uptight manner made him unattractive to many Americans and limited his ability to elicit public sympathy. Not even Lincoln in the darkest days of the Civil War had faced such intense dissent and public doubts about his course of action.[60]

College students expressed the most powerful opposition to the Vietnam War. They began with teach-ins, which involved long discussions about the war with many participants. In the mass demonstrations that followed, students taunted Johnson with the refrain, "Hey, hey, LBJ, how many kids did you kill today?"[61] Johnson's desire to win, a trait cultivated in his childhood, caused him to pursue the war effort in the face of mass dissension. Withdrawal meant defeat to him, and that was unthinkable.

What Johnson saw as a moral war, much of the public condemned as immoral. Then as the leader of the war effort, he attempted to hide the war's realities, hoping the public would rally to the effort.[62] Falling victim to the classic moral fallacy that the end justifies the means, Johnson created a "false impression . . . believing his cause and eventually that of the nation would benefit."[63] The public saw both the war and Johnson's handling of it as morally repugnant.[64]

Television contributed immensely to Johnson's fall in two ways. First, Johnson was not adept at television, a relatively new medium of communication. For Kennedy, television was like a bright fishing lure enticing public support. For Johnson, it was a microscope magnifying his warts and wrinkles to the public. Second, the American public saw and heard the awful brutality of war for the first time on television. The My Lai massacre and other atrocities sickened the public and weakened the war's moral standing. To many the Vietnam War was a sign of moral depravity.[65] According to Robert Dallek:

> Johnson's failure to understand that this was a civil war which had nothing to do with consequential U.S. interests resulted in divisions at home and distrust of presidential authority that won't go away.
>
> The war brought out the worst in Johnson. His failure to deal effectively with the conflict partly rested on his character flaws: his grandiosity that could overcome every obstacle and his impulse to view criticism of his policies as personal attacks which he would overcome by increasing his efforts to make his policies succeed.[66]

Johnson's political career crumbled and collapsed. In March 1968, after the humiliating results of the New Hampshire presidential primary at the hands of U.S. Senator Gene McCarthy, a Vietnam War dove who won 42 percent of the vote, Johnson acted. He withdrew from the presidential race and simultaneously halted the bombing of North Vietnam "in order to devote his full energies to achieving peace."[67]

Final Thoughts

Ultimately Johnson lost two wars and the presidency. His War on Poverty at home and his Vietnam War overseas became a kind of military pincers movement against him. They cost him his dream of a Great Society and a place in the pantheon of presidential greatness.[68]

The two wars also proved damaging to the country in many other ways. First, public trust in government and public officials plunged, and it has never recovered. Second, the taxes required to finance the two wars created high inflation and soaring budget deficits, and only recently has the country enjoyed some reprieve from them. Third, the two wars split the Democratic Party, breaking up the Roosevelt coalition of the solid South, big-city political machines, and big labor unions. Captured by U.S. Senator George McGovern and others, the Democratic Party turned against such traditional leaders as Chicago mayor Richard J. Daley and AFL-CIO president George Meany. Fourth, the two wars and the Democrats' divisions handed powerful issues to the Republican Party. Both Southern Democrats and many traditional New Deal Democrats converted to the Republican Party. Fifth, the two wars contributed to an erosion of civil discourse in America. Respect for others lessened, and tensions mounted, making agreement on national goals difficult, sometimes impossible. America began to resemble two armed camps firing volleys of cannon fire over a mountainous divide. Sixth, Johnson pushed a grandiose moral agenda in part because it fit his character. His ambition exceeded his grasp, leaving the public to suffer for it. Seventh, the public learned the hard way that presidents are not invincible and that constitutional restraints on presidential actions are important.

Cruel irony afflicts Lyndon B. Johnson's reputation. The irony is particularly apparent in civil rights: blacks greatly admire John F. Kennedy, but Lyndon B. Johnson did more for them than any president since Abraham Lincoln. Image triumphed over substance. Johnson's legislative success is rivaled only by Franklin Roosevelt's. Roosevelt ranks among the greatest presidents, Johnson among the worst. He attempted too much and fought one too many wars. His moral crusades at home and abroad failed; what he intended as moral the public considered immoral.

RICHARD M. NIXON, 1969–1974

Who Is the Real Richard Nixon?

Historians, journalists, political scientists, psychologists, and psychoanalysts, fascinated by the Nixon psyche, enjoy putting him on the proverbial psychologist's couch. Perhaps only Woodrow Wilson has endured more psychological analysis. For that, Nixon leaves behind a legacy of a small publishing industry.

Psychoanalyst David Abrahamsen in *Nixon v. Nixon* (1977) described him as "a man torn by inner conflict, lonely, hypersensitive, narcissistic, suspicious, and secretive."[69] Historian Bruce Mazlish, trained in psychoanalysis, said in *In Search of Nixon* that the "predominant characteristic of the 'real' Nixon behind the public figure was a fear of passivity, of appearing soft, of being dependent on others."[70] Historian Fawn Brodie wrote in *Richard Nixon: The Shaping of His Character* (1981) that Nixon "lied to gain love, to shore up his grandiose fantasies, to bolster his ever-wavering sense of identity. He lied in attack, hoping to win. . . . And always he lied, and this most aggressively, to deny that he lied."[71]

Where did this complex figure come from? A poor family in Whittier, California. Throughout life, Richard Nixon classified himself as a "have not" person, working hard to advance. His father, Frank Nixon, reinforced this view by repeatedly telling Richard and his brothers how fortunate they were to advance by getting an education.

Fear of rejection haunted Richard Nixon. He failed to make the Whittier College football team, "thus flunking one of the established tests of orthodox American males."[72] His difficulty in attracting the opposite sex also made him feel like a failure. Further marking his psyche was his father, who "volatile, cantankerous, loud, and not much of a provider, may have embarrassed the young Richard."[73] Nixon, who lacked a very close relationship with his mother, said that "in her whole life I never heard her say to me or to anyone else, 'I love you.'"[74] Perhaps these experiences contributed to feelings of inadequacy and poor self-esteem.

According to journalist Tom Wicker, Nixon pretended "to be *less* than he was—less thoughtful, less introverted, less skeptical and analytical, less cerebral—to present himself deliberately as an Average American; patriotic, conventionally religious and responsible, gregarious, sports-loving, hardworking, and hard-nosed."[75] In reality, Nixon was a studious introvert. A college acquaintance said that Nixon "had a room up over the garage that was his room where he could be alone to study. . . . He liked to be alone to study."[76]

In political life, too, Nixon preferred the quiet of his study to the boisterousness of a political rally. On election night in 1968 at New York's Waldorf Astoria Hotel, Nixon closeted himself in one room, leaving his wife and daughters in another. Seclusion and silence, reflection and meditation away from family, friends, advisers, and crowds typified Nixon's behavior during major moments in his presidency.[77]

This penchant for isolation from others hurt his presidential leadership. It limited his ability to reach out for advice and counsel, and it prevented him from receiving the personal consolation and encouragement of others. Standing alone, he made decisions affecting the world. Direct counsel from advisers, family, and friends might have steered Nixon in different directions on Watergate and allowed him to survive longer than he did relying solely on his own ability and determination.

"Never quit was not only the central theme of Nixon's political career, it was the core of his being," according to Stephen E. Ambrose.[78] This determination can be seen in his reaction after the debates with Kennedy during the 1960 presidential campaign. Television, more than anything else, cost Nixon the 1960 election. According to radio listeners, Nixon won the first debate, but television viewers declared Kennedy the winner. Nixon determined that he would correct his poor physical appearance on television in 1968. Using television to Nixon's advantage, his campaign presented images of the candidate as he wanted the public to know him.[79]

"I Am Not a Crook"

President Nixon dealt with moral issues thrust upon him and also those of his own making. The Vietnam War, inherited from Presidents Kennedy and Johnson, challenged him first. Nixon knew that he would suffer Johnson's fate if he could not find a solution to the war. In the end, Nixon wrapped the Vietnam mantle over his own shoulders. A war that belonged to his predecessors' legacies became his war, doing as it had to Johnson—

damaging his moral authority.

Nixon wanted to reduce American commitments in Vietnam but without sacrificing South Vietnam's noncommunist government. He decided to steadily reduce American involvement in the war but to expand America's war effort into neighboring Cambodia and Laos, a strategy called by critics "widening down" the war.[80]

Guiding his decisions was the Nixon Doctrine: to reduce American casualties, withdraw troops, and turn the fighting over to Vietnamese. To ensure the success of his Vietnamization program and to protect the reduced ranks of American soldiers, Nixon had seventy thousand American and South Vietnamese troops strike enemy sanctuaries and supply lines along the Cambodian border on April 10, 1970. However, he failed to obtain his main objective, capturing Cambodian Communist headquarters.[81] Nixon's action inflamed the passions of America's antiwar protest movement. At Kent State University in May 1970, when two thousand angry demonstrators gathered, Ohio National Guardsmen, fearing violence, fired into the throng, killing four and wounding nine.

Congressional pressure to end American participation in the Vietnam War began to increase. The 1970 Cooper amendment restricted presidential warmaking powers in Southeast Asia, prohibiting action by American combat troops in Laos and Thailand.[82] Soon thereafter the Cooper-Church amendment banned the deployment of American forces in Cambodia. Then the Eagleton amendment called for a halt in all American military operations in Laos, Cambodia, and Vietnam after August 15, 1973.[83] Finally, in 1973, Congress passed the War Powers Resolution, which required American presidents to obtain congressional approval within sixty days for any military action.[84] Congressional action in the early 1970s reflected popular disapproval of the war, the loss of its moral underpinnings, and the desire to restrain presidents from unfettered action in foreign military conflicts.

Nixon negotiated an end to America's military presence in Vietnam with the Paris Peace Accords in January 1973, bringing to a conclusion talks that had begun almost five years earlier. The war itself continued, but without American combat involvement, resulting in a Communist victory over South Vietnam. The war cost Americans $110 billion, 58,000 American soldiers dead, and 304,000 wounded.[85]

Nixon, sometimes considered a miscast secretary of state, saw the need to alter America's foreign obligations, recognizing that a multipolar world had replaced a bipolar world. The United States must now share power with emerging economic powers, such as Japan, Germany, and others. The Soviet Union and the United States could no longer dominate the world. He also recognized that communism was a fractured, not a united, front.

President Nixon succeeded with his New China Policy. In 1972 he "set aside his long-standing hostility to Communist China to try to broaden scientific, cultural, and trade contacts between the two governments."[86] Becoming the first American president to visit China, he laid the groundwork for full diplomatic recognition, educational exchanges, and economic trade.

Domestically, Nixon had a surprisingly successful and foresighted agenda. He fought for two crime bills. The Organized Crime Control Act authorized severe penalties for "dangerous special offenders" and barred the use of organized-crime money in legitimate businesses.[87] The Drug Abuse Control Act reduced penalties for simple possession but increased penalties for trafficking.

Nixon also became the first president since the 1930s to devolve some national government power to state and local governments. His revenue sharing between the national government and state and local governments highlighted his federalism agenda. By addressing such issues as welfare and the environment, he anticipated the agendas of later presidents.

Unfortunately, Watergate overshadowed Nixon's domestic and foreign affairs foresight. On June 17, 1972, during the presidential campaign, the police arrested five employees of the Committee to Reelect the President (CREEP) for burglary at the Watergate headquarters of the Democratic National Committee. The burglary capped a series of political dirty tricks that began in the fall of 1971. Approved by Attorney General John Mitchell, White House chief of staff H. R. Haldeman, and White House counsel John Dean, these activities intended to disrupt the Democratic presidential primary campaigns of U.S. Senators Edmund Muskie and George McGovern. The clandestine endeavors included stolen documents, false news stories, forged letters, and spy missions.[88]

What the White House dismissed as "a third-rate burglary attempt" unraveled into one of America's worst constitutional, legal, and political scandals, eventually forcing the president to resign.[89] By June 20, 1972, the truth emerged: the Watergate burglars had White House ties. Nixon denied personal involvement, contending that he did not authorize the

Watergate burglary, but the investigation successfully targeted him for its cover-up.

Apparently, White House officials authorized the payment of hush money to Watergate defendants. Although Nixon vowed his innocence, he refused to turn over subpoenaed tapes of White House meetings to Congress, citing executive privilege. The Supreme Court, however, unanimously ordered him to release the tapes. One tape contained a mysterious eighteen-minute gap—deliberately erased, according to sound experts.[90] A federal grand jury named Nixon as an unindicted coconspirator in the Watergate scandal.

By July 1974, the House Judiciary Committee had approved three articles of impeachment against President Nixon for (1) obstruction of justice: making false or misleading statements to investigators, withholding evidence, condoning and counseling perjury, interfering with lawful investigations, approving payment of hush money, and attempting to misuse the Central Intelligence Agency; (2) abuse of power: misusing the Internal Revenue Service, the Federal Bureau of Investigation, and the Secret Service; and maintaining an unlawful secret investigative unit (plumbers) within the Office of President; and (3) failure to comply with congressional subpoenas.[91]

Realizing he faced almost certain impeachment by the House and conviction by the Senate, Nixon resigned on August 9, 1974, admitting errors of judgment but not illegal actions. He resigned, according to his farewell statement, because "to continue to fight through the months ahead for my personal vindication would almost totally absorb the time and attention of both the President and Congress in a period when our entire focus should be on the great issues of peace abroad and prosperity without inflation at home."[92]

Nixon's need and desire for power corrupted his administration and legacy by introducing "a paranoid style of politics that viewed the struggle for power as a form of warfare against enemies. It countenanced the use of dirty tactics on a scale not previously accepted."[93] Getting and maintaining power overrode ethical and moral considerations. Power became an end in itself.

To maintain himself in power once news of the scandal broke, Nixon followed the same fivefold strategy later used by Clinton: (1) *delay* giving investigative authorities subpoenaed evidence, (2) *discredit* those conducting the investigation, (3) *deny* involvement in the scandal, (4) *deflect* attention from the scandal by traveling widely, and (5) *diminish* the scandal's importance by belittling its significance. Nixon even fired Attorney General Elliot Richardson because he would not dismiss the independent prosecutor chosen to investigate the scandal, Archibald Cox.

Ironically, Nixon probably could have sustained his presidency if he had publicly admitted and apologized for his involvement when news of the scandal broke. Instead, he looked at the scandal as a war with his enemies. Throughout his presidency, he used subordinates, such as Vice President Spiro Agnew, to attack his enemies, including the press and the Democratically controlled Congress.

Conclusion

Events of the 1960s and early 1970s eroded public confidence in political institutions, leaving a dark tarnish on the presidency, Congress, the media, and other public institutions. In addition, investigative reporting intensified after Watergate. The government and the press looked more like enemies than friendly adversaries. Muckraking grew into a major industry, rewarding reporters with Pulitzer Prizes and hefty book contracts.

Before Vietnam and Watergate, presidents had room to maneuver, flexibility in making decisions. The public treated them with more deference. Vietnam and Watergate put presidents on a tight leash. If presidential conduct had become too imperial before those events, afterwards presidents were forced to act with more restraint. Today people still expect much of presidents, but they lack the latitude to perform. For some years after Watergate, presidents were caught in a vise between high demands and low support.

Presidents were not alone in feeling these restraints; the national government, too, faced the prospect of a diminished role in American federalism. Political leaders and presidents began to call for reducing the power of the national government and increasing the power of state and local governments. For several decades presidents had advanced centralized national solutions to problems. Beginning with President Nixon, the call for decentralized solutions mounted. No longer did the public look upon the national government as a universal savior.

The 1960s and early 1970s were an age in transition from the feel-good innocence of an earlier era to a period that trampled on traditions, crushing cherished ideas and ideals. Kennedy, Johnson, and Nixon reflected and contributed to society's changing moral values. Common to these three presidents were unfettered personal ambition; lavish attention to image making; brazen renunciation of political principles for political pragmatism; callous manipulation of the media; unbridled obsession with power; and the dangerous gratification of personal desires. The "me generation" entered the White House through the front door. Presidents failed to demonstrate what Philip G. Henderson says a president must have: "deep and abiding principles, a clear and compelling vision, and a commitment to uphold the constitutional order and the dignity of office."[94]

6

POSTMODERN PRESIDENTIAL MORALITY

> Moral codes for dealing with sex, money, and power were rooted in
> common spiritual and aesthetic assumptions; today we share no com-
> mon assumptions from which we can interpret any sort of moral code.
> —Suzanne Fields, "Long Fall from Lee's Code
> to Clinton's," *Richmond Times-Dispatch*

Few issues command more attention than the physical environment.
"Save the Earth" and other campaigns generate much interest among
politicians, policymakers, interest groups, and the public. Ironically, as the
nation focuses on the battle to save "Mother Earth," another danger
looms: moral disintegration. Presenting obstacles more challenging and
dangerous than acid rain and nuclear waste, this threat strikes at the heart
of who and what America is.

The American presidency, the most visible embodiment of American
values, offers striking evidence of the deteriorating moral climate. Like
urban skyscrapers that endure and redirect wind currents, presidents func-
tion within the moral atmosphere, reflecting and redirecting moral currents. Unlike skyscrapers, however, presidents may reflect more than they
redirect. History records how moral turbulence influenced Presidents Gerald Ford, Jimmy Carter, Ronald Reagan, George Bush, and Bill Clinton.

THE PROCESS OF MORAL POLLUTION CONTINUES

The moral environment of the 1990s is a product of gradual pollution. Since
the 1960s, layers of social and political unrest have slowly accumulated on

the surface of American society, eating away bit by bit at the nation's moral foundations. The attack on the bulwarks of American society continues unabated.

As the black and white lines of right and wrong blended into gray, a moral haze formed over society. After President Nixon's resignation, America turned to Gerald Ford to rebuild national harmony and to reestablish presidential trust. Unfortunately, he could not answer the public's cry for help, and in 1976 the public turned to Jimmy Carter, who campaigned on the theme "You can trust me," to lead the nation out of a terribly exhausting decade. The 1970s offered no end to the controversies created by Vietnam, Watergate, rock and roll and disco music, and increases in illegal drug use and crime rates. America could not get off the treadmill of moral change.

In the 1980s, the haze that already hovered over the moral environment of America began to descend. Though Ronald Reagan stressed the importance of family values, even he could not stop the erosion of traditional family life, an accepted and expected American norm. Homosexuals came out of the closet in growing numbers. A dreaded virus, AIDS, came on the scene and spread primarily through gay and drug-using populations. Politically, the two-party system began to fail. Loyalty to one's party no longer commanded strong support, and parties turned to other criteria for the selection of party candidates. The 1980s ended with George Bush as president and with moral turmoil abounding.

LIFE IN THE 1990s: THE SMOG IS BLINDING

James Q. Wilson points out, "Many Americans worry that the moral order that once held the nation together has come unraveled. Despite freedom and prosperity—or worse, perhaps because of freedom and prosperity—a crucial part of the moral order, a sense of personal responsibility, has withered under the attack of personal self-indulgence."[1] The chaos of recent decades has created a formidable belief that objectivity is a delusion. The blinding smog that engulfs America's moral environment limits the nation's ability to decipher truth. Without accepted standards to measure behavior, truth becomes relative, the invitation to question authority routine, instability commonplace, and tolerance the watchword. After all, who dares make a moral judgment if there are no accepted standards?

Examples of today's moral smog abound, especially in the entertainment industry. Movies, music, and television now subvert rather than reinforce traditional moral standards.

By the 1980s, Hollywood had become part of America's moral crisis. Rather than using its influence to reaffirm traditional values, the movie industry romanticized moral decay. In fact, Hollywood reflected an America in crisis. The public rage and fear of the 1970s found its way onto the big screen in such horror movies as *Halloween* and *Friday the 13th*. These new creations offered more violence than their earlier counterparts. Just as Vietnam and Watergate undermined public trust, movie moguls shattered America's moral armor.

Horror movies were not the only films to strike at America's moral innocence. In the early 1980s, *Porky's, National Lampoon's Animal House,* and other movies pictured society with little sexual discipline and no moral guidance. These sexually explicit, vulgar, and profane movies were new to Hollywood. By allowing such images to play on the big screen, Hollywood justified the loss of American values. Casual sex, uncivil language, and random acts of violence became acceptable, even desirable, based on the themes of these movies. The once majestic and glamorous world of Hollywood fell victim to the pollution of the new national moral environment.

Realism did not decline in the 1990s, but became more telling, if that is possible. *Forrest Gump* is the best revelation of this disturbingly realistic portrayal of American society. This award-winning epic traces the life of a simple, yet innocent, man from his birth in the 1950s through his coming of age in the 1990s. Though Forrest, played by Tom Hanks, is not very intelligent, the audience learns much from his experiences in a world even more lost than this foolish man.

Forrest lives through the confusion of the 1960s and observes his childhood playmate, Jenny, become addicted to drugs and alcohol. He also serves during the Vietnam War and experiences the pain of a nation that rejected its veterans. Forrest is like an uncontaminated soul, offering a clear vision of these tragedies. His simple, but prophetic, questions probe the state of American society. In two hours on the screen, all of the corruption of three and a half decades passes by.

At the end, Forrest has not changed, but he realizes that the world around him has. Jenny, who becomes his wife, dies of AIDS, leaving Forrest as a single father trying to comprehend a confusing world. The lesson of Forrest Gump is both simple and profound: Simplicity and family values are desirable ideals, not guarantees of a life of boredom.

Like movies, the music industry parallels the pollution of the moral environment. In the 1950s and early 1960s, buoyant, cheerful music and light rock and roll were the norm. However, as America became less idealistic, so did its music. After Vietnam and Watergate, heavy metal found its way into the mainstream of American radio. Anger and violence became the main messages of this new musical genre, which revealed the gloom of society. Performers such as Ozzy Osbourne took their anger on tour. Osbourne became notorious for killing animals on stage and biting off the heads of bats. Alarmingly, these displays of unethical and disgusting behavior attracted large audiences. Society had begun to breathe in the smog of moral destruction.

In the 1980s, the temporary hope brought by the Reagan era produced some upbeat music. Teen bands like Menudo and New Kids on the Block became popular, and country music attracted larger audiences. Though more upbeat, the music of the 1980s was often racy. Madonna gained great popularity by recording such controversial songs as "Papa Don't Preach" and "Like a Virgin," which dealt with sexually explicit material.

At the same time, the relatively new medium of the music video became extremely popular, and artists magnified their messages with visual interpretations. The video for "Papa Don't Preach" received a lot of attention from media critics because it dealt with the sensitive issue of teenage pregnancy. In the video, Madonna and a male actor portray two young people very much in love but scared by the challenges of an unplanned child. Critics complained that the video romanticized such circumstances and made sexual promiscuity seem "cool" or appropriate behavior. However, Music Television (MTV) did not quit airing the piece, which rose to the top of MTV and radio charts.

The music of the 1990s has continued along the same destructive path, falling, like other areas of society, to dangerous lows. Music of the 1990s lacks true roots or meaning. Its synthetic sounds mimic the moral moods of a synthetic society. Rap and alternative music are the most popular with American teenagers, because they express the turmoil and confusion of the modern era. Song titles of the 1990s reveal the impact of moral pollution on the music industry. "I Want to Sex You Up" and "Cop Killer" expose an industry that glorifies sex and lacks social responsibility.

Television also depicts the state of America's moral decline, mirroring the society it entertains. Whereas viewers of the 1950s and 1960s watched *Leave It to Beaver,* today's television faithful see such programs as *Melrose Place* and *Party of Five.* TV began to touch upon delicate social issues in the 1980s, when shows like *Dallas, Falcon Crest,* and others began to air scripts containing sexually explicit messages and images. These evening soap operas were the first shows to openly defy television's traditional moral code against such programs during family viewing hours. They portrayed America as it was, not as it should be. Viewers apparently liked what they saw. In 1984, *Dallas* became the most watched television program in America.[2] This popularity convinced networks that Americans were ready for "no holds barred" programming. Today, that is exactly what America gets! On *Melrose Place,* young characters address moral decisions with the same passion that they order lunch. *Party of Five* presents a family torn apart, struggling to survive in a society that discriminates against the traditional family unit. Television in the 1990s walks a fine line between entertaining a society with few moral guidelines and trying to maintain a respectable image.

Movies, music, and television demonstrate how moral pollution has affected modern culture. America's highest institution also suffers. Each modern president has had to address moral issues on national and personal levels.

Americans suffered the cruel irony in the 1980s of becoming more prosperous but worse off. The selfishness and greed of the "me" decade followed a natural course of individualism begun in the 1960s, with their open rebellion against traditions and the government. Social discord in the 1980s resulted from over twenty years of stubborn independence and the decline of traditional morality. The decline in American family life and the decreased significance of religion magnetized America's moral compass, rendering it useless.

In these circumstances presidential leadership becomes more difficult. A selfish society may turn to the president to solve its problems but withhold two key supports for presidential leadership: deference and sacrifice. Presidents who either oppose popular desires or call upon the public to sacrifice short-circuit their leadership. President Jimmy Carter learned that lesson the hard way when he said that Americans would have to learn to get along with less. Accustomed to the theme of "have it your way," the public rejected President Carter and his solemn warning.

The media, political parties, and religion, which serve as extensions and reflections of society, have contributed to society's gradual decline. Television's power and influence over society allows it to affect public perceptions of the presidency. For example, the amount of positive press that a president receives may drastically affect his popularity rating, while negative media attention can destroy a president's image. Thus, politicians and presidents in particular have had to win over the media to preserve their political livelihood. If they ignore the power of the press, politicians doom themselves to a career of constant inquiry and controversy. Image creation becomes more important than moral leadership.

America's political parties also contribute to moral pollution. Responding to changes in American society, Democrats and Republicans overhauled their systems of presidential-candidate selection during the 1960s and 1970s. Their old systems, which emphasized party leaders, seniority, and party loyalty, gave way to an emphasis on media savvy, money, and charm. A candidate's character became less important and electability more important. In a society devoid of moral standards, that creates a dangerous situation. So political parties have unintentionally brought moral issues to the attention of the public by selecting individuals without significant regard for character and virtue and sending them into a political arena filled with predatory media. Keith Whittington puts it this way: "In minimizing the distance between the president and the populace, the modern rhetorical presidency has minimized the significance of stature. Presidents are merely popular individuals whose particular arena of celebrity is political."[3]

Ironically, religion—or the lack thereof—is the third agent of moral pollution. Once dominant, Christianity, though still the most popular religion in America, no longer speaks with significant moral authority. Membership losses in the millions have moved mainstream Christian denominations onto the sidelines of American culture. Their vacuous moral pronouncements receive little or no hearing in American society. More vigorous conservative denominations now vie to replace mainstream Christianity, but even they are no match for the cultural power of the media, music, and the movie industry.

A moral vacuum has replaced the once powerful practices of prayer, Bible reading, posting of the Ten Commandments, and Christmas celebrations in the public schools and American life generally. Public schools, for example, now wrestle with how to teach morality, but they lack a moral base. Absent respect for authoritative and authentic moral standards, such as the Ten Commandments, morality moves into the realm of the relative. Church activities, once the soul of cultural life in American communities, are no longer dominant. The bastions of commerce and entertainment now attract larger followings on Sunday than the church, which was once the center of family life. America lost a great moral voice in that exchange.

How can a leader lead without followers? The postmodern era lacks traditional and historical standards to give moral direction, and moral decay has decimated the ranks of people willing to follow an authentic moral voice. How can a president lead with moral authority when society has none? If the people elect a president who represents their interests and desires, then logically that president will not speak with historic moral authority.

GERALD R. FORD, 1974–1977

Watergate and the events surrounding Richard Nixon's resignation, which placed moral issues squarely on the public agenda, caused many Americans to lose faith in their government and political leaders. Restoring public trust after one of the biggest scandals in presidential history became the centerpiece of President Ford's agenda. Ford himself came to the presidency after being chosen to replace Nixon's scandal-plagued vice president, Spiro Agnew, who had resigned amidst charges of tax evasion and accepting bribes. Since Democrats and Republicans held Ford in high regard, both houses of Congress overwhelmingly confirmed him to replace Agnew pursuant to the Twenty-fifth Amendment.

Ford, who brought a reassuring presence to the vice presidency and then to the presidency, confronted an especially delicate task. Coming to office during a national crisis and without the benefit of an election, Ford faced a wary nation. Wanting to soothe the anxieties of a public that had not elected him and looked askance at Watergate, he said: "I will remain my own man, fly my own course, and speak my own convictions."[4]

When he took office on August 9, 1974, he became—and remains—the only person to attain the presidency without ever having won a national election for any office. James Cannon points out that Ford "became President not because he was popular with the American public, not because he campaigned for the job, but because of his character."[5]

His impeccable integrity paved his path to the presidency. "He was the perennial good guy, a product of traditional midwestern conservatism."[6] Born in Omaha, Nebraska, he grew up in Grand Rapids, Michigan, played football for the University of Michigan, and then earned his law degree at Yale. After serving as lieutenant commander in the Navy during World War II, he returned to Grand Rapids, resumed his law practice, and entered Republican politics. In 1948, he married Elizabeth Bloomer Warren.

Having grown up during a much more peaceful time, Ford appreciated the importance of character. Known for integrity and respect for tradition, he held to the values of the past and remained steadfast in his religious convictions.

These character traits made it difficult for Ford to accept the events of Watergate. He believed that "the morality of politicians and the government itself—reflects the cross section of people who go to the polls."[7] He wondered how a popularly elected administration could so easily fall prey to immoral acts. He believed the Nixon administration was an indictment of the times that brought him to power, a product of an immoral atmosphere. Nixon, he thought, represented too much of the bad and not enough of the good in America. In the wake of Watergate, America needed a president who was what Nixon was not. The public wanted honesty, trustworthiness, and loyalty.

Ford's presidency began beautifully. At his swearing-in he assured the public that "our long national nightmare is over. Our Constitution works. Our great Republic is a government of laws and not of men."[8] He then asked the nation to "let brotherly love purge our hearts of suspicion and hate."[9] Ford set out to restore confidence in the presidency and to grant the nation time to heal.

The public embraced Ford, giving him very high marks early in his administration. The honeymoon ended, however, almost before it began. On September 8, 1974, Ford shocked the nation by granting a full pardon to former president Richard Nixon. Though he had the legal authority to take such an action, "that one stroke destroyed the credibility of Ford's presidency."[10] Support from an angry and suspicious public plummeted, and the press stoked the fires of public outrage. Almost immediately, the press reported rumors of a "deal" between Ford and Nixon.

Although Ford testified before Congress that these rumors were untrue, he could not fully restore his reputation. Instead of healing the nation after the Watergate tragedy, Ford's goal, the pardon reopened the wound. In effect, in pardoning Nixon, he sacrificed his presidency, for without the pardon he would likely have won the 1976 presidential election.

Although Ford's pardon of Nixon surprised the public, it should not have. The product of an era that believed in forgiveness, he thought the nation should forgive and not consume itself in hate and recrimination:

> We are not vengeful people, forgiveness is one of the roots of the American tradition. And Nixon, in my opinion, had already suffered enormously. I was not motivated by sympathy for his plight or by concern over the state of his health. It was the state of the country's health at home and around the world that worried me.[11]

Perhaps Ford foresaw frightening consequences of a continued obsession with Watergate. In any event, the public reacted vehemently. Hugh Sidey notes:

> Perhaps the national reaction was so severe because the public so much wanted to believe that Gerald Ford would solve their own problems, put credibility back into leadership, and ride through their midst like a man on a white horse. No man could have lived up to the hopes that grew wildly in the wake of Nixon's departure. So when Ford's human dimensions became so starkly visible at the time of the pardon, the disappointment was magnified.[12]

Ford's press secretary, J. H. terHorst, opposed the pardon and resigned, stating, "Jerry, I regret this, I think you've made a mistake. But I respect your views. I'm sorry if there was any misunderstanding."[13] Only Ford himself seemed comfortable with his decision:

> Finally it was done. It was an unbelievable lifting of a burden from my shoulders. I felt very certain that I had made the right decision, and I was confident that I could now proceed without being harassed by Nixon or his problems anymore. I thought I could concentrate 100 percent of my time on the overwhelming problems that faced me and the country.[14]

However, the media attention the pardon attracted made it difficult, if not impossible, for Ford to redirect his attention to matters he found more pressing. His ability to forgive and forget left him open to attacks on his frailties. Common mistakes, magnified by the media, transformed the Ford presidency into comedy material for the nightly news. For instance, on a 1975 trip to Australia, the president slipped on the stairs of Air Force One.

Reporters and cameramen shared the incident with the world. "The image of klutz would never fade away. Every time he stumbled, bumped his head, fell to the snow on his skis, the image was compounded. Ford became famous for his gaffes, whether real or exaggerated."[15]

Personal character, his strength, paved the way to his political defeat. Chosen and confirmed as vice president for his character, he lost the presidency because of what he considered an important moral act in the national interest. Ford's fate illustrates what happens to a president who acts with moral courage in the national interest but against the will of the public. Ford stood by his moral conviction but paid the supreme political price: "He pardoned Nixon knowing that this would almost surely cost him any chance he had to win, but he still felt it was the right thing to do. It was the character for which he was chosen, but it was an element of his character that created the issue that caused him to be defeated."[16] Ford did not become president because of popularity with the American people, but he lost the presidency for lack of it. In recognition of Ford's unselfish service, President Jimmy Carter began his inauguration speech by thanking him for "all he has done to heal our land."[17]

JIMMY CARTER, 1977–1981

Ford's pardon of Nixon gave Jimmy Carter the edge he needed to win the 1976 presidential election. Carter, a stranger to most of the American people before his run for the presidency, came from a small southern town, Plains, Georgia, the son of a farmer and a nurse. With popular distrust of Washington running high, Carter's background as an outsider helped him to win the presidency. Lack of political skills honed in Washington, however, eventually cost him the support of his party and also of the people.

After attending public schools, he enrolled in the Georgia Institute of Technology before transferring to the U.S. Naval Academy, from which he graduated. His naval career lasted eleven years, and he rose to the rank of lieutenant. In 1946, he married Rosalyn Smith. His political career began in 1962 when he won a seat in the Georgia Senate. In 1966, he lost a race for governor, but won that office four years later. Then, in 1974, he announced his candidacy for president of the United States.

By electing Jimmy Carter in 1976, the American people sent a strong political message. Gerald Ford had betrayed the public's trust when he adhered to his own ethical code. However, America did not realize that Jimmy Carter was equally fervent in character. Hendrick Hertzberg says Carter was "a moral leader more than a political leader."[18] This characteristic of Carter's leadership explains both his presidential failures and his postpresidential success. Jimmy Carter was the first president to wear his religion on his sleeve. In more than one instance, his open identification as a Christian sparked moral controversies. Richard G. Hutcheson writes:

> In certain identifiable ways Carter's presidency was probably handicapped or weakened by his deep religious faith. The sense of national malaise on the part of the individual who sees human sin as inevitable, and humility as the appropriate response, is theologically accurate. But it is politically treacherous, and perhaps even dangerous.[19]

His first major moral controversy arose during the 1976 campaign when *Playboy* interviewed him. The interview, an attempt to expand Carter's constituency beyond its narrow southern and evangelical Christian base, backfired when he referred to the sin of "lust in the heart." Obviously, Carter did not know his audience when he described the wickedness of extramarital fantasies. Opponents and supporters chastised his political foolishness. Critics laughed aloud, while his supporters hoped that the issue would soon pass, which it did, but not without damaging his reputation.

The image cast an unfortunate shadow on religion. Many Americans looked at the controversy as evidence of hypocrisy. Where Carter had hoped to revitalize American interest in religion, his efforts had failed. Like the rest of his presidency, he had good intentions, but poor execution. Carter did have a moral message to share; unfortunately for Americans, they missed that message completely.

After shaking the media's initial stigma, Carter began work on his presidential goals. His desire was "to give the Country a Government as good and as competent and as compassionate as are the American people."[20] Unfortunately, the president had overestimated the American people. He seemed unaware of the moral pollution that would set boundaries on his goals.

Carter had little opportunity to do what he did best. He could not utilize his moral ideology, because the nation was in the backwash of a moral crisis. His problems in the domestic arena were not moral but essentially managerial. Carter's valuable ability to distinguish between right and wrong became irrelevant. He noted later that: "There was no right or wrong way to solve these problems; just effective and ineffective ways."[21]

Carter chose to focus on foreign policy because he believed that he could harness his morality to prevent war, preserve peace, and protect human rights. Above all, Carter wanted world peace. He thought it necessary to avoid war at all costs, because he believed the rewards of violence were short term. He urged Americans to consider foreign relations in a broader sense by advocating a "higher cause"—peace. Carter's desire for peace reflected his concern for moral principles. While some criticized his policies as weak and timid, "he considered morality in foreign policy to be an expression of the essential character of this nation, not a weakness."[22] Though he attempted to apply his religious and ethical values in foreign policy, the results were the same. Carter failed to convince the nation that his foreign policy was effective. For example, during debate over the Panama Canal Treaty, public disapproval was well publicized. Carter knew that the people did not want to return the canal. However, he chose to go through with it: "He thought it was the right thing to do, he did it and he made it stick."[23] Again, Carter acted as a moral leader, not a politician.

The president openly addressed the problems he saw plaguing the nation in July of 1979, when he spoke about the public's "crisis of confidence." However, his efforts were too little, too late. Rather than ease the minds of the American public, the speech simply acknowledged that the country was lost—politically and spiritually. His call for personal sacrifices in the national interest fell on deaf ears. He could not rejuvenate America's moral spirit.

Carter also chose to take the moral high ground when Iranian terrorists took American embassy personnel and visitors on November 4, 1979. Against the public's will, Carter for many months refused to take military action. When the president finally attempted to rescue the Americans in a secret military mission, his effort failed. It was the last straw. Leaders from the Left and the Right accused Carter of compromising his values. Though Carter's "moral character remained unquestioned, the image of weakness became too strong to overcome."[24]

In 1980 Jimmy Carter lost to Republican Ronald Reagan. Carter's presidency, filled with ethical dilemmas, allowed him to apply his spiritual faith in making moral decisions. However, moral pollution made success difficult. Americans wanted a president with a vision like their own and a man who would not flaunt his religion or push his beliefs on others. America wanted leadership based upon something other than just principles of right and wrong. So, Jimmy Carter left the White House "to take up once more the only title in our democracy superior to that of President, the title of citizen."[25] Ronald Reagan would be the next man to try to release the country from its own terrifying grasp.

RONALD REAGAN, 1981–1989

Ronald Reagan, resembling a hero from one of his cowboy movies, strode into the world's most prestigious office intent on saving the day. Unlike his two predecessors, Reagan appeared more aware of the nation's moral deficiencies and projected greater personal and political strength. Plagued by political miscalculations and weak images, Ford and Carter lost their respective elections in 1976 and 1980. Reagan exuded assurance and confidence in himself and his conservative political principles.[26]

Bred a Democrat by family influence and the New Deal's attraction, Reagan actively supported the party until he became disenchanted with the excesses of its liberal policies, campaigning in 1948 for Harry Truman. Reagan's father, a salesman, passionately expressed his beliefs, just as the younger Reagan would later as a conservative Republican. When a hotel refused lodging to Jews, his father slept in his car rather than stay there.[27] His mother, active in the Christian Church, inculcated biblical principles in Reagan at an early age; Reagan graduated from Eureka College, founded by his mother's church. His conversion to conservative Republicanism was like a rebirth of his childhood values.

> It might be said that the heyday of modern political liberalism, in its American manifestation, was the 1960's, when the Great Society began and the Kennedys were secular saints and the costs of enforced liberalism were not yet apparent. And that is precisely when Reagan came down hard right for Goldwater in 1964. It wasn't exactly a career enhancing move, but Reagan thought the conservatives were right. So he joined them, thinking that he was right and thinking that sooner or later he and the country were going to meet in a historic rendezvous.[28]

Reagan was right that he and the nation would meet again, but could he convince America that it needed his help?

Reagan's visions were grand. He saw a nation that lacked the moral guidance of his youth, but he did not believe it was lost forever. His initiatives for the nation included strengthening the family, reducing government bureaucracies, and restoring American pride. Reagan brought to his dreams the courage to fight for them. Reagan speechwriter Peggy Noonan said: "At the core of Reagan's character was courage, a courage that was ultimately contagious. The whole country caught his courage."[29] Reagan's confidence and vision were like a tranquilizer to a public reeling from two decades of social and moral turbulence. He appeared like a throwback to the tranquil 1950s.

He expressed courage, charm, and compassion in unusual ways. Just after an assassin's bullet hit him in 1981, he quipped to his wife, "I forgot to duck." Then to his doctors he joked, "I hope you're Republicans." Reagan often appeared at his best during national tragedies, such as comforting the nation after the *Challenger* disaster and following the return of caskets bearing soldiers who had given their lives to the nation's service. His personal touch with people during tragedies communicated his compassion to the nation.

Reagan's leadership style was reminiscent of the "realpolitik" era. He called the Soviet Union the "evil empire," successfully fought for increased defense spending to challenge communism, and told Soviet Premier Gorbachev at the Berlin Wall, "Tear down this wall." He saw himself conducting a moral crusade against the communist menace. However, the administration only rarely used force, and then with restraint. For example, Reagan ordered a swift and surgical invasion of Grenada to stop a communist uprising. He did not open itself up to liberal criticism by using force in the battle against communism.[30]

Reagan's terms, while often romanticized, were not without controversy. Domestically, critics chastised him for supporting supply-side economics, calling it "Reaganomics" and "voodoo economics." Believing that the economy would grow if the government removed restraints on the private sector, Reagan fought for large tax cuts to promote consumer spending and investment. He also reshaped the federal budget, intending to reduce wasteful spending on social programs.

Democrats scoffed at his actions and accused him of insensitivity to the needs of the poverty-stricken. His motives, however, were probably a pure reflection of his childhood values and his firm belief in the traditional American dream. He believed that individual determination and hard work, not reliance on government programs, were the keys to a better life for Americans. Reagan thought that welfare and other social programs perpetuated dependence on the government and reduced personal responsibility.

The Iran-Contra affair in 1986 raised moral issues. That affair involved secretly selling arms to Iran in exchange for the return of American hostages in Lebanon and diverting funds from the sales to Nicaraguan Contras in violation of a congressional prohibition on such aid. Iran-Contra raised questions about two issues: secrecy in foreign and military operations, and presidential versus congressional authority.

Public concern about the scandal contributed to Democrats retaking control of the U.S. Senate. Reagan himself, who remained almost unscathed by Iran-Contra, earned the nickname the "Teflon president." His openness in handling Iran-Contra issues helped him overcome the controversy. Pledging full cooperation with the investigation, neither he nor his administration hid behind executive privilege.

Reagan's clear political and moral visions of the future contributed to his success. "He knew what he thought and he knew it in a serious way."[31] Often called "the Great Communicator," Reagan spoke convincingly and reassuringly to the public about his ideas. Inheriting the presidency as America's moral fabric unraveled, Reagan offered a needle and thread. He assured people that hard work and firm principles paid off. After all, he was a former Hollywood actor turned president of the United States.

Reagan steadfastly rejected the postmodern notion that absolute truth is nonexistent and that all truth is relative. He argued that simple truths exist all around us, but government and bureaucracy cannot lead us to them. Instead, individuals must pierce the moral smog. Bob Schieffer said, "God, Home, and Country—that's what Reagan believes in." The magic of his presidency was that he made Americans believe in them too.

Questions about Reagan's ability to make moral decisions differed from those that faced President Carter. Critics found Carter too concerned with moral issues and Reagan, not enough.[32] Hutcheson concluded about Reagan that "the Iran/Contra affair perhaps epitomized the lack of moral sensitivity that marked certain aspects of the presidency."[33]

Both conservatives and liberals criticized Reagan. Conservatives thought he sold out some of his principles and platforms, such as failing to abolish the Department of Education and to fully support the pro-life movement and prayer in the public schools. Liberals criticized him for disregarding congressional intent during the Iran-Contra scandal. Amazingly high popularity ratings, however, overshadowed these criticisms. With towering popularity, Reagan left the White House in 1989 to his vice president, the newly elected George Bush.

Reagan addressed America's moral crisis, but he left behind a record of mixed success. Hutcheson notes that: "President Reagan seemed initially to be moving the country out of its sense of moral crisis. . . . But large numbers were still concerned about the deeper moral vacuum, the nakedness of the public square."[34] The public respected Reagan's political and moral integrity, but as president he could not single-handedly reverse America's moral decline. At best he managed to slow the rate of moral pollution, at least for a time.

GEORGE HERBERT WALKER BUSH, 1989–1993

Succeeding a popular president and leading the country into the century's last decade challenged George Bush. He brought to the challenges a different background from Ronald Reagan's. Raised in the home of an international investment banker and U.S. senator from Connecticut, Bush graduated from a prestigious preparatory school and Yale University. Between prep school and Yale, he became, at age eighteen, the youngest pilot in Navy history. During World War II he married Barbara Pierce while on home rotation.

Graduating from Yale in three years after the war, Bush declined a position in his father's firm and moved to Texas, where he made his own fortune in the oil business. There he entered politics, ultimately holding many appointive and elective positions in the national government and the Republican Party.

When tapped by Ronald Reagan as his vice presidential nominee in 1980, Bush enthusiastically supported the Reagan agenda, even changing some of his own positions to do so. For example, he became a firm opponent of abortion and supported Reagan's economic policies. Bush's unflinching support of President Reagan earned him credibility in the Republican Party but raised the eyebrows of critics, especially in the press, who considered him a chameleon. Outwardly, he captured public support, but inwardly, Bush struggled with a simmering moral conflict. In conservative Texas and as Reagan's vice president, Bush sometimes took positions with which he was personally uncomfortable and that made him appear more conservative than he really was.

During his campaign in 1988, Bush proclaimed with his "Read my lips" pledge, "No new taxes!" His "no new taxes" declaration assured conservatives that he remained true to their cause. After winning the presidency, however, Bush compromised, accepting a slight increase in taxes during intense budget negotiations with the Democratically controlled Congress. That compromise, which cost him support among both conservatives and the general electorate, foreshadowed his 1992 defeat.

Was failure to keep his word a character flaw or an act of courage in the national interest? Arguments run both ways. Presidents do and should change their minds on occasion. Inflexibility in pursuit of a goal is not always morally right. Circumstances and needs change, sometimes making flexibility the proper moral course. In this instance, Bush exercised courage in an effort to balance the budget, but his promise and change of mind placed him in a moral vise that in the end squeezed the life out of his presidency. His change of mind betrayed core supporters and raised doubts among the public about his character. Politically either he should not have made the promise or, once he had made it, he should have kept it. This episode represents a moral dilemma common to presidents and presidential candidates who do not have a clear ideological agenda to govern their decisions. In Bush's shoes, Reagan, guided by his clearly conservative agenda, would likely have kept his word. Bush's centrist tendencies sometimes caused him to deviate from a clearly conservative course.

Bush performed best on the international stage. As a former director of the CIA and President Nixon's diplomatic representative to China, he had excellent foreign affairs credentials and contacts throughout the world. Few presidents ever brought to the presidency as much experience in foreign affairs. Bush, who loudly echoed Reagan's convictions about communism, benefited from what Reagan had set in motion, the collapse of Soviet communism and its client states. Since this great moral success culminated on his watch, Bush receives partial credit.

Desert Storm and the Gulf War outshone all of Bush's other successes. He built an international consensus, including even some Arab countries, for action against Iraq. Then an international military action removed Iraq from Kuwait and damaged the Iraqi warmaking machine. Critics said he should have toppled the Iraqi leader, Saddam Hussein, but Bush believed that the instability created by Hussein's downfall would create a greater crisis for the Iraqi people. He also feared that some Arab allies might withdraw their support from his large international coalition.

Bush demonstrated the will to use the American military in selective instances to achieve moral purposes. In Panama, for example, he ordered a successful invasion to overthrow the corrupt Noriega government. Again substantial advance planning went into this endeavor, and he received significant international support.

After the Gulf War, Bush's popularity skyrocketed to over 90 percent. Unsure of how to invest his popularity dividends, he lost them by failing to offer a compelling vision for America's future, especially at home. What he achieved on the international stage he lost on the domestic stage. Bush set the stage for his own defeat in 1992. His "no new taxes" pledge handed Ross Perot an issue, and his failure to convert his popularity dividends into a compelling moral vision for America gave Bill Clinton an issue.

Bush did not realize how much America's moral values had changed. He pitted his World War II record with that generation's solid moral values against the values of a candidate from the 1960s. He offered vast experience in national and international politics against two candidates with minuscule resumes. Bush could not fathom how someone with Bill Clinton's checkered morality and limited experience could win the presidency. Nor could he comprehend how someone without any elective political experience, such as Ross Perot, could win 20 percent of the vote. His campaign looked much like the campaign of someone running for high school student body president: "Vote for me, because I am the best candidate." He relied on character and experience, and he lost. Clinton beat Bush with his vision for America and with his emphasis on the economy, and Perot undercut Bush by addressing ticklish budget issues that Bush avoided.

Bush wanted to convince America that "family, faith, and friends are what matters. We should help one another to strengthen the American family."[35] Bush wanted Americans to see and experience these values for themselves, but he was not able to communicate his ideas to a nation that appeared unable to recall his view of American tradition and culture.

Why did Ronald Reagan succeed and George Bush fail with the same moral message? First, Bush's compromises on such issues as taxes clouded his message. Second, his communication skills did not measure up to Reagan's. Third, Bush failed to take advantage of his opportunities, especially his popularity after the Gulf War. Fourth, Reagan's presidency now looks like a blip on the moral radar screen. The values of the 1960s loom larger in American life than those of the World War II generation. Shades of gray have replaced the moral clarity of black and white, right and wrong. Fifth, Bush failed to understand the importance of vision, especially during unstable times. The public receives reassurance and confidence from candidates who articulate compelling visions. Sixth, Bush's centrist tendencies sometimes conflicted with the reigning conservative ideology in his party, creating a crisis of credibility for him on some issues. Seventh, the values of the World War II generation are apparently passing away with it.

George Bush now appears as a transitional president, the last of the World War II generation to serve as president. He brought to the presidency the moral values of his generation—dignity, honor, integrity, sacrifice, and respect. As president in a society undergoing moral challenges and changes, Bush could not adapt to emerging moral values.

WILLIAM JEFFERSON CLINTON, 1993–2001

William Jefferson Clinton won the three-way presidential race in 1992 with 43 percent of the vote. Elected at the age of forty-six, Clinton is the first president born after World War II; he came of age during the turbulent 1960s. He was born William Jefferson Blythe IV in the small town of Hope, Arkansas, three months after his father's death in an automobile accident. His mother, a nurse, remarried and Bill took his sometimes-abusive, hard-drinking stepfather's name. Clinton's mother dealt with her pain by escaping reality. An emotionally fragile woman, she lived her life in fantasies through gambling, card playing, and other ways. In this environment, Bill Clinton learned to strive for attention any way possible. He had a need, not just a desire, to surround himself with friends.

From elementary school through college, Clinton came into contact with thousands of people, making special efforts to remember their names, their histories, and interests. As a teenager in Arkansas, he sometimes invited friends to his house to watch him finish a crossword puzzle.[36] This need for constant company motivated him to meet others and fanned the flames of his political aspirations.

Clinton graduated from Hot Springs (Arkansas) High School and attended Georgetown University, graduating in 1968 with a degree in foreign service. He then won a Rhodes Scholarship to study at Oxford

University in England. At the height of the Vietnam War, he managed to get a draft deferment. Returning to the United States, he entered Yale Law School, where he met Hillary Rodham, whom he married in 1975. She brought to their marriage firm resolve, sharply honed political instincts, a keen awareness of policy issues, and a willingness to maintain her own political agenda while helping with his. The match appeared made for politics.

In 1974, Clinton made an unsuccessful bid for a seat in Congress as representative of Arkansas's Third District. He was elected attorney general of Arkansas in 1976 and governor in 1978. He lost the governorship in 1980 but was reelected in 1982 and served until 1992.

Even in Arkansas, allegations of Clinton's "womanizing" surfaced. From the beginning, the relationship between Bill and Hillary Clinton was not monogamous. Former aides note that during Clinton's first campaigns, one of his Arkansas girlfriends would leave by the side door just as his fiancée, Hillary, came through the front door.[37] During the 1992 presidential campaign, Gennifer Flowers went public with her claim that she had been in a twelve-year extramarital relationship with Clinton in Arkansas. On national TV, candidate Clinton admitted that he had "caused pain" in his marriage.

Clinton's candidacy for the presidency moved the baby-boomer generation that came of age in the 1960s into the mainstream of American politics. Both his platform and his personal problems illustrate the prominence of this new generation. He strove to be all things to all people. He admitted using marijuana but denied that he inhaled. He dodged the military draft but said that was not his intent. He told women and minorities that he "felt their pain," but he pulled back from fully supporting their agendas.

Candidate Clinton said he wanted to "reinvent" government. He argued that Republican cynicism had dampened the American spirit and threatened the American dream. Also he said he wanted to give the people a government they could trust. His first two actions as president, although popular with some people, created great controversy and shortened his presidential honeymoon. Having promised in the campaign to "lift the ban" on homosexuals serving in the military, he started discussions on the issue that, after much discussion and ill feeling, resulted in the current "don't ask, don't tell" policy; and he ended the restrictions instituted in the Bush administration on federal funding of transplantation research using fetal tissue from induced abortions.

Clinton again broke new ground by naming his wife to chair a major commission on health care. No president's wife had ever before held such a powerful policy position. He had promised in his campaign that if the public elected him, it would get two presidents for the price of one. Clinton acknowledged neither the limitations of his electoral mandate nor the precedents and traditions governing a first lady's performance. Early in his administration he remained true to form, extending, exceeding, and blurring the boundary lines around him.

Clinton has had nothing comparable to either Franklin Roosevelt's New Deal or Lyndon Johnson's Great Society. Neither his electoral mandate in his first term nor the nation's budgetary problems would allow major policy initiatives. His only major policy proposal, health-care reform, failed. The most significant social policy reform during his administration was welfare, a Republican initiative with which he cooperated.

Clinton's calls for federal subsidies to local governments and school districts to hire police officers and teachers were minor when compared to the ambitious social agendas of Roosevelt and Johnson. They are instructive, however, in learning about Clinton's success. Following chief political adviser Dick Morris's advice, Clinton gained maximum political mileage by offering small proposals on large issues like education and crime, which the public considered two of the most important issues facing the nation. This approach is a major reason why he won reelection in 1996.

Clinton's legacy also includes a balanced budget and a healthy economy, but as with welfare reform, he must share the credit with the Republican congressional majority. The greatest benefit to Clinton occurred in 1995 when congressional Republicans forced the shutdown of the executive branch during a budget dispute. When that happened, Clinton's popularity had dropped to under 40 percent. The president took advantage of the shutdown, arguing that Republicans were insensitive to the needs of the American people. His popularity then began to rise and remained at consistently high levels.

This popularity persisted in spite of the continuing controversies and investigations that have run throughout his two terms. Early in his administration, he angered many by high-handedly replacing the White House travel office staff with Clinton loyalists in what came to be known as Travelgate. Questions also arose about his and his wife's involvement in a land deal in Arkansas, Whitewater. Filegate, the misuse of secret FBI files on political enemies, also created controversy.

Seven independent counsels named by the attorney general to investigate scandals in the Clinton administration have not had a major impact on public opinion. One of them, Judge Kenneth Starr, obtained convictions of over a dozen of Clinton's appointees. He also won seventeen appeals brought by the White House, which attempted to use the doctrine of executive privilege to shield the president from providing subpoenaed information and to keep subordinates from testifying. President Clinton claimed executive privilege more times than Presidents Carter, Reagan, and Bush during their sixteen years in office.[38]

Also, Paula Jones, a former Arkansas government employee, sued Clinton for sexual harassment, the first time in history a citizen sued a sitting president. A Supreme Court ruling permitted the suit to go forward during Clinton's term rather than delaying proceedings until after Clinton left office. While the president and Jones eventually settled out of court, the blemish remains on his record. He paid her $850,000 to settle the case.

The confluence of the Paula Jones and Whitewater investigations eventually brought to light Clinton's affair with Monica Lewinsky, a twenty-one-year-old White House intern. It was this relationship that led to impeachment proceedings against Clinton (see chapter 7).

When allegations surfaced in 1999 that Chinese intelligence agents had captured important nuclear secrets, fate smiled kindly upon President Clinton. Republican predecessors shared responsibility for the scandal.

Foes contend that Clinton's actions have consumed his time and the nation's time, causing the judicial system and the Congress to absorb themselves in investigations of his imprudence. The centerfold of the Bill Clinton saga, Monica Lewinsky, represents more than marital infidelity to Clinton's opponents. To them, trust is the issue. If you cannot trust a president to keep the sacred vows of marriage, then can you depend on him to keep the public trust? Marvin Olasky puts it this way: "Journalists and voters who do not scrutinize candidates' sexual flings are negligent. . . . Small betrayals in marriage generally lead to larger betrayals, and leaders who break a large vow to one person find it easy to break relatively small vows to millions."[39]

Certainly, Clinton's friends (and former friends) have suffered from his failings. "FOB," Friend of Bill, a coveted designation when Bill Clinton won the presidency, brought with it unusually trying and frightening experiences. David Maranis points out that as Clinton struggled to survive his White House scandals, he became "a study of presidential loneliness."[40] In fact, a look at Clinton's administration proves that an FOB may have more headaches than laughs. Vince Foster, his boyhood friend and White House legal adviser, committed suicide. William Hubbell, longtime friend and former deputy attorney general, served time in the federal penitentiary. George Stephanopoulos, friend and senior White House political adviser, felt betrayed and left the White House. Dick Morris, longtime friend and political adviser, lost his White House entrée when he attributed the president's sexual misconduct to Mrs. Clinton's unwillingness to participate in marital relations.

The list of former friends turned foes does not end there. In fact, the office has brought Clinton "nothing but drudgery and daily loss of friends."[41] Press Secretary Mike McCurry, though loyal to the president, decided to abandon the Clinton White House. His daily beatings by the press left him battered and ready to rid himself of the scandals associated with the administration. Where does Clinton turn when longtime friends and advisors leave? To his family?

Perhaps suffering more than anyone during the Clinton chronicles is his daughter, Chelsea. Her father's admitted relationship with Monica Lewinsky, someone about her age, humiliated the family and soiled family devotion. Thus, during his trying times the president found himself estranged from family and distanced from friends. In this low and lonely position, he had fewer outlets to satisfy his craving for friendship. Ironically, when he needed friends and family more, his actions had reduced their circle of consolation.

The Politician

In the face of all these scandals, what accounts for Clinton's staying power? Several factors external to Clinton influence his success: a healthy economy, the popular appeal of small policy initiatives on large issues, Republican miscalculation in shutting down the government, shared blame with Republicans on the issue of Chinese espionage, and no notable policy disasters, except health care. Both at home and overseas, Clinton had only minor setbacks. Circumstances have looked kindly upon him except in his personal life.

On a personal level, the reasons for Bill Clinton's political rise and threatened fall are the same. First, Clinton's abilities and illusions of invincibility set him apart from most politicians. Rarely has he suffered setbacks. His rise from a small, rural, southern state to the White House almost defies reality. Along the way his alleged misbehavior either went unchecked or unchallenged. A brilliant mind and splendid use of the English language enabled him to artfully dodge difficult questions and situations. An aura of invincibility seemed to surround him.

Second, his drives to excel and to exceed blurred the boundary lines around him. At each stage of his political career, Clinton found himself anxious for more than his duties allowed. Never satisfied with the status quo, he used his positions to fulfill an inner need for constant activity. A desire for more and a tendency toward excess are the defining elements of Clinton the politician. Just as marriage could not satisfy his desire for women, no political office could quench his thirst for advancement. He lives in perpetual motion. If Clinton sees himself as invincible, it is no wonder that his appetite for life far exceeds the normal human capacity.

Third, his constant restlessness and overactive appetites revealed themselves in the form of promiscuity and a hunger for power. The governor's office provided him with many opportunities to travel and to escape from the normal realities and boundary lines of life. He even participated in highway patrol raids to "scope out" women. While on road trips, he visited nightclubs in the company of adoring "groupies." As president, his relationship with Monica Lewinsky reflected his need for attention and inner peace. With each political advancement, he found new privileges of office. To appease his need for acceptance, Clinton often abused those privileges, and sometimes his abuses fed other needs.

Fourth, Clinton's success also rests on another foundation, redefining himself. By changing as situations dictate, he "is able to continually reinvent himself, flexibly adapting his ideology, his behavior, and his very personality to the needs of the moment."[42]

One aspect of Clinton's presidency that continues to plague him is his tendency to get caught in inconsistencies. During his campaign for the presidency, Clinton's stories about the draft were constantly evolving. Also, his reversal on the middle-class tax cut gained some media attention. Such discrepancies continued through his presidency.

Flip-flops on Bosnia, Whitewater, Vince Foster, and Somalia inspired columnist Bob Herbert to write about "Mr. Clinton's more or less fluid conception of what's real."[43] Herbert even suggests that the White House staff "make a concerted effort to heighten Mr. Clinton's regard for the objective truth."[44]

The president's apparent disregard for the truth probably stems from a combination of many factors. His mother focused on the present and paid little heed to the past:

> Her world view taught, ultimately, that people are not to be judged by their actions, but are endlessly free to reinvent themselves, to be whatever the moment demands . . . since the "irrelevant" past does not really exist . . . the actions of the moment cease to exist once the moment becomes past, and cannot be held against one later.[45]

Another factor in the president's creative approach to truth is his need for adoration. This trait, though helpful in his political endeavors, makes him "peculiarly vulnerable to the universal temptation of political life—to tell people what they want to hear."[46] The result of this need for constant reaffirmation is a man of little substance. Michael Kelly describes a "hollowness to the Clinton Presidency" and notes that "it lacks a center because the man at its center lacks one of his own."[47]

These characteristics of Clinton the politician raise several questions about the intersection of personal morality and his fitness for presidential leadership: If he has not learned the moral traits of loyalty, trust, and respect, can the public trust him as a leader? If he is unwilling to place national and group needs above his personal drives, is he worthy of leadership? If he ignores and disrespects the laws and their application to him personally, can the public trust him to enforce laws fairly?

These questions emphasize the importance of personal moral leadership in the presidency. President Clinton avoided close scrutiny of his personal moral behavior for much of his career. When his character did come into question, he successfully evaded the questions and issues, leaving behind a pathway to power strewn with moral and ethical destruction.

The public's willingness to overlook Clinton's behavior raises serious questions: Is the public apathetic? Does the public approve of his behavior? Is the president merely a reflection of the public's own morality? Has the nation's educational system failed to teach standards of morality? Does the public see no relationship between personal morality and leadership?

Effects on the Presidency

During the Clinton presidency, which without scandal seems rather dull, the institution itself has evolved for better or worse. "Until relatively recently, the American presidency was more about myths than about mischief. Now the mischief itself has become the stuff of myth. In both cases, the danger is to the larger truth."[48] Therefore Clinton has brought the office of the presidency to a new and seemingly lower level.

Can the presidency recover from Bill Clinton and what he represents? William J. Bennett says: "He is bringing us down. Through his tawdry, reckless, irresponsible conduct, he has plowed salt in America's civic soil."[49] However, others state that never before has a president so embodied the state of the nation. Is Bill Clinton, successes and failures combined, America? Does Clinton symbolize a nation completely void of any moral guidance or consideration?

The Clinton presidency wonderfully illustrates the effect that moral pollution has had on the nation's highest office. "The President's essential character flaw isn't dishonesty so much as a-honesty [amorality]. He is an existential President living with absolute sincerity in the passing moment."[50] The president is a product of his times. His truth is not absolute, it is in the moment and is always fleeting. In turn, he must follow where it goes. Perhaps that is why pinning down this elusive president and his beliefs is difficult.

Elected at age forty-six, Bill Clinton is the first president to have grown up during the decay of the moral environment. He was a teenager during the 1960s and experienced firsthand the turmoil of the following decades. When Clinton entered the office in 1992, he vowed to do away with the "drift and deadlock" of the past. Instead, he spoke of an American renewal, based on the dream and ideals of a new generation. Unfortunately, like his generation, Clinton lacked the focus and the ideals to accomplish such a monumental task.

More than anything else, Clinton has created controversy. His personal and political actions have heralded numerous public relations nightmares. Personally, Clinton is famous for his sexual indiscretions. In Arkansas, his romantic involvement with Gennifer Flowers earned him a reputation as a womanizer. His alleged advances towards Paula Jones also earned him legal attention. Perhaps the most disturbing personal allegation made about the president is the controversy surrounding former

White House intern Monica Lewinsky. She alleged that the two had sexual relations while she was an intern. The president's numerous and insistent denials finally crumbled in the face of advancing truth, and then he faced allegations of asking her to lie about their involvement.

When Americans elected Bill Clinton to office, they elected themselves, according to Edith Efron: "The voters . . . saw Clinton's narcissism as a reflection of their own self-preoccupations, well aware of his appetites for hard women and soft money, they were happy to send him to Washington as a representative of their collective moral confusion."[51]

Though Clinton acts without moral consideration, his intentions are not all bad. In fact, this is the scariest thing of all. He simply lacks the moral education that once was fundamental to American life. The president is a man of "unfinished and contradictory character—scholarly and shallow, outgoing and shy, principled and craven, the mood depending on the motive."[52] His character is incomplete without an ethical code. He lacks the confidence, discipline, and compassion necessary to lead the nation out of its moral despair. Yet he lacks these things in part because society's moral pollution has deprived him of them.

THE PRESIDENTIAL PUZZLE

What now? The pollution of America's moral environment goes on apace, leaving presidents caught in the middle. If they exercise traditional moral leadership, they swim upstream against the flow of American society. President Jimmy Carter learned that lesson the hard way. If they go with the flow of society, then they contribute to society's moral pollution, the legacy of President Bill Clinton. Emerging from the moral state of America, presidents confront severe restraints in exercising moral leadership. As the products of democracy, they cannot impose morality. Yet, they bear a responsibility for moral leadership. Like correcting the course of a ship at sea, correcting the nation's moral course requires time and effort. Ironically, those primarily responsible for moral contamination, such as the media, are also the principal checks on immorality. Successful moral leadership by presidents requires a willingness to lead by personal example and to use the "bully pulpit" appropriately in convincing the media and others to make a course correction.

7

THE SEAMLESS GARMENT OF MORALITY

We urge the society as a whole to take account of the ethical commitments necessary for a civil society and to seek the integrity of both public and private morality.

—Declaration Concerning Religion, Ethics,
and the Crisis in the Clinton Presidency

Combatants in the debate about the investigations of President Clinton
agreed on at least one point: They hurt the country. Clinton's supporters
denounced their debilitating effects on presidential leadership, while his
antagonists agonized over their inability either to indict him or to remove
him from office. Democrats considered the investigations a partisan witch
hunt, while Republicans contended that Democrats bloc-voted against
impeachment charges despite their merits and that the White House
stonewalled the independent counsel's investigation. The truth, resting
between the two extremes, reveals the paradox of impeachment, the myth
of Clinton's victory, and the irony of democracy. Or as Aristotle said:
"Virtue is the golden mean between two extremes."

THE PARADOX OF IMPEACHMENT

In defense of her husband, Mrs. Clinton said that his offenses "do not rise
to the level of impeachment." The Constitutional standard for impeachment in Article 2, Section 4 reads: "The President . . . shall be removed
from Office on Impeachment for, and Conviction of, Treason, Bribery, or
other high Crimes and Misdemeanors." Was Mrs. Clinton right?

History

Impeachment wears a political lining inside the cloak of constitutionality.[1] Dating to English history in 1380, impeached officials faced such charges as "making uncivil addresses to a woman" or "appointing someone known to be a person of ill fame and reputation." In 1386, when the first impeachment comparable to modern usage occurred, "high crimes and misdemeanors" included common-law offenses and other charges, such as "advising the King to grant liberties and privileges to certain persons to the hindrance of the due execution of laws." Other impeachable offenses included "granting offices to unfit persons, and misspending public funds." From then until the mid-seventeenth century, "high crimes and misdemeanors" expanded to include negligence and improprieties in office. In 1680 the impeachment sword fell on Chief Justice William Scroggs for browbeating witnesses, cursing and drinking to excess, and generally bringing "the highest scandal on the public justice of the kingdom." Further expansion of impeachment occurred in the eighteenth century, when "high crimes and misdemeanors" began to include purely political offenses. The Earl of Oxford faced the charge of "violation of his duty and trust" in 1701, and the governor general of India, Warren Hastings, faced charges of maladministration, corruption in office, and cruelty toward the people of India.

The Founding Fathers drafted the American Constitution with this history in mind and with the guidance of William Blackstone's *Commentaries on the Laws of England* in hand. Perjury and the subornation of perjury, according to Blackstone, received the punishment of "six months imprisonment, perpetual infamy, and a . . . Fine, or to have both ears nailed to the pillory." Blackstone lists bribery just after perjury in his order of impeachable offenses. Other influences on the Founding Fathers' view of impeachment included William Hawkins's *Treatise on the Pleas of the Crown,* which reads: "perjury . . . Is of all crimes whatsoever the most infamous and detestable." Another person influencing the Founding Fathers' consideration of impeachment, Samuel Pufendorf, wrote: "Perjury appears to be a most monstrous sin, in as much as by it the forsworn wretch shews that he at the same time condemns the divine and yet is afraid of human punishment; that he is a daring villain towards God, and a sneaking coward towards men."

Gary McDowell concludes: "Based on the historical record, the common law, the expressed intent of the Framers, and the writings of the principal legal authorities relied upon by the Framers, there should be no doubt that perjury should properly be deemed a 'high crime and misdemeanor' in an impeachment trial under the Constitution." McDowell's analysis accords with that of Supreme Court justice Joseph Story, who said that "it is not only crimes of a strictly legal character that are impeachable offenses, but also political offenses, growing out of personal misconduct . . . so various that they must be examined upon very broad and comprehensive principles of public policy and duty." Together, McDowell and Story underscore former president Gerald Ford's contention when he served as minority leader in the U.S. House of Representatives that "an impeachable offense is whatever a majority of the House of Representatives considers it to be at a given moment in history."

So, was Mrs. Clinton right? Constitutionally, she was wrong. By his own testimony, the president committed acts that fit within the precedents governing impeachment. Politically, she was right. Impeachment depends upon public opinion and the political action of the U.S. House of Representatives and U.S. Senate, whose members respond to the pressures of politics and public opinion.

Politics

Often considered a blunt instrument, the impeachment process requires an indictment by a majority vote of the House of Representatives, conviction by a two-thirds majority vote of members present in the Senate, and then removal from office.[2] The U.S. House of Representatives has only impeached three presidents, and the U.S. Senate has convicted none. President Andrew Johnson survived the Senate's trial of his impeachment by one vote. President Richard M. Nixon resigned after the House Judiciary Committee approved articles of impeachment, realizing that he lacked sufficient votes to prevent impeachment by the House and conviction in the Senate. President Clinton, indicted by a slim majority on a nearly straight party-line vote in the House, easily survived a comparable partisan vote in the Senate on conviction.

Why did Clinton survive politically? Obviously, he had the support of his party, but that was not a given from the outset. A combination of White House strategy and Republican miscalculations enabled the president to turn the issue into partisan warfare. Once the issue became political, only time stood in the way of his victory.

First, Democrats and Republicans refused to cooperate and to compromise in the U.S. House of Representatives. Democrats wanted to narrow the scope of impeachment charges, but Republicans preferred to consider their full breadth and effect. Had the two parties cooperated in reaching a compromise, they would have had an opportunity to approve less ambitious bipartisan articles of impeachment in the House of Representatives. In politics, timing is often everything: Once the time for cooperation and compromise passed, impeachment became a political football game. By contrast, Democrats and Republicans cooperated during the impeachment of President Nixon, creating a broad bipartisan consensus.

Second, Republicans failed to recognize an important fundamental of American politics: The middle governs. Throughout impeachment deliberations, Republicans isolated themselves from the middle of American politics, jeopardizing their chances for impeaching, convicting, and removing President Clinton. Public opinion polls showed that Americans, while disapproving of presidential actions, wanted him to remain in office. As the impeachment process progressed, the president became more popular and Republicans less popular. In the end, Republicans stood alone against both Democrats and the broad mainstream of American politics.

Third, the roles of victim and villain were reversed: Clinton became the victim, while Republicans and independent counsel Kenneth Starr became the villains. Two crucial events ensured this reversal of roles. Rather than taking Clinton's grand jury testimony in secret, Starr agreed to a prime-time public airing. In that, the White House outfoxed him like Brer Rabbit in the briar patch. Starr allowed Clinton to perform publicly on his home turf, the White House, and to do what he does best, communicate with the public. Starr and his assistants hardly laid a hand on the president during four hours of testimony. Then, when the supposedly confidential Starr report came to the House Judiciary Committee, Republicans appeared too eager to release it.

Fourth, wanting more rather than less said about the evidence for impeachment, the White House gambled and won on two goals of their strategy: trivializing the evidence and tiring the public. The more both sides said about the evidence, the more commonplace it appeared, supporting French minister Talleyrand's well-known observation: "What becomes excessive becomes irrelevant." Finally the incessant airing of the dirty linen fatigued a long-suffering public, which said: "Let's get it over."

Fifth, at the same time that the White House pursued these goals, it projected the president on center stage doing the public's business. The president's common refrain was, "I want to get about doing what you elected me to do."

Economics

"It's the economy, stupid" played well twice for Clinton: first in his 1992 campaign against George Bush and then throughout the impeachment deliberations. Public perceptions of a bad economy helped him win in 1992, and then the public's good economic perceptions helped him survive in 1999. Between Nixon's Watergate and Clinton's Whitewater, the economy stands out as the primary reason Nixon failed and Clinton survived. Nixon, who won one of history's greatest landslide victories in 1972, retained high job approval ratings until the economy soured. For example, during 1971 and 1972 inflation hovered at a modest 3.4 percent but jumped to 8.8 percent in 1973 and then to 12.2 percent in 1974. By early 1974, surveys showed that about 70 percent of the public believed the economy was in serious condition. Nixon's job approval ratings correspondingly dropped. By contrast, Clinton's job approval ratings remained high even though the public rates him below all modern presidents except Carter in leadership ability and Nixon in integrity.

Options

Ironically, most members of Congress believed that the president's actions warranted severe rebuke, but they lacked a clearly constitutional means for doing so. The Constitution offers only one option for removing a president, the rarely used process of impeachment and conviction. A vote of no confidence, frequently used in the United Kingdom and other parliamentary democracies, allows a parliamentary majority to sanction the prime minister without removing him from office. If successful, a vote of no confidence leads to a new election in which the prime minister can stand for reelection. In a parliamentary democracy, the parliament's majority elects the prime minister, unlike America's presidential democracy, with its separation of powers and separate electoral constituency for the president.

A vote of no confidence cuts swiftly and surgically, while impeachment proceedings cut slowly and jaggedly, leaving many scars and requiring a long time for healing. Were the United States a parliamentary democracy, Congress could have let the public clear the putrid air of charges against Clinton following a vote of no confidence. The public in the election following a majority vote of no confidence could have either removed the president or reinstated their faith in him without allowing the storm clouds of impeachment to hang overhead.

Although Congress, and especially Democrats, searched for other options to punish President Clinton short of removal, they could not agree on an alternative.[3] Three options seriously pursued—censure, finding of fact, and impeachment without a Senate trial—illustrate how Congress tried to craft an acceptable alternative short of conviction on charges of impeachment. A censure resolution verbally reprimands a president, while censure-plus adds a monetary fine. A finding of fact declares a president guilty based on the facts. Impeachment by the House without a Senate trial would have the effect of censure, enabling Congress to rebuke a president but not remove him from office. Congress has censured only one president, Andrew Jackson in 1833. Censure-plus, finding of fact, and impeachment without a trial, never before used or considered by Congress, reveal the extraordinary difficulties presented by President Clinton's case. Censure-plus and finding of fact would probably have raised constitutional issues for the U.S. Supreme Court to decide. Could Congress force a president to pay a fine, or would that violate separation of powers? Would a finding of fact jeopardize a president's right to a fair trial in either a criminal or a civil case against him?

These three options also lacked permanence. In 1833 a Whig-controlled Senate by a vote of 26 to 20 censured President Andrew Jackson after he fired the secretary of the treasury for removing deposits from the national bank. The resolution censured President Jackson "for assuming authority and power not conferred by the Constitution and laws in removing deposits." Senator Henry Clay accused Jackson of tyranny, while Jackson likened the U.S. Senate to the Roman Senate: "a corrupt and venal Senate that overturned the liberty of Rome before Caesar reached her gates." In 1834 Jacksonian Democrats retook Congress and overturned the censure.

President Clinton survived congressional action against him for several reasons. First, many members believed that Congress should only use the one method of punishment constitutionally spelled out, impeachment by the House and trial by the Senate. Second, others, tiring of deliberations, wanted to end congressional action by the final vote on impeachment in the Senate. Third, many Democrats viewed the Senate's impeachment vote as a final partisan vindication of their efforts to protect a Democrat in the White House. Fourth, also for partisan reasons, many Republicans did not want to let Democrats off the hook by first voting against impeachment and then voting for a lesser form of punishment. Fifth, Republicans refused to compromise with Democrats and accept an option short of removal from office. Sixth, members wanting a permanent form of punishment looked askance at options other than impeachment and conviction.

Clinton demonstrated that a determined president, when backed by popular opinion, can withstand the action of a congressional majority that either fails to win bipartisan support to impeach and convict or cannot agree on another form of punishment.

THE MYTH OF PRESIDENT CLINTON'S VICTORY

After public revelations of the Monica Lewinsky affair, many analysts predicted President Clinton's imminent political demise. But the predictions were premature, and the president emerged as the ever savvy politician, a political Houdini who snatched victory out of the jaws of defeat. Only a slim partisan majority of the House of Representatives approved articles of impeachment against the president, the Senate did not even come close to convicting him, and the independent counsel began to look like a punching bag. But President Clinton's victory was a mirage; he lost while winning.

Personal Character and Job Approval Ratings

Public opinion revealed a double paradox about personal character and job approval ratings. First, the more the independent counsel and congressional Republicans investigated Clinton, the higher his job approval ratings rose. By February 1999, they reached a phenomenal 79 percent. Of course, the White House used job approval ratings to argue that the public supported President Clinton and his retention in office. Second, his personal character ratings dropped as his job approval ratings rose. The same public opinion poll that revealed high job approval ratings also discovered that the public disapproved of his character:

- 63.2 percent said they would not like for their children to look up to President Clinton as a personal role model.

- 58.2 percent said they would not hire a person who had consensual sex with subordinates.

- 66.7 percent considered it immoral for a U.S. president to have consensual sex with a twenty-one-year-old intern.

- 88.8 percent considered it immoral for a spouse to have sex with someone he or she supervised.[4]

The Congressional Dilemma

Strewn along the President's congressional victory march were the spoils of a loser. The impeachment process alone left a permanently damaging record developed in the hearings and reports of the House Judiciary Committee and in the debates on the floors of the House and Senate. However, as members of Congress in both parties, but especially Democrats, searched intently for a way to find the president guilty without removing him from office, they also left a damaging record. For example, a strong supporter of Clinton, Senator Dianne Feinstein (D–Calif.), introduced the following resolution of censure:

Whereas William Jefferson Clinton, President of the United States, engaged in an inappropriate relationship with a subordinate employee in the White House, which was shameless, reckless and indefensible;

Whereas William Jefferson Clinton, President of the United States, deliberately misled and deceived the American people, the members of his Cabinet and his staff;

Whereas William Jefferson Clinton's conduct in this matter is unacceptable for a President of the United States, does demean the Office of the President as well as the President himself, and creates disrespect for the laws of the land;

Whereas President Clinton fully deserves condemnation and censure for engaging in such behavior;

Whereas future generations of Americans must know that such behavior is not only unacceptable but also bears grave consequences, including loss of integrity, trust and respect;

Whereas William Jefferson Clinton's conduct in this matter has brought shame and dishonor to himself and the Office of the President; and

Whereas William Jefferson Clinton through his conduct in this matter has violated the trust of the American people;

Now, therefore, be it resolved that:

The United States Senate does hereby censure and condemn William Jefferson Clinton, President of the United States, in the strongest possible terms for his conduct.[5]

Then, Senators Pete Domenici (R–N.M.) and Olympia Snowe (R–Maine) put forward this finding of fact:

The Senate finds that:

The President of the United States, William Jefferson Clinton, on August 17, 1998, swore to tell the truth, the whole truth, and nothing but the truth before a United States grand jury. Contrary to that oath, William Jefferson Clinton willfully provided false and misleading testimony to the grand jury.

The President of the United States, William Jefferson Clinton, wrongfully engaged in conduct to delay the discovery and to cover up the existence of evidence and to alter testimony related to a federal civil rights lawsuit and a United States grand jury investigation.[6]

Three political factors combined to defeat these approaches. First, they came late in Senate deliberations, not long before the Senate voted on articles of impeachment. Second, Senate Democrats, knowing the president would remain in office, did not want to declare him guilty through either a finding of fact or a resolution of censure. His job approval ratings, fundraising potential for Democrats, and power to punish wayward Democrats kept them in line. Third, Republicans, not wanting to let Democrats avoid voting on impeachment charges, opposed the two alternatives.

Ironically, while Clinton won the impeachment battle, the full record of congressional action condemned rather than absolved him of guilt. He lost trust, the most important ingredient of successful leadership.

Presidential Greatness

While great presidents stand for great causes and policies that redefine the course of history, Clinton sacrificed his potential for greatness on the altar of immediate personal gratification. His immersion in scandal removed whatever opportunity he might have had to pursue an ambitious agenda. He had to reconcile himself to the pursuit of small policies and projects during his second term.

Scandal-prone presidents rank low on the scales of presidential greatness. Ulysses S. Grant and Warren G. Harding, perhaps the two most scandal-prone presidents other than Clinton, vie for bottom honors. Even presidents with ambitious and sometimes successful agendas may find their ranking lowered. Lyndon B. Johnson's failure to tell the truth about Vietnam helped to earn him an early departure from the White House and lowered his standing on the scale of presidential greatness.

Clinton, who promised the "most ethical administration in history," may cause students of presidential greatness to add morality as a specific measure of presidential greatness. The standard criteria for measuring presidential greatness focus on: (1) leading the nation successfully during critical times, such as a war or a depression; (2) serving the nation effectively and making sound decisions; (3) understanding presidential power and how to use it in the national interest; (4) providing sound administrative leadership; (5) selecting excellent personnel; (6) projecting a publicly attractive personality; (7) leaving a favorable impact on the presidency; and (8) influencing history positively. Clinton's record makes a compelling case to add an unmistakably moral dimension to the criteria: possessing sound moral character.

Lost Trust and Presidential Power

President Clinton, recognizing that presidential greatness scales tip in favor of powerful presidents with great agendas, modeled himself after such presidents. Ironically, however, not only did his personal immorality prevent him from pursuing an activist's agenda, but it also damaged the public trust and the power of the office. Under Clinton the public trust in the government and politicians hit its lowest point in 40 years. In 1963, about 75 percent of Americans said they trusted the government in Washington either "just about always" or "most of the time." By Clinton's last term in office, that percentage plummeted to 20 percent. In 1952, only 35 percent of Americans said they believe public officials ignore what ordinary people think. By 1998, 60 percent answered "yes."[7] Only 20 percent of Americans expressed satisfaction with the state of the nation at the midpoint of President Clinton's second term.[8] While Clinton does not bear full responsibility for these data, they did occur on his watch. The only reversal of this forty-year downward trend in public trust occurred during Reagan's administration. Ironically Clinton, who wanted to increase presidential power, weakened the presidency.

Judge Starr's Ironic Victory

The White House pummeled and pilloried independent counsel Kenneth Starr for several months, making him anathema to the public and putting pressure on Congress to abolish the position of independent counsel. Although losing the battle for public opinion, Starr won the constitutional and legal battle to define presidential power. Hiding behind the doctrine of executive privilege, President Clinton refused to produce important evidence and rejected requests for the depositions and testimony of key advisors and other staff, such as the Secret Service. Starr won over a dozen appeals against Clinton and the White House, curtailing the doctrine of executive privilege and reducing the power of future presidents. Historically, presidents have claimed executive privilege to protect the confidentiality of communications with their advisors. Starr's victories have placed pressures on Congress to address five serious questions about the nature and extent of presidential power.

1. What rules should govern when, if ever, a private citizen can sue a sitting president?

2. If Congress grants presidential immunity from civil suits, should a statute of limitations allow a private citizen to sue a former president?

3. What boundary lines should Congress draw to protect the doctrine of executive privilege for a president in his communications with personal staff, government attorneys, the Secret Service, and others?

4. Should Congress protect a sitting president from standing trial in a criminal court against his will?

5. Should Congress reform the Office of Independent Counsel to correct its deficiencies or establish another entity or procedure to ensure that a president's Department of Justice does not sweep presidential scandals under the rug?

Vice President Gore: Victor and Victim

Vice President Gore earned President Clinton's support for the Democratic presidential nomination by steadfastly supporting him during the depths of presidential scandals. For that, however, he paid a price. Gore made his mark in public life by carefully cultivating the image of a principled politician, willing to stand courageously on principle for a just and an honorable cause. His support of President Clinton however, tarnished that image.

Political IOUs

When the battle raged against President Clinton, African-Americans, feminists, and homosexuals did not retreat but stayed on the front lines, supporting their man. No one fought harder for the president than these three groups. Politically they had no choice. Clinton had fought for their agendas, including the appointment of many to high positions in his administration. They paid their political debts to the president, and that done, he owed them his political life.

To support the president they had to turn a blind eye to his behavior, even sacrificing some of their own principles. For example, the National Organization for Women and other feminists fought hard against U.S. Senator Bob Packwood (R–Ore.) and the then nominee for the U.S. Supreme Court, Clarence Thomas, who stood accused of the same shenanigans as Clinton. When then-senator Gary Hart (D–Colo.) found himself in similar compromising circumstances during his campaign for the Democratic presidential nomination in 1988, columnist Ellen Goodman said his adultery reveals "his capacity for deception . . . impulsiveness, [lack of] self-control, even his ability to compartmentalize ethics." Gloria Steinem concluded Hart had "a character problem." Suzannah Lessard observed that "if a man abuses his wife by womanizing, there could be something abusive in his nature."[9] But Clinton presented a different story. Here they sacrificed their convictions on the altar of political expedience.

Principle and Power

By his own admission President Clinton lied to his cabinet and to his personal staff, but not one of them resigned. Not only did he lie to them, but he also sent them forth to peddle his lies as the truth. After a cabinet meeting on January 26, 1998, Secretary of State Madeleine Albright, Secretary of Health and Human Services Donna Shalala, and Secretary of Commerce William Daley stood before the television cameras and forthrightly declared their belief in the president's word. Only moments before he had lied to them about the Monica Lewinsky affair. Secretary of the Treasury Robert Rubin declared on CNBC, "I absolutely believe" the president.[10] Did not their abhorrence of sexual harassment demand action based on conscience and conviction? Did they not value truthfulness in judicial proceedings? They sacrificed their principles on the altar of power.

Presidential Strategy: The Achilles' Heel

President Clinton demonstrated that he could survive with a fivefold strategy: delay, hoping the public and the press would shift their attention to something else; deny, recognizing he could use the moral authority of the presidential office to deny charges of moral turpitude; discredit, using the power of the presidential bully pulpit to undermine the character of the opposition; deflect, turning the public's attention from his moral crises by taking the offensive on other issues; and diminish, lessening the impact of his immorality by diminishing its seriousness, admitting to doing something "inappropriate," but never confessing that it was wrong, harmful, damaging, or sinful. The strategy worked: The president, a political escape artist, remained in office. However, to the extent that he won politically, he lost morally. The strategy revealed him for what he is: a successful politician but a man without a moral compass.

Hillary: The Ultimate Winner

How did Hillary Rodham Clinton survive a failed national health-care proposal, missing legal billing records, a near brush with criminal indictment by the independent counsel, testimony before a federal grand jury investigating her, and less-than-honorable behavior by her husband? During President Clinton's first term, Mrs. Clinton's approval ratings suffered for several reasons, but particularly because of her humiliating failure to win congressional support for her national health-care plan. As the point guard and playmaker for this plan, she became entwined with its success or failure. Then as the Whitewater debacle unfolded, she became the first first lady to testify before a grand jury. Even now, no compelling explanation exists for the missing billing records from Little Rock's Rose law firm that mysteriously appeared one day in the private quarters of the White House. Finally, not only did her husband face his own legal difficulties, but he also lied to her about his adultery.

Mrs. Clinton's ride on the roller-coaster of public opinion ended with soaring ratings. She became the victimized woman who stood by her man. Using her rising stature and the White House platform, she traveled widely and addressed important issues, building a solid personal political base independent of her husband. Behind the scenes of his tenuous presidency, she orchestrated his legal and political strategy, becoming the linchpin of his survival. Perhaps more than anyone else, she cemented the support of African-Americans, feminists, and homosexuals during her husband's darkest hour. She reached out to key leaders in each of these constituencies, such as Jesse Jackson, to ensure their abiding support.

Presidential Personality and Character

When President Clinton faced an uphill battle during the 1992 New Hampshire presidential primary, longtime and high-ranking Clinton staffer George Stephanopoulos snapped this picture of Clinton's personality needs:

> I was sure all was lost, but Clinton demonstrated the power of pure will. He was determined to talk to and touch every voter in New Hampshire. . . . This was all about Clinton—his pride, ambition, anger, his need to be loved and his drive to do good. Watching him made me wonder if you had to be a little crazy to become president. What did it do to you to want something so badly?[11]

Stephanopoulos's analysis reveals either explicitly or implicitly a relationship between the president's personality needs and behavior. He appeared to live life either on the verge of success or the brink of destruction. The needs identified are:

1. **Attention.** President Clinton's desire for attention caused him to crave "pressing the flesh" and getting media attention. He looked for the dramatic moment and used the style that would guarantee attention. Throughout his presidency, he looked like a whirling dervish,

constantly in motion. Moments of quiet, meditation, and reflection appeared hard to find in his daily schedule, especially when contrasted with the schedules of Presidents Ford, Carter, Reagan, and Bush.

2. **Dominance.** A thirst for the highest position of power and the manipulation of circumstances and people to achieve and retain that power revealed a need for dominance. For example, to remain in office in 1996, he skirted campaign fund-raising laws to attract large sums of Chinese and other foreign money.

3. **Achievement.** Wanting to go down in history as a great president, he cultivated an open style of leadership to reach out to more people and to obtain new ideas. This open style produced both good and bad results. He worked closely with Republicans and against most Democrats to obtain passage of welfare reform and the North American Free Trade Agreement, but he also linked himself with people of questionable motives, in such areas as campaign fund-raising. Risk taking was his stock in trade.

4. **To be liked.** His insatiable thirst for others to like him caused him to work hard to establish networks of friends, to have a high tolerance for compromise, and to maintain unsavory friendships and relationships.

5. **Personal gratification.** Lack of discipline and self-control allowed his desire for personal gratification to reign unchecked at critical moments. His legacy will now always bear the marks of daring affairs that risked his marriage, family, personal friendships, and presidency.

Clinton lacked the necessary judgment, discernment, discipline, propriety, and self-control to keep his behavior within acceptable bounds.

Presidential Nomination Process

For most of American history, a person with President Clinton's background would not have become president. Party leaders, who once controlled the presidential nomination process, began to lose their dominance with the advent of television and presidential primaries. These changes brought so-called retail politics to presidential nominations, allowing a candidate from a small state to emerge victorious. When political leaders controlled the nomination process, they looked for candidates from states with large blocs of electoral college votes who would help the party nationwide, but particularly in critical areas. While no system can guarantee the nomination of electable and moral candidates, the value of having party leaders make the selection is that they are more likely to consider personal character, morality, and the party's future. Clinton, a product of the reformed nomination system, presided over a significant decline in his party's following: the Democratic Party lost control of Congress, many governorships, and state legislatures.

Clinton reveals that decay and decomposition may rest beneath the surface of an apparently successful and victorious presidency. The evidence of this decay and decomposition, at least in the case of President Clinton, confirms the importance of a national debate on the future of the American democracy.

The Irony of Democracy

Democracy, which means "people govern," from the two Greek root words *demos* and *kratis,* requires truth, trust, and tolerance in sufficient measures to form an epoxy bonding a people together. Truth fosters trust between the people and their leaders. Trust encourages people to defer to their leaders in making decisions. Tolerance encourages people and groups to respect one another and their differing opinions without breaking apart.

Moral scandals test this democratic bond by simultaneously chipping away at truth, trust, and tolerance. By its nature, democracy requires an open society with such rights as freedom of religion, freedom of speech, and freedom of the press. These and other freedoms magnify democracy's flaws. Democracy's very strengths create weaknesses. Perhaps that is why Winston Churchill said: "Democracy is the worst form of government except for all the rest." Democracy contains the seeds of both its own destruction and its reconstruction. The destructive seeds of moral scandals undermine truth, trust, and tolerance, but the same freedoms that reveal moral scandals can also show how to correct them. Focusing on the nation's moral scandals reveals several important lessons about democracy and presidential morality.

Challenging the Cycle of Correction

In the ebb and flow of American politics, the tide usually runs in favor of presidents with impeccable moral credentials after a president with a loose moral record. Following the scandals of President Warren Harding, Americans turned to presidents with high moral standards, Calvin Coolidge and Herbert Hoover. Then, after the scandals of Presidents Johnson and Nixon, the public had two presidents with records of integrity, Gerald Ford and Jimmy Carter. The cycle of correction, therefore, suggests that Americans can expect a period of high integrity in the White House during the new millennium.

The question arises, however, whether today's American democracy can expect a cycle of correction to last very long or even to begin. The answer to this question hinges on yet another: by what standard can American society say something is right or wrong? If Americans have no clear and consistent standard for measuring the morality of behavior, then the determination of right and wrong rests on moral quicksand. The increasing diversity of approaches to morality in America makes the definition of morality more difficult, and raises questions about either the existence or the duration of a cycle of correction early in the millennium.

Seven approaches to morality now exist in America: divine morality, utilitarian morality, natural rights morality, contractual morality, legal realism morality, values clarification morality, and primitive morality.

Moral conflict exists on two fronts: between divine morality and other moral approaches that do not stipulate the certainty of an external moral reference point, and among all approaches over what should determine morality. The competing definitions of morality not only complicate presidential leadership but also offer more lines of moral defense for presidential decisions. In short, increased moral complexity produces more moral confusion.

America's Culture War

Debate about presidential morality is part of a larger debate about the future of American culture. Economic, ideological, political, religious, and social conflict engulf American society. As the only nationally elected leader, a president stands on top of a powder keg of cultural change.

Economically, Max Weber's Protestant ethic, with its emphasis on sacrifice, savings, and self-denial, no longer is viewed as the major economic determinant of human happiness. Contemporary Americans look much more to spending and self-fulfillment. Earlier, America had a reputation as a nonideological society when compared with the United Kingdom and other European countries with their sharp ideological tensions. Today America has sharper ideological cutting edges that make agreement more difficult. For example, ideological public policy research think tanks, hardly known before the 1960s, are now commonplace. Politically, the two major political parties find compromise between them more difficult to achieve. Today their party platforms present many more clear policy differences, and the parties in Congress no longer communicate and compromise as effectively. When House Speakers Sam Rayburn (D–Texas) and Joe Martin (R–Mass.) held the speakership for over two decades between the 1930s and the early 1960s, they worked closely together both personally and politically. Since the 1960s, however, both congressional leaders and rank-and-file members have found working relationships more strained. Religiously, the once-dominant voice of mainstream Protestantism faces serious internal strife between conservative and liberal elements and external challenges from both Roman Catholics and the emerging evangelical and fundamental Protestants. The substantial Jewish contribution to American religious and political life continues, but it also reflects its own divisions between conservatism and liberalism. The Islamic influence, though increasing in some states and in larger cities, has not yet emerged as a significant national force. Socially, the powerful emergence of African-Americans, feminists, and homosexuals as important voting blocs has altered the landscape of Americn society.

The cultural stability that once undergirded a president's political leadership no longer exists. As voices become more strident in America, they speak with greater assurance about the morality of their respective causes and positions. People and groups become less willing to compromise when they believe that their ideas occupy the moral high ground. These moral crosscurrents make presidential leadership more difficult and tenuous.

The Seamless Garment of Morality

The Clinton scandals began a national debate about the importance of personal morality in American public life. This debate benefited the nation by producing many articles, books, and media commentaries on the subject, none more important than a declaration signed by 140 scholars of religion and public life. These scholars sounded a clarion call to action.

> As scholars interested in religion and public life, we protest the manipulation of religion and the debasing of moral language in the discussion about presidential responsibility. We believe that serious misunderstandings of repentance and forgiveness are being exploited for political advantage. The resulting moral confusion is a threat to the integrity of American religion and to the foundations of a civil society.[12]

As a pièce de résistance, their declaration forcefully proclaims that personal morality undergirds the survival of American democracy. The declaration finds that President Clinton's behavior subverted essential moral underpinnings of a healthy society.

1. **Presidential manipulation of religious symbols:** "We fear that the religious community is in danger of being called upon to provide authentication for a politically motivated and incomplete repentance that seeks to avert serious consequences for wrongful acts."

2. **Presidential avoidance of personal responsibility:** "When the President continues to deny any liability for the sins he has confessed, it suggests that his public display of repentance was intended to avoid political disfavor."

3. **Presidential accountability and political survival:** "We are aware that certain moral qualities are central to the survival of our political system, among which are truthfulness, integrity, respect for the law, respect for the dignity of others, adherence to the constitutional process, and a willingness to avoid the abuse of power. We reject the premise that violations of these ethical standards should be excused so long as a leader remains loyal to a particular political agenda and the nation is blessed by a strong economy. . . . By his own admission, the President has departed from ethical standards by abusing his presidential office, by his ill use of women, and by his knowing manipulation of truth for indefensible ends. We are particularly troubled about the debasing of the language of public discourse with the aim of avoiding responsibility for one's actions."

4. **Presidential behavior and society's future:** "We maintain that in general there is a reasonable threshold of behavior beneath which our public leaders should not fall, because the moral character of a people is more important than the tenure of a particular politician or the protection of a particular political agenda. Political and religious history indicate that violations and misunderstandings of such moral issues may have grave consequences. The widespread desire to 'get this behind us' does not take seriously enough the nature of transgressions and their social effects."

5. **Presidential morality, public and private:** "We urge the society as a whole to take account of the ethical commitments necessary for a civil society and to seek the integrity of both public and private morality. While partisan conflicts have usually dominated past debates over public morality, we now confront a much deeper crisis: whether the moral basis of the constitutional system itself will be lost."

This declaration continues a commentary that has been ongoing for at least the past thirty years about the dubious state of the American character and moral condition. From Andrew Hacker's *End of the American Era* in 1970 to William Bennett's *Death of Outrage* in 1999,[13] many scholars and commentators have pictured the American character and moral condition in a state of decline. Ironically, Clinton as a candidate for president in 1992 said: "The people whose character is really an issue are those who would divert the attention of the people and divide the country we love."[14]

Mirror of Society

As the only nationally elected public official, President Clinton, more than anyone else, represents all Americans. No other single person offers a better view of the state of the American character and moral condition. In presidential history, Clinton's legacy includes the longest list of moral scandals: Whitewater; Webster Hubbell; Gennifer Flowers; Paula Jones; Juanita Broaddrick; Kathleen Willey; Julie Hyatt Steele; "Travelgate"; "FBI Filegate"; Monica Lewinsky; illegal foreign fund-raising; Chinese espionage; personal vacations paid for by wealthy contributors with significant financial interests in the president's policies; lying to his cabinet, staff, and family; and others. These scandals reveal defects and deficiencies not only in the president but also in the moral order: the corruption of political power, the diminution of the public trust, the decline in respect for the law, and the degeneration of personal morality.

Never before in American history have Americans heard so much about morality. Clinton's conduct precipitated a multimillion-dollar morality industry, publishing articles and books and producing television and other media programs. His life and administration offer convincing proof of the seamless garment of personal and public morality.

NOTES

CHAPTER 1

1. *The Writings of George Washington*, ed. John C. Fitzpatrick (Washington, D.C.: U.S. Government Printing Office, 1940), 35: 229.

2. Michael Novak, *Choosing Our King* (New York: Macmillan, 1974), xv.

3. Clinton Rossiter, *The American Presidency* (New York: New American Library, 1960), 239.

4. James Reston, quoted in Thomas E. Cronin, "The Textbook Presidency and Political Science," *Congressional Record*, 91st Congress, October 5, 1970, S17106.

5. Fred Greenstein, *The Hidden-Hand Presidency* (New York: Basic Books, 1982).

6. On Kennedy, see Thomas C. Reeves, *A Question of Character* (New York: Free Press, 1991); and Seymour Hersh, *The Dark Side of Camelot* (Boston: Little, Brown, 1997). On Roosevelt, see Doris Kearns Goodwin, *No Ordinary Time* (New York: Simon & Schuster, 1994).

7. Mortimer B. Zuckerman, "Where Have Our Values Gone?" *U.S. News and World Report*, August 8, 1994, 88.

8. William J. Bennett, "How to Teach Values," *Ladies Home Journal*, September 1994, 142.

9. Benjamin M. Spock, *A Better World for Our Children: Rebuilding American Family Values* (Bethesda, Md.: National Press Books, 1984), 93.

10. As stated by Geraldine Ferraro on *Larry King Live,* CNN, July 27, 1998.

CHAPTER 2

1. Robert N. Bellah, *The Broken Covenant: American Civil Religion in Time of Trial* (New York: Seabury Press, 1975), 45.

2. Alexis de Tocqueville, *Democracy in America* (New York: Vintage Books, 1954), 311.

3. Bellah, *Broken Covenant*, 12.

4. Richard Hofstadter, *The American Political Tradition* (New York: Knopf, 1948), 16.

5. Alexander Hamilton, James Madison, and John Jay, *The Federalist Papers,* ed. Clinton Rossiter (New York: New American Library, 1961), 346.

6. Hamilton, Madison, and Jay, *Federalist Papers,* 353.

7. Hamilton, Madison, and Jay, *Federalist Papers,* 231.

8. Hamilton, Madison, and Jay, *Federalist Papers,* 40.

9. Hamilton, Madison, and Jay, *Federalist Papers,* 471.

10. *Resolution Relative to the Alien and Sedition Laws,* 1798.

11. John Locke, "An Essay Concerning the True Original Extent and End of the Civil Government," in *Works,* ed. J. A. St. John (London: G. Bell, 1908), 5: 1–13.

12. John Locke, "The Reasonableness of Christianity as Defined in the Scriptures," in *Works,* vol. 7, reprinted in William Ebenstein, *Great Political Thinkers* (New York: Holt, Rinehart & Winston, 1969), 390–400.

13. William Blackstone, "Of Laws in General," in *Commentaries on the Laws of England* (Chicago: University of Chicago Press, 1979), 3–62.

14. Daniel J. Elazar, "Political Theory of Covenant: Biblical Origins and Development" (paper presented at the annual meeting of the American Political Science Association, New York, September 1980).

15. Louis I. Bredvold and Ralph G. Ross, eds., *The Philosophy of Edmund Burke* (Ann Arbor: University of Michigan Press, 1960), 157.

16. In Carl Brent Swisher, *The Growth of Constitutional Government* (Chicago: University of Chicago Press, 1963), 77.

17. Swisher, *Growth of Constitutional Government,* 77.

18. In Alpheus T. Mason, *The Supreme Court from Taft to Warren* (New York: Norton, 1964), 15.

19. Mason, *Supreme Court,* 15.

20. Hamilton, Madison, and Jay, *Federalist Papers,* 292–93.

21. Harvey Mansfield, *The Spirit of Liberalism* (Cambridge: Harvard University Press, 1978), 39.

22. Alexis de Tocqueville, *Democracy in America,* as cited in Ellis Sandoz, "Classical and Christian Dimensions of American Political Thought," *Modern Age* 25, 21.

23. Harold C. Syrett, ed., *American Historical Documents* (New York: Columbia University Press, 1960), 110–13.

24. For these and many other quotations and studies of this subject, see James H. Hutson, *Religion and the Founding of the American Republic* (Washington, D.C.: Library of Congress, 1998); M. E. Bradford, *A Worthy Company: Brief Lives of the Framers of the United States Constitution* (Plymouth, Mass.: Plymouth Rock Foundation, 1982); Syrett, *American Historical Documents*; *Letter from Plymouth Rock* (Plymouth, Mass.: Plymouth Rock Foundation, 1983); William J. Federer, ed., *America's God and Country: Encyclopedia of Quotations* (Coppell, Texas: Fame Publishing, 1994); and Charles Wallis, ed., *Our American Heritage* (New York: Harper & Row, 1970).

25. Samuel Eliot Morison, *The Oxford History of the American People* (New York: Oxford University Press, 1965), 74.

26. Joshua O. Haberman, "America's Safety Belt in the Bible Belt," *World,* October 19, 1987, 8.

27. Timothy Dwight, *A Discourse on Some Events of the Last Century*, delivered in the Brick Church in New Haven, Wednesday, January 7, 1801 (New Haven, Conn., 1801), 17–23, 28–30, 32–34, 45–47.

28. John D. Richardson, ed., *A Compilation of Messages and Papers of the Presidents: 1780–1897* (Washington, D.C.: U.S. Government Printing Office, 1986), 1: 64.

29. *The Public Papers and Addresses of Franklin D. Roosevelt*, ed. Samuel I. Rosenman (New York: Random House, 1938), 4: 449.

30. Aleksandr I. Solzhenitsyn, *A World Split Apart* (New York: Harper & Row, 1978), 49.

31. For an extended analysis of these points, see Charles W. Dunn, *American Political Theology: Historical Perspective and Theoretical Analysis* (New York: Praeger, 1984); and Charles W. Dunn, ed., *Religion in American Politics* (Washington, D.C.: Congressional Quarterly Press, 1989).

32. *Engel v. Vitale* (1962) and *Abington School District v. Schempp* (1963).

33. John Dunphy, "A Religion for a New Age," *Humanist*, January/February 1983, 26.

34. Alexis de Tocqueville, *Democracy in America*, as cited in Robert S. Alley, *So Help Me God* (Richmond, Va.: John Knox Press, 1972), 21.

35. Allan Bloom, *The Closing of the American Mind* (New York: Simon & Schuster, 1987), 146.

36. Alexis de Tocqueville, *Democracy in America* (New York: HarperPerennial, 1988), 479.

37. Dan Quayle, "Restoring Basic Values," *Vital Speeches*, June 15, 1992, 517.

38. Dan Quayle, "The Family Comes First," *Vital Speeches*, September 15, 1992, 711.

39. Bill Clinton, "A Bridge to the Future," *Vital Speeches*, August 15, 1992, 642.

40. Hillary Rodham Clinton, "A Bridge to the Future," *Vital Speeches*, September 15, 1996, 707.

CHAPTER 3

1. Gail Collins, *Scorpion Tongues: Gossip, Celebrity, and Politics* (New York: William Morrow, 1998), 25.

2. Collins, *Scorpion Tongues*, 25.

3. Collins, *Scorpion Tongues*, 23.

4. Collins, *Scorpion Tongues*, 24.

5. Collins, *Scorpion Tongues*, 25.

6. Ken Burns, "Too Human to Be Heroes?" *USA Weekend*, July 31, 1998, 5.

7. Jack Shepherd, *The Adams Chronicles* (Boston: Houghton Mifflin, 1975), 188.

8. Shepherd, *Adams Chronicles*, 201.

9. Shepherd, *Adams Chronicles*, 196.

10. Garret Wood Sheldon, *The Political Philosophy of Thomas Jefferson* (Baltimore: Johns Hopkins University Press, 1991), 70.

11. Collins, *Scorpion Tongues*, 28.

12. Collins, *Scorpion Tongues*, 28.

13. Collins, *Scorpion Tongues*, 29.

14. Collins, *Scorpion Tongues*, 29.

15. Burns, "Too Human to Be Heroes?" 5.

16. Thomas Jefferson, *Jefferson's Papers*, ed. Julian P. Boyd (Princeton, N.J.: Princeton University Press, 1950), 2: 217.

17. David Whitney, *The American Presidents* (Garden City, N.Y.: Doubleday, 1967), 44.

18. Ian Elliot, ed., *James Madison, 1751–1836* (Dobbs Ferry, N.Y.: Oceana Publications, 1971), 10.

19. Elliot, *James Madison*, 46.

20. Elliot, *James Madison*, 46.

21. Elliot, *James Madison*, 77.

22. Elliot, *James Madison*, 77.

23. Adrienne Koch, *Madison's "Advice to My Country"* (Princeton, N.J.: Princeton University Press, 1966), 137.

24. Whitney, *American Presidents*, 51.

25. David Gilman, *James Monroe* (New Rochelle, N.Y.: Arlington House, 1970), 78, 98.

26. Noble E. Cunningham, *The Presidency of James Monroe* (Lawrence: University Press of Kansas, 1996), 68–69.

27. Collins, *Scorpion Tongues*, 31.

28. Shepherd, *Adams Chronicles*, 216.

29. Shepherd, *Adams Chronicles*, 285.

30. Shepherd, *Adams Chronicles*, 283.

31. Shepherd, *Adams Chronicles*, 292.

32. Shepherd, *Adams Chronicles*, 292.

33. Shepherd, *Adams Chronicles*, 286.

34. Shepherd, *Adams Chronicles*, 229.

35. Collins, *Scorpion Tongues*, 31.

36. Collins, *Scorpion Tongues*, 31.

37. Shepherd, *Adams Chronicles*, 217.

38. Shepherd, *Adams Chronicles*, 302.

39. Hal Morris, "The American Whig Party," Database Online <http://www.odur.let.rug.nl/~usa/Euswhig/whigs01.htm>.

40. Collins, *Scorpion Tongues*, 45.

41. Collins, *Scorpion Tongues*, 45.

42. Morris, "Whig Party."

43. Morris, "Whig Party."

44. Collins, *Scorpion Tongues*, 33.

45. Collins, *Scorpion Tongues*, 39.

46. Collins, *Scorpion Tongues,* 38.

47. Collins, *Scorpion Tongues,* 43.

48. Samuel Eliot Morison, *The Oxford History of the American People* (New York: Oxford University Press, 1965), 428.

49. Whitney, *American Presidents,* 85.

50. Whitney, *American Presidents,* 85.

51. Collins, *Scorpion Tongues,* 45.

52. Collins, *Scorpion Tongues,* 48.

53. Whitney, *American Presidents,* 86.

54. Whitney, *American Presidents,* 86.

55. Whitney, *American Presidents,* 92.

56. Collins, *Scorpion Tongues,* 46.

57. Collins, *Scorpion Tongues,* 46.

58. David Durfee, ed., *W. H. Harrison, 1773–1841/J. Tyler, 1790–1862* (Dobbs Ferry, N.Y.: Oceana Publications, 1970), 63.

59. Paul Bergernon, *The Presidency of James K. Polk* (Lawrence: University Press of Kansas, 1987), 207.

60. Collins, *Scorpion Tongues,* 46.

61. Whitney, *American Presidents,* 109.

62. Whitney, *American Presidents,* 111.

63. John Farrell, ed., *Zachary Taylor 1784–1850/Millard Fillmore 1800–1874* (Dobbs Ferry, N.Y.: Oceana Publications, 1971), 55.

64. Collins, *Scorpion Tongues,* 46.

65. Collins, *Scorpion Tongues,* 46.

66. Collins, *Scorpion Tongues,* 46.

67. Whitney, *American Presidents,* 122.

68. Irving J. Sloan, ed., *Franklin Pierce, 1804–1869* (Dobbs Ferry, N.Y.: Oceana Publications, 1968), 15.

69. Collins, *Scorpion Tongues,* 49.

70. Collins, *Scorpion Tongues,* 51.

71. Irving Sloan, ed., *James Buchanan, 1791–1868* (Dobbs Ferry, N.Y.: Oceana Publications, 1968), 11.

72. Sloan, *James Buchanan,* 47.

73. Sloan, *James Buchanan,* 16.

74. Sloan, *James Buchanan,* 17.

75. David Herbert Donald, *Lincoln* (New York: Simon & Schuster, 1995), 299.

76. Donald, *Lincoln,* 299.

77. Donald, *Lincoln,* 420.

78. Abraham Lincoln, *Collected Works,* ed. Roy P. Basler (New Brunswick, N.J.: Rutgers University Press, 1953), 5: 388–89.

79. Phillip Shaw Paludan, *The Presidency of Abraham Lincoln* (Lawrence: University Press of Kansas, 1994), 79.

80. Donald, *Lincoln,* 270.

81. Donald, *Lincoln,* 95.

82. Collins, *Scorpion Tongues*, 55.

83. Collins, *Scorpion Tongues,* 55.

84. Donald, *Lincoln*, 268.

85. "Andrew Johnson," *North Carolina Encyclopedia,* State Library of North Carolina <http://statelibrary.dcr.state.nc.us/nc/bio/public/johnson.htm>.

86. "Andrew Johnson."

87. Collins, *Scorpion Tongues*, 56.

88. "The Whiskey Ring," *The American Presidency* <http://gi.grolier.com/presidents/ea/side/whisring.html> (accessed July 29, 1999).

89. Michael Barone, "Grant and the Historians," *Weekly Standard,* August 8, 1998, 31.

90. Collins, *Scorpion Tongues*, 58.

91. Margaret Leech and Harry Brown, *The Garfield Orbit* (New York: Harper & Row, 1978), 168.

92. David C. Whitney, *The American Presidents,* 7th ed., rev. and updated by Robin Vaughn Whitney (New York: Prentice Hall, 1990), 157.

93. Harry Barnard, *Rutherford B. Hayes and His America* (New York: Bobbs-Merrill, 1954), 169.

94. Barnard, *Rutherford B. Hayes,* 169.

95. Whitney, *American Presidents,* 7th ed., 162; and obituary, *New York Times,* January 18, 1893 <http://starship.python.net/crew/manus/Presidents/rbh/rbhobit.html> (accessed July 29, 1999).

96. Barnard, *Rutherford B. Hayes,* 169.

97. Whitney, *American Presidents,* 7th ed., 162–63.

98. Whitney, *American Presidents,* 7th ed., 163.

99. Howard Furer, ed., *James Garfield, 1831–1881/Chester Arthur, 1830–1886* (Dobbs Ferry, N.Y.: Oceana Publications, 1970), 45.

100. Furer, *James Garfield/Chester Arthur,* 16.

101. Furer, *James Garfield/Chester Arthur,* 14.

102. Collins, *Scorpion Tongues,* 75.

103. Collins, *Scorpion Tongues*, 75.

104. Harry Sievers, *Benjamin Harrison, 1833–1901* (Chicago: Regnery, 1968), 20.

105. Mural Halstead, *The Illustrious Life of William McKinley: Our Martyred President* (Chicago: n.p., 1901), 154.

106. Charles Olcott, *American Statesman: William McKinley* (Boston: Houghton Mifflin, 1916), 336.

107. Olcott, *American Statesman,* 7

108. Lewis L. Gould, *The Presidency of William McKinley* (Lawrence: Regents Press of Kansas, 1980), 52.

109. Gould, *Presidency of McKinley,* 52.

110. Gould, *Presidency of McKinley,* 250.

111. Gould, *Presidency of McKinley,* 250.

112. Gould, *Presidency of McKinley,* 162.

113. Gould, *Presidency of McKinley,* 161.

114. Gould, *Presidency of McKinley*, 182–83.

115. Gould, *Presidency of McKinley*, 156

116. Gould, *Presidency of McKinley*, 156.

117. Gould, *Presidency of McKinley*, 251.

118. Gould, *Presidency of McKinley*, 252.

119. Sidney Milkis and Michael Nelson, *The American Presidency: Origins and Development* (Washington, D.C.: Congressional Quarterly, 1990), 191.

120. William White, *A Puritan in Babylon* (New York: Macmillan, 1939), 59.

121 Milkis and Nelson, *American Presidency*, 219.

122. Milkis and Nelson, *American Presidency*, 223.

123. William B. Gatewood Jr., *Theodore Roosevelt and the Art of Controversy* (Baton Rouge: Louisiana State University Press, 1970), 5.

124. Collins, *Scorpion Tongues*, 109.

125. Collins, *Scorpion Tongues*, 111.

126. Milkis and Nelson, *American Presidency*, 209–10.

127. "William Howard Taft: Twenty-Seventh President, 1909–1913" <http://www.whitehouse.gov/WH/glimpse/presidents/html/wt27.html>.

128. Milkis and Nelson, *American Presidency*, 78–85.

129. Collins, *Scorpion Tongues*, 114.

130. Collins, *Scorpion Tongues*, 121.

131. Woodrow Wilson, *The New Freedom* (Princeton, N.J.: Princeton University Press, 1913), 247.

132. John Morton Blum, *Woodrow Wilson and the Politics of Morality* (Boston: Little, Brown, 1956), 79.

133. Wilson, *New Freedom*, 258.

134. Milkis and Nelson, *American Presidency*, 247.

135. Francis Russell, *The Shadow of Blooming Grove* (New York: McGraw Hill, 1968), 498.

136. Russell, *Shadow of Blooming Grove*, 498.

137. Russell, *Shadow of Blooming Grove*, 525.

138. Carl Anthony, "A President of the People," *Washington Post*, June 7, 1998, F1–F4.

139. Russell, *Shadow of Blooming Grove*, 529.

140. Russell, *Shadow of Blooming Grove*, 529.

141. Anthony, "President of the People."

142. Anthony, "President of the People."

143. Russell, *Shadow of Blooming Grove*, 532.

144. Anthony, "President of the People."

145. Anthony, "President of the People."

146. Collins, *Scorpion Tongues*, 127.

147. Collins, *Scorpion Tongues*, 127.

148. Russell, *Shadow of Blooming Grove*, 168.

149. Russell, *Shadow of Blooming Grove*, 168.

150. Edward Connery Latham, *Meet Calvin Coolidge* (Brattleboro, Vt.: Stephen Greene Press, 1960), 10.

151. John Sutherland Bonnell, *Presidential Profiles: Religion in the Life of American Presidents* (Philadelphia: Westminster Press, 1971), 196.

152. Claude M. Fuess, *Calvin Coolidge: The Man from Vermont* (Hamden, Conn.: Archon Books, 1965), 467–68.

153. White, *Puritan in Babylon*, 393.

154. White, *Puritan in Babylon*, 323.

155. White, *Puritan in Babylon*, 397.

156. David Burner, *Herbert Hoover: A Public Life* (New York: Knopf, 1979), 33.

157. Burner, *Hoover: Public Life,* 33.

158. Burner, *Hoover: Public Life,* 215.

159. Burner, *Hoover: Public Life,* 213.

160. Burner, *Hoover: Public Life,* 214.

161. Arnold Rice, ed., *Herbert Hoover, 1874–1964* (Dobbs Ferry, N.Y.: Oceana Publications, 1971), 11.

162. William J. Barber, *From New Era to New Deal* (Cambridge: Cambridge University Press, 1985), 99.

163. Rice, *Herbert Hoover,* 15.

164. Rice, *Herbert Hoover,* 80.

165. Rice, *Herbert Hoover,* 26.

166. Burner, *Hoover: Public Life,* 219.

CHAPTER 4

1. James E. Combs and Dan Nimmo, *Mediated Political Realities* (White Plains, N.Y.: Longman, 1993), 112.

2. Combs and Nimmo, *Mediated Political Realities,* 114.

3. Michael Curtiz, director, *Casablanca* (United Artists, Warner Bros. Pictures, Inc., 1942).

4. Combs and Nimmo, *Mediated Political Realities,* 116.

5. Doris Kearns Goodwin, "Franklin D. Roosevelt, 1933–1945," in *Character above All,* ed. Robert A. Wilson (New York: Simon & Schuster, 1995), 14.

6. Goodwin, "Franklin D. Roosevelt," 13.

7. Goodwin, "Franklin D. Roosevelt," 15.

8. Goodwin, "Franklin D. Roosevelt," 15.

9. Goodwin, "Franklin D. Roosevelt," 16.

10. Rexford G. Tugwell, *The Democratic Roosevelt* (Garden City, N.Y.: Doubleday, 1957), 247.

11. Goodwin, "Franklin D. Roosevelt," 17.

12. Goodwin, "Franklin D. Roosevelt," 23.

13. Tugwell, *The Democratic Roosevelt,* 343.

14. Goodwin, "Franklin D. Roosevelt," 15.

15. Goodwin, "Franklin D. Roosevelt," 15.

16. Goodwin, "Franklin D. Roosevelt," 13.

17. Tugwell, *The Democratic Roosevelt*, 11.

18. Goodwin, "Franklin D. Roosevelt," 17.

19. Gerald W. Johnson, *Roosevelt: Dictator or Democrat?* (New York: Harper, 1941), 254.

20. Johnson, *Roosevelt: Dictator or Democrat?* 33.

21. Johnson, *Roosevelt: Dictator or Democrat?* 35.

22. Thomas H. Greer, *What Roosevelt Thought* (East Lansing: Michigan State University Press, 1958), 5.

23. Greer, *What Roosevelt Thought,* 4–5.

24. Tugwell, *The Democratic Roosevelt*, 342.

25. Tugwell, *The Democratic Roosevelt*, 342.

26. Tugwell, *The Democratic Roosevelt*, 342.

27. Goodwin, "Franklin D. Roosevelt," 18.

28. Henry F. Graff, ed., *The Presidents: A Reference History,* 2nd ed. (New York: Charles Scribner's Sons, 1996), 520.

29. Graff, *The Presidents,* 515.

30. Gary L. Gregg, "Liberals, Conservatives, and the Presidency," *Intercollegiate Review* 33, no. 2 (Spring 1998): 26–32.

31. Gregg, "Liberals, Conservatives, and the Presidency," 26–32.

32. Goodwin, "Franklin D. Roosevelt," 18.

33. Goodwin, "Franklin D. Roosevelt," 35.

34. Goodwin, "Franklin D. Roosevelt," 18.

35. Joseph Alsop, *FDR, 1882–1945: A Centenary Remembrance* (New York: Viking, 1982).

36. Alsop, *FDR,* 511.

37. Graff, *The Presidents,* 524.

38. Tugwell, *The Democratic Roosevelt,* 404.

39. William A. DeGregorio, *The Complete Book of U.S. Presidents,* 4th ed. (New York: Barricade Books, 1993), 506.

40. David McCullough, *Truman* (New York: Simon & Schuster, 1992), 324.

41. McCullough, *Truman,* 326.

42. McCullough, *Truman,* 349.

43. Gregg, "Liberals, Conservatives, and the Presidency," 26–31.

44. David McCullough, "Harry S. Truman, 1945–1953," in *Character above All,* ed. Robert A. Wilson (New York: Simon & Schuster, 1995), 52.

45. McCullough, "Harry S. Truman," 41.

46. McCullough, *Truman,* 83.

47. Harry S. Truman, *Mr. Citizen* (New York: Bernard Geis Associates, 1960), 141.

48. Truman, *Mr. Citizen,* 135.

49. McCullough, *Truman,* 326.

50. McCullough, "Harry S. Truman," 58.

51. McCullough, "Harry S. Truman," 53.
52. McCullough, "Harry S. Truman," 58.
53. Robert S. Donovan, *Tumultuous Years: The Presidency of Harry S Truman* (New York: Norton, 1982), 114.
54. Donovan, *Tumultuous Years,* 114.
55. Jules Abels, *The Truman Scandals* (Chicago: Regnery, 1956) 7.
56. William E. Pemberton, *Harry S Truman, Fair Dealer and Cold Warrior* (Boston: Twayne, 1989), 167.
57. McCullough, "Harry S. Truman," 53.
58. McCullough, *Truman,* 357.
59. Margaret Truman, *Harry S Truman* (New York: Morrow, 1972).
60. McCullough, "Harry S. Truman," 46–47.
61. Merle Miller, *Plain Speaking* (New York: Berkley, 1974), 116.
62. Pemberton, *Fair Dealer,* 143.
63. Pemberton, *Fair Dealer,* 143.
64. Pemberton, *Fair Dealer,* 144.
65. McCullough, "Harry S. Truman," 50.
66. McCullough, "Harry S. Truman," 51.
67. McCullough, "Harry S. Truman," 51.
68. McCullough, *Truman,* 442.
69. McCullough, *Truman,* 443.
70. McCullough, *Truman,* 443.
71. DeGregorio, *Complete U.S. Presidents,* 519.
72. DeGregorio, *Complete U.S. Presidents,* 519.
73. McCullough, "Harry S. Truman," 50.
74. McCullough, *Truman,* 915.
75. McCullough, "Harry S. Truman," 57.
76. Graff, *The Presidents,* 459.
77. Graff, *The Presidents,* 459.
78. Graff, *The Presidents,* 460.
79. Graff, *The Presidents,* 460.
80. Fred Greenstein, *The Hidden-Hand Presidency* (New York: Basic Books, 1982), 19.
81. Stephen E. Ambrose, "Dwight D. Eisenhower, 1953–1961," in *Character above All,* ed. Robert A. Wilson (New York: Simon & Schuster, 1995), 79.
82. Greenstein, *Hidden-Hand Presidency,* 19.
83. Greenstein, *Hidden-Hand Presidency,* 18.
84. Greenstein, *Hidden-Hand Presidency,* 19.
85. Greenstein, *Hidden-Hand Presidency,* 30.
86. Graff, *The Presidents,* 461.
87. Graff, *The Presidents,* 461.
88. Graff, *The Presidents,* 461.
89. Graff, *The Presidents,* 461.
90. Ambrose, "Dwight D. Eisenhower," 59.

91. Russell Porter, "Eisenhower Bids U.S. Stay Powerful to Protect Peace," *New York Times,* April 26, 1946, 18.

92. Ambrose, "Dwight D. Eisenhower," 80.

93. Ambrose, "Dwight D. Eisenhower," 80.

94. Ambrose, "Dwight D. Eisenhower," 80.

95. DeGregorio, *Complete U.S. Presidents,* 531.

96. DeGregorio, *Complete U.S. Presidents,* 531.

97. DeGregorio, *Complete U.S. Presidents,* 538.

98. DeGregorio, *Complete U.S. Presidents,* 539.

99. "Transcript of President Eisenhower's Press Conference, with Comment on Indo-China," *New York Times,* April 8, 1954.

100. DeGregorio, *Complete U.S. Presidents,* 539.

101. Graff, *The Presidents,* 475.

102. Graff, *The Presidents,* 475.

103. Graff, *The Presidents,* 475.

104. Graff, *The Presidents,* 466.

105. Greenstein, *Hidden-Hand Presidency,* 218.

106. Graff, *The Presidents,* 467.

107. Robert T. Donovan, *Eisenhower: The Inside Story* (New York: Harper & Bros., 1956).

108. Arthur M. Schlesinger Jr., *The Imperial Presidency* (Boston: Houghton Mifflin, 1989), 152.

109. Ambrose, "Dwight D. Eisenhower," 79.

CHAPTER 5

1. Mel Elfin, "A Kinder Judgment Day for LBJ," *U.S. News and World Report,* April 23, 1990, 35.

2. Richard G. Hutcheson, *God in the White House: How Religion Has Changed the Modern Presidency* (New York: Macmillan, 1988), 59.

3. Hutcheson, *God in the White House,* 62.

4. Hutcheson, *God in the White House,* 61.

5. Henry F. Graff, ed., *The Presidents: A Reference History,* 2nd ed. (New York: Charles Scribner's Sons, 1996), 479.

6. Thomas C. Reeves, *A Question of Character* (New York: Free Press, 1991), 236.

7. Richard Reeves, "John F. Kennedy, 1961–1963," in *Character above All,* ed. Robert A. Wilson (New York: Simon & Schuster, 1995), 82.

8. Reeves, "John F. Kennedy," 82–83.

9. Reeves, "John F. Kennedy," 87.

10. Graff, *The Presidents,* 485.

11. Reeves, "John F. Kennedy," 94.

12. Victor Lasky, *JFK, The Man and the Myth* (New York: Macmillan, 1963), 68.

13. Reeves, *Question of Character*, 152.
14. Reeves, *Question of Character*, 158.
15. Reeves, *Question of Character*, 158.
16. Seymour M. Hersh, *The Dark Side of Camelot* (Boston: Little, Brown, 1997), 22.
17. Hersh, *Dark Side of Camelot*, ix.
18. Lasky, *JFK,* 496.
19. Lasky, *JFK,* 496.
20. Lasky, *JFK,* 495.
21. Reeves, *Question of Character*, 166.
22. Hersh, *Dark Side of Camelot,* 24.
23. Reeves, *Question of Character*, 241.
24. Hersh, *Dark Side of Camelot*, 103.
25. Hersh, *Dark Side of Camelot*, 106.
26. Hersh, *Dark Side of Camelot*, 106.
27. Bruce Miroff, *Pragmatic Illusions* (New York: David McKay, 1976), 250.
28. William A. DeGregorio, *The Complete Book of U.S. Presidents,* 4th ed. (New York: Barricade Books, 1993), 557.
29. DeGregorio, *Complete U.S. Presidents,* 557.
30. DeGregorio, *Complete U.S. Presidents,* 555.
31. Reeves, *Question of Character,* 277.
32. Reeves, *Question of Character,* 257.
33. Graff, *The Presidents,* 492.
34. Reeves, *Question of Character*, 257.
35. DeGregorio, *Complete U.S. Presidents,* 558.
36. Graff, *The Presidents,* 495.
37. Robert Dallek, "Lyndon B. Johnson, 1963–1969," in *Character above All,* ed. Robert A. Wilson (New York: Simon & Schuster, 1995), 105.
38. Dallek, "Lyndon B. Johnson," 108.
39. Dallek, "Lyndon B. Johnson," 108.
40. Dallek, "Lyndon B. Johnson," 112.
41. Dallek, "Lyndon B. Johnson," 113.
42. Lyndon B. Johnson, *My Hope for America* (New York: Random House, 1967), 51.
43. Doris Kearns Goodwin, *Lyndon Johnson and the American Dream* (New York: Random House, 1967), 211.
44. DeGregorio, *Complete U.S. Presidents,* 574.
45. Marvin E. Gettleman and David Mermelstein, eds., "The War on Poverty Is a Movement of Conscience," in *The Great Society Reader* (New York: Random House, 1967), 205.
46. Gettleman and Mermelstein, "War on Poverty," 208.
47. Dallek, "Lyndon B. Johnson," 116.
48. Johnson, *My Hope for America,* 17.
49. Lyndon B. Johnson, *The Vantage Point: Perspectives of the Presidency, 1963–1969* (New York: Holt, Rinehart, & Winston, 1971), 70.

50. DeGregorio, *Complete U.S. Presidents*, 574.

51. Dallek, "Lyndon B. Johnson," 117.

52. Hugh Sidey, *A Very Personal Presidency: Lyndon Johnson in the White House* (New York: Atheneum, 1968), 172.

53. Sidey, *Very Personal Presidency*, 164.

54. Hutcheson, *God in the White House*, 63.

55. Graff, *The Presidents*, 506.

56. Graff, *The Presidents*, 506.

57. Graff, *The Presidents*, 506.

58. DeGregorio, *Complete U.S. Presidents*, 576.

59. Graff, *The Presidents*, 508.

60. Graff, *The Presidents*, 509.

61. Graff, *The Presidents*, 509.

62. Sidey, *Very Personal Presidency*, 181.

63. Sidey, *Very Personal Presidency*, 181.

64. Hutcheson, *God in the White House*, 64.

65. Hutcheson, *God in the White House*, 64.

66. Dallek, "Lyndon B. Johnson," 119.

67. DeGregorio, *Complete U.S. Presidents*, 576.

68. DeGregorio, *Complete U.S. Presidents*, 581.

69. DeGregorio, *Complete U.S. Presidents*, 581.

70. DeGregorio, *Complete U.S. Presidents*, 581.

71. DeGregorio, *Complete U.S. Presidents*, 581.

72. Tom Wicker, "Richard M. Nixon, 1969–1974," in *Character above All*, ed. Robert A. Wilson (New York: Simon & Schuster, 1995), 135.

73. Wicker, "Richard M. Nixon," 135.

74. Richard M. Nixon, *In the Arena* (New York: Simon & Schuster, 190), 94.

75. Wicker, "Richard M. Nixon," 135.

76. Wicker, "Richard M. Nixon," 135.

77. Wicker, "Richard M. Nixon," 131.

78. Stephen E. Ambrose, *Nixon: Ruin and Recovery, 1973–1990* (New York: Simon & Schuster, 1991), 403.

79. Ambrose, *Nixon*, 403.

80. DeGregorio, *Complete U.S. Presidents*, 595.

81. DeGregorio, *Complete U.S. Presidents*, 595.

82. Graff, *The Presidents*, 522.

83. Graff, *The Presidents*, 522.

84. Graff, *The Presidents*, 522.

85. DeGregorio, *Complete U.S. Presidents*, 596.

86. DeGregorio, *Complete U.S. Presidents*, 596.

87. DeGregorio, *Complete U.S. Presidents*, 597.

88. Graff, *The Presidents*, 530.

89. DeGregorio, *Complete U.S. Presidents*, 597.

90. DeGregorio, *Complete U.S. Presidents*, 598.

91. DeGregorio, *Complete U.S. Presidents,* 598.

92. DeGregorio, *Complete U.S. Presidents,* 599.

93. Graff, *The Presidents,* 532.

94. Philip G. Henderson, "The Presidency, Then and Now," *Perspectives on Political Science* 26 (Summer 1997): 133.

CHAPTER 6

1. James Q. Wilson, *Moral Judgment: Does the Abuse Excuse Threaten Our Legal System?* (New York: Basic Books, 1997), 1.

2. See Floyd Rogers, *Television in American Society* (New York: Ebb & Ross, 1990); Les Brown and Savannah Waring Walker, *Fast Forward: The New Television and American Society* (Kansas City: Andrews & McMeel, 1983); Glenn Alan Cheney, *Television in American Society* (New York: Watts, 1983); Aletha C. Huston, *Big World, Small Screen: The Role of Television in American Society* (Lincoln: University of Nebraska Press, 1992); and Jeffrey Scheuer, *The Sound Bite Society: Television and the American Mind* (New York: Four Walls Eight Windows, 1999).

3. Keith Whittington, "The Rhetorical Presidency, Presidential Authority, and President Clinton," *Perspectives on Political Science* 26, no. 4 (Fall 1997): 199.

4. Richard Reeves, *A Ford, Not a Lincoln* (New York: Harcourt Brace Jovanovich, 1975), 54.

5. James Cannon, "Gerald Ford," in *Character above All,* ed. Robert A. Wilson (New York: Simon & Schuster, 1995), 146.

6. "Gerald R. Ford: Thirty-Eighth President" <http://www.whitehouse.gov/WH/glimpse/presidents/html/gf38.html> (accessed August 19, 1999).

7. "President Ford: The Man and His Record," *Congressional Quarterly,* August 1974, 59.

8. "Gerald R. Ford: Thirty-Eighth President."

9. "Gerald R. Ford: Thirty-Eighth President."

10. "Gerald R. Ford: Thirty-Eighth President."

11. Gerald Ford, *A Time to Heal* (New York: Harper & Row, 1975), 77.

12. Hugh Sidey, *Portrait of a President* (New York: Harper & Row, 1975), 77.

13. Ford, *Time to Heal.*

14. Ford, *Time to Heal.*

15. Sidey, *Portrait of a President,* 63.

16. *Character above All,* PBS Broadcast transcript, May 29, 1996.

17. "Gerald R. Ford: Thirty-Eighth President."

18. Hendrick Hertzberg, "Jimmy Carter, 1977–1981," in *Character above All,* ed. Robert A. Wilson (New York: Simon & Schuster, 1995), 180.

19. Richard G. Hutcheson, *God in the White House: How Religion Has Changed the Modern Presidency* (New York: Macmillan, 1988), 235.

20. "James E. Carter, Jr. Biography," *The Hall of Public Service Web Page* <http://www.achievement.org/autodoc/page/car)bio-1>.

21. "James E. Carter, Jr. Biography."

22. Hutcheson, *God in the White House*, 221.

23. *Character above All*, PBS broadcast transcript, May 29, 1996.

24. Erwin Hargrove, *Jimmy Carter as President* (Baton Rouge: Louisiana State University Press, 1988).

25. Hertzberg, "Jimmy Carter," 174.

26. "Presidency of Ronald Reagan" <http://grid.let.rug.nl/^welling/usa/ch8/p.22.html>.

27. Peggy Noonan, "Ronald Reagan, 1981–1989," in *Character above All*, ed. Robert A. Wilson (New York: Simon & Schuster, 1995), 205.

28. Noonan, "Ronald Reagan," 205.

29. Noonan, "Ronald Reagan," 205.

30. "Presidency of Ronald Reagan."

31. *Character above All*, May 29, 1996.

32. Hutcheson, *God in the White House*, 234.

33. Hutcheson, *God in the White House*, 234.

34. Hutcheson, *God in the White House*, 234.

35. "George Bush" <http://www.achievement.org/autodoc/page/bus0int-1> (accessed August 19, 1999).

36. David Maranis, "It's Lonelier than Usual for the Man at the Top," *Washington Post*, February 16, 1998, A1.

37. David Maranis, "Clinton's Personality Patterns," *Washington Post*, February 2, 1998, 6.

38. William J. Bennett, "What We Know," *Wall Street Journal*, April 16, 1998.

39. Marvin Olasky, "Sex and the Presidency," *New York Times*, A18.

40. Olasky, "Sex and the Presidency."

41. Olasky, "Sex and the Presidency."

42. Gene Edward Veith, " A Post-Modern Scandal," *World*, February 21, 1998, 24.

43. Lynne Cheney, *Telling the Truth* (New York: Simon & Schuster, 1995), 187.

44. Cheney, *Telling the Truth*, 187.

45. Cheney, *Telling the Truth*, 189.

46. Cheney, *Telling the Truth*, 189.

47. Cheney, *Telling the Truth*, 189.

48. David M. Shribman, "The Heroes at 1600," *State (Columbia, S.C.)*, January 1, 1998, D4.

49. Bennett, "What We Know."

50. Marc Levinson, "Telling the Truth," *Newsweek*.

51. Edith Efron, "Can the President Think?" *Reason* 194 (November 1994): 21–44.

52. Efron, "Can the President Think?"

CHAPTER 7

1. Gary L. McDowell, "The True History of High Crimes and Misdemeanors," *Wall Street Journal,* January 25, 1999, A19.

2. Robert H. Bork, "Read the Constitution: It's Removal or Nothing," *Wall Street Journal,* February 1, 1999, A21.

3. David E. Rosenbaum, "Gray Area: The Sense of Congress," Week in Review, *New York Times,* December 6, 1998, 3.

4. <http://www.georgecosborn.com/oped1021.htm>.

5. *Wall Street Journal,* February 8, 1999, A22.

6. *Wall Street Journal,* February 8, 1999, A22.

7. "Poll: Clinton Approval Rating Up Despite Videotape Release" <http://cnn.com/ALLPOLITICS/stories/1998/09/22/clinton.poll/>.

8. *New York Times,* March 10, 1998, A15.

9. Peter Beinart, "Private Matters," *New Republic,* February 15, 1999, 21.

10. Holman W. Jenkins Jr., "For Their Own Good, Democrats Must Do the Walk of Shame," *Wall Street Journal,* February 3, 1999, A23.

11. "The Not-So-White House," review of *All Too Human: A Political Education,* by George Stephanopolous, *The Economist,* March 20, 1999, 89.

12. Gabriel Fackre, ed., *Judgment Day at the White House: A Critical Declaration Exploring Moral Issues and the Political Use and Abuse of Religion* (Grand Rapids, Mich.: Eerdmans, 1999), 1.

13. Andrew Hacker, *The End of the American Era* (New York: Atheneum, 1970), 146; and William J. Bennett, *The Death of Outrage: Bill Clinton and the Assault on American Ideals* (New York: Free Press, 1999).

14. Robert Shogan, *The Double-Edged Sword* (Boulder, Colo.: Westview Press, 1999), 4.

INDEX

ABOUT THE AUTHOR

Charles W. Dunn is dean of the School of Arts and Letters and professor of political science at Grove City College. He was formerly professor of political science at Clemson University. He received a B.S. from Illinois State University and an M.S. and Ph.D. from Florida State University. His books include *American Government in Comparative Perspective* (2nd ed., 2000), *The Conservative Tradition in America* (2nd ed., 1996), *Religion in American Politics* (1989), *Constitutional Democracy in America* (1987), *American Political Theology* (1984), *American Democracy Debated* (2nd ed., 1982), and *The Future of the American Presidency* (1975). His articles have appeared in numerous journals, including the *American Journal of Political Science, American Politics Quarterly, Modern Age,* and *PS.* He has appeared as a political commentator on radio and television and has lectured widely. From 1989 to 1993 he was a member of the William J. Fulbright Foreign Scholarship Board, serving four terms as its chairman. For his efforts on behalf of the Fulbright program, he received the United States Information Agency's Award for Outstanding Service.